THE MIND OF PAUL VI

On the Church and the World

THE MIND OF PAUL VI

On the Church and the World

Introduction by Augustin, Cardinal Bea

Edited from the works of Cardinal Montini
by JAMES WALSH S.J.

Translated by ARCHIBALD COLQUHOUN

GEOFFREY CHAPMAN - LONDON 1964

NIHIL OBSTAT: JOANNES M. T. BARTON, S.T.D., L.S.S., CENSOR DEPUTATUS
IMPRIMATUR: GEORGIUS L. CRAVEN, EPUS. SEBASTOPOLIS, VIC. GEN.
WESTMONASTERII, DIE 9A APRILUS, 1964

MADE AND PRINTED IN GREAT BRITAIN BY
RICHARD CLAY AND COMPANY LTD., BUNGAY, SUFFOLK
FOR THE PUBLISHERS, GEOFFREY CHAPMAN LTD., 18 HIGH ST.,
WIMBLEDON, LONDON, S.W.19

ACKNOWLEDGEMENTS

The material in this book has been selected and translated from works originally published and copyrighted by L'Ufficio Studi Arcivescovile di Milano.

Selections have been taken from the following works:
Discorsi per il Natale e l'Epifania (1955–61); *Discorsi su la Chiesa* (1957–62); *Discorsi per la Settimana Santa e la Pasqua* (1955–61); *Sul senso religiosi* (1957); *Sul senso morale* (1961); *Per la famiglia cristiana* (1960); *Il cristiano e il benessere temporale* (1963); *Religione e lavoro* (1960).

The publishers are indebted to Messrs Darton, Longman & Todd to quote from their edition of *Man's Religious Sense*, on pp. 77–84 and pp. 143–57.

Scriptural quotations throughout are taken from the *Revised Standard Version*

CONTENTS

INTRODUCTION

The image of Paul VI in the light of the first months of his government

SELDOM WAS the familiar phrase 'difficult succession' to a pontificate rich in prestige and in works so true as after the death of Pope John XXIII. 'Good Pope John' had acquired a widespread popularity even outside the Catholic Church; he had decided upon, prepared, and begun the vastest and the best-prepared council of all time; he had set the Church in motion towards a rediscovery of the traces of her more fervent youth, towards the revelation of her conquering power to the men of today; by his encyclicals and especially by the council, he had attracted the interest and admiration of world opinion. Now he was dead, his work just begun, and there was universal grief and consternation.

The vacancy of the Apostolic See, with the inevitable and numerous conjectures as to his probable successor, was far from creating a halo of prestige for whoever should succeed Pope John and receive his heritage. Conjectures, while partly assisting the more perspicacious minds to a discernment of persons and of their qualities, are always largely equalizing, at least as regards the various likely candidates, because conjectures—even when calmly voiced, which is not generally the case—tend to exalt one's own candidate by criticizing those of others. For all these reasons, it was certainly no empty word when Paul VI himself, the day after his election, spoke of his 'spirit trembling before the vastness of the task' imposed upon him, and of the weighty legacy received from his predecessor.

However, the Pope declared in the same speech that the primary sentiment welling up in his heart was 'one of certain trust in the omnipotent help of the Lord'. In fact, from the very outset his actions were marked by an immense, serene, and confident vigour. What strength of will in the solemn announcement to the entire world less than twenty-four hours after the election—and we know how full and burdensome those hours were—of the precise pro-

Note: The texts of speeches quoted or referred to have been published in *La Civiltà Cattolica*, 1963, Vol. III–IV; 1964, Vol. IV.

gramme of his pontificate! Hardly a week later, even before the coronation, he had already established the date for the reopening of the council. Then came in rapid succession those other decisions of which we recall merely the solemn announcement of the Curia reform and the history-making decision regarding his pilgrimage to the Holy Land.

These acts and decisions gradually made an impression on us and little by little formed in us a picture of Paul VI. It is therefore extremely interesting for us all to reflect a little in order to syn-thesize this multitude of traits and acts and of our own impressions, and attempt to create a mental portrait of Paul VI. This is what we wish to do in these introductory pages. This mode of procedure will have the advantage of avoiding not only empty words and the suspicion of flattery, which would be unworthy, but also the danger of forcing Paul VI into the measure of what he was and did during his long career in the Secretariat of State and subsequently in the Metropolitan See of Milan, and as a Cardinal. Although in fact all this evidently constitutes the 'stuff' of which Christ gradually formed his Vicar on earth and therefore it is a help to us, in a certain sense, in understanding Pope Paul VI also, nevertheless it is still *merely* the expression of Giovanni Battista Montini's personality and not yet that of Paul VI. In this introduction, on the contrary, we shall seek to create for ourselves a portrait of Paul VI, drawing for evidence on how he has acted as pope.

Let us consider, first of all, the Pope's *programme*. He mentioned it at the time of his first radio message, summarizing it in these four items: the council, pre-eminent task of his pontificate; the reform of Canon Law; world peace; Christian unity. In his coronation dis-course he added dialogue with the modern world. In September he completed it by solemnly announcing his intention of reforming the Roman Curia to fit it to the times. Let us look at some of its details.

In making *peace* one of the principal aims of his pontificate, the Pope linked himself both with the pontificate of Pius XI whose motto was 'the peace of Christ in the kingdom of Christ' and also, more immediately, with that of Pope John, whose encyclical on peace had awoken such deep echoes throughout the world. Of peace, the Pope affirms that it is today the supreme need of humanity, 'the insuppressible need in the conscience of the new generations'. He expresses the hope, therefore, that true peace may reign in the world 'in truth, in justice, in liberty and love' and he formulates the prayer 'to all men of good will, yes, to all responsible persons in the cultural and political field to regard the problem of peace as fundamental'. As for himself, he goes as a pilgrim to the Holy Land 'to implore divine mercy in favour of peace among men'.

As regards *dialogue with the modern world*, Paul VI's vision of this world and of the Church's attitude towards it is quite characteristic. In the first place, there is full recognition of progress and success in the fields of science and technology. He recognizes moreover that this modern world, which may appear remote from everything of a religious and spiritual order, nevertheless ardently yearns after justice and not only technical but also human progress, after lasting peace. The Pope adds that in the service of these ideals the world shows itself capable of practising to an amazing degree the virtues of fortitude and courage, the spirit of enterprise, of dedication, of sacrifice. And he adds emphatically: 'All this is ours.' In his message from Bethlehem, the Pope again declares: 'We look out over the world with immense sympathy.' Perhaps it is just this sympathy with the world which enables the Pope to perceive its weak and painful side. 'We know that man is tormented by atrocious doubts, we know that in his soul there is much darkness, much suffering.' Despite all this, the Church regards the world with deep under-standing and with the desire to serve and aid it. 'The Pope, like the Church, considers himself the enemy of no one. The only language he knows how to use is that of friendship and trust.' It is precisely for this reason that the Church is trying to regain vigour in the council, in order to be a much more efficacious instrument for the salvation of humanity and to foster unity among all men. The Pope's first Christmas radio message, devoted chiefly to the problem of hunger in the world, that is, to the fact that 'more than half the human race is without sufficient bread' and that 'entire generations of children are still dying and languishing today in indescribable indigence' reveals the extreme practicality of this solicitude on the part of the Pope for the welfare of men.

Quite characteristic, too, is Paul VI's attitude towards the question of *Christian unity*. While fully pursuing his predecessor's line, the Pope is adding much that is his own, much that is personal. He explicitly affirms that between Catholics and non-Catholic Christians a certain unity *already* exists, bestowed by baptism, by the same fundamental faith in Christ and love for him. This unity must be manifested right now, wherever possible. Paul VI, moreover, reveals with ever new expressions his own respect, esteem, and love for non-Catholic Christians, for all they have that is characteristic and proper to themselves. Not only does he assure them that they will be able to keep all this and use it to the full in visible unity with the Church of Rome which 'sublimates and endows with new splendour the treasures of their history, their cultural patrimony, their religious heritage', but he says, 'We wish neither to absorb nor to restrict this great blossoming of Oriental Churches.' The Pope then adds an exhortation to these Churches to cherish perseverance 'in the most complete fidelity to their origins'. But along with fidelity to what is their own, there must be eagerness and vigorous action for the re-establishment of unity. 'The voice would like to sound as an angel's trumpet proclaiming: "Come, let us break down the barriers which separate us; let us explain the points of doctrine on which we differ . . . let us endeavour to render our Creed unanimous and stable, to link and firmly cement our hierarchical unity".'

Nevertheless, desire and nostalgia for unity do not obscure his realistic vision of the problem's vastness and the gravity of the obstacles, which leads him to declare that nobody knows how long the preparation for unity will take. When, however, historic reality threatens his hopes with disillusionment, he considers Christ's words: 'What is impossible to man's powers is possible to God' (Luke 18, 27). Finally, he declares to the non-Catholic observers at the council: 'Hope is our guide, prayer is our strength, charity our method in the service of divine truth which is our faith and our salvation.'

Let us turn our gaze from the programme to the person of the Pope. By now it is well known how very human and of what an extreme *simplicity* he is in his dealings with men. We cite an example. Seated in an arm-chair in the midst of the non-Catholic observers in the audience granted them on 17 October, the Pope said, in simple words: 'To approach one another, to meet, to greet, to know each other, to speak to each other—what could be simpler, more natural, more human? Certainly this is so. But here we have something more: we are listening to one another, praying for one another and, after many years of separation, after painful controversies, we are beginning again to love one another.'

These words give us already an example of his oratory, for which a better word would be his 'conversation', so pleasant and spontaneous

is it. Thus, from the simplest and most obvious things, with extreme
facility and almost imperceptibly, he passes to profound considerations and expands in visions of unsuspected breadth and vastness.

This simplicity, however, is based on a profound and at the same
time quite natural *modesty and humility*, not only in words. Certainly
he can speak of himself as the least worthy among the brethren, in
tones so sincere as to be convincing. Nevertheless, it is understandable that in the modern world many remain sceptical of
sayings like these. But here we have facts. We have that decision, as
unusual as it was courageous, of remaining to lunch with the
Cardinals immediately after his election and instead of taking the
highest place, staying in the one he had occupied as a Cardinal.
Again, his undoubted acceptance as his own of practically the entire
programme of his predecessor is the unmistakable indication of a
man who, oblivious to self, looks solely to the welfare of the Church
and to what he believes to be the will of God.

Then we have that *request for pardon* at the opening of the second
session of the council. In the most solemn setting of the council,
before over two thousand council Fathers from all parts of the
world, before about sixty non-Catholic observers from almost the
whole of Christendom, indeed before the entire world which was
listening-in by radio or television, and lastly, before history itself,
the Pope solemnly declared: 'If we are in any way to blame for this
separation, we humbly beg God's forgiveness and ask our brothers'
pardon for any injuries they feel they have sustained from us. For our
part, we willingly forgive whatever injuries the Catholic Church has
suffered and forget the grief she has endured as a result of the long
years of dissension and separation.' Those who were present or who
listened to the radio are aware how his voice trembled with emotion
and, as we learned later, many among the non-Catholic Christians
were touched.

Not satisfied with this, the Pope repeated the plea for pardon in the
audience granted to the non-Catholic observers at the council,
which we have already mentioned: 'We dared (note the word) in our
speech of 29 September, to appeal first of all to Christian forgiveness, mutual if possible. *Veniam damus petimusque vicissim.* Our souls
need this tranquillity if they are to establish friendly contact and
enter into calm conversations.' For the same reason he said that for his
own part he wished to follow St Paul's rule of forgetting what he
had left behind, intent on what lies before him (cf. Phil. 3, 13, etc.),

forgetting the past, that is, and fixing his attention on what can be and what remains to be done.

The Pope was animated by the same spirit of Christian humility when he returned the visit of the Orthodox Patriarchs in Jerusalem, of the Ecumenical Patriarch Athenagoras, of the Patriarch Benedictos of Jerusalem, of the Armenian Orthodox Patriarch Jegishe Derderian. Passing above the protocol in force for centuries, the Pope wished to be just the servant of the servants of God, seeking like Jesus not to be served but to serve.

Connatural complement to humility in the doctrine and the life of the Pope is his *Christocentricism*. This is the attitude of one who recognizes by faith that he has received from Christ all that he has and must look to him for everything. A splendid example of this is the declaration made at the opening of the second session of the council, that for all the council seeks and proposes to do, the reply and the solution are to be found in Christ: 'Christ our starting point, Christ our leader and our way, Christ our hope and our goal.' And he went on, fervently: 'May this ecumenical council have a clear realization of that bond which binds us to Jesus Christ—a bond that is one yet manifold, stringent yet compelling, mysterious yet manifest, tightly drawn yet most welcome. It binds us, the living, holy Church, to Christ from whom we come, through whom we live, toward whom we tend. May this present assembly shine with no other light than Christ, the light of the world. May our minds seek no other truth than that proclaimed by the words of the Lord, our only teacher. May our sole ambition be to give whole-hearted, loyal obedience to his commands. May no other confidence sustain us than that which strengthens our own poor frailty—relying on his words: "And behold I am with you all through the days that are coming, until the consummation of the world."'

It is this total confidence in Christ and dependence upon him which echoes again and again through Paul VI's speeches; this is the reason for his repeated exhortation to prayer, penance, and sacrifice united to purity of life and charity towards others, as the principal means for ensuring the success of the council. 'We solemnly affirm, Venerable Brethren, that in this abundance of prayer of Christian penance are to be placed our hopes of an abundant spiritual harvest from the council which is principally the work of the Holy Spirit.'

Moreover, he himself furnished a remarkable example of this in his pilgrimage to the Holy Land. In fact, its principal aim was precisely that of offering prayer and penance for the happy success of the council: 'We are so deeply convinced that for the happy outcome of the council prayers and works must be intensified, that we have decided, after mature reflection and not a little prayer, to go ourselves in pilgrimage to the land of our Lord Jesus.'

All this might lead some people to suppose that the Pope has a winning manner, if not exactly like Pope John's, nevertheless with at least some facility and success. But this is not the case. His slim and rather austere figure, the vigour which shines in his face, tense in recollection or in reaching for the goals which his will proposes, even the rather dark complexion of his face, do not tend to popular appeal. Again, his long sojourn in the Secretariat of State, whose extremely delicate work exacts great prudence and circumspection, too easily leads many people to suspect that this or that word, this or that gesture or attitude, is studied and calculated, rather than the spontaneous expression of his mind.

All this is obviously an obstacle to his conquest of men's hearts. Yet we must say that Paul VI has succeeded in overcoming even this obstacle and in dissipating by degrees and in good measure even these suspicions. For example, his spontaneous visit on Christmas Day to a very poor little paralysed girl in a suburb of Rome touched the Romans; his visit to a crippled Moslem in Jerusalem and all his spontaneous and profound piety during his visit to the Holy Places, a piety observed by millions of televiewers throughout the world, succeeded in breaking the ice. After the pilgrimage to the Holy Land, the human sympathy of millions and millions of men was turned towards the Pope. Experience shows, moreover, that a sympathy which grows by degrees and with a longer interior action is deeper and more lasting.

In his radio message on the day following his election, Pope Paul at once recalled his three immediate predecessors who, he said, 'have left us a sacred and glorious spiritual heritage: Pius XI, with his indomitable strength of mind; Pius XII, who illuminated the Church with the light of a teaching full of wisdom; and lastly, John XXIII, who gave to the entire world an example of singular goodness'. It was thought, and with some reason, that this commemoration could be seen as a sort of key to the personality of Pope Paul VI and his pontificate. In fact, not only do these three pontificates cover the period of his direct service to the Church, but they must necessarily have made a deep impression on his personality, since he worked at the very centre of the Church's activity, in the Secretariat of State and, moreover, in ever closer collaboration with the Pope himself.

More than once the great similarity between Paul VI and Pius XII has been remarked, even to the slender figure and the gestures. While Paul VI has in common with Pius XI and Pope John a clear grasp of goals and great strength and rapidity of decision—a quality already mentioned above—yet he is distinguished from them by his extraordinary regularity and practical vigour in dealing with business, going straight to the object in view without any prolixity, which is reminiscent of Pius XII. After dealing for several years with Pope John, one noticed from the first audience the great difference in his regard between Paul VI and his immediate predecessor. Paul VI has Pius XII's depth of thought, although he is more spontaneous, more simple, and more accessible in expressing it, so that its profundity nearly escapes one, and this recalls rather the manner of Pius XI and Pope John. Lastly, as has already been said, one cannot fail to observe the increasingly obvious similarity of Pope Paul to Pope John in the matter of goodness.

From what we have said, it is evident that the personality of Paul VI is not easily understood. Any help towards a better and more exact understanding is therefore welcome. The present book will be a valuable aid in this direction. It will lead to a deeper understanding of the ideas, aspirations, and apostolic yearnings of Paul VI, since it will enable the study of the Pope's pronouncements in the light of the speeches and sermons of the then Archbishop and Cardinal Montini. Naturally, in considering the declarations of the Pope in this broader light the reader must be careful to bear in mind, so to speak, the 'hierarchy' existing between the various declarations reproduced in the book. The declarations of the Pope are indeed the determining ones, whereas those made prior to the pontificate are subsidiary, an aid towards the fuller understanding of the former and not to be used for the purpose of interpreting in any other than their true sense the acts and words of the Pontiff. May this introduction assist the reader to discern the main and determining lines of the Pope's teaching, while the introduction will receive abundant light from the precious and numerous extracts reproduced in the book itself.

My wish, then, for this book, is that it may achieve a well-merited success and the widest circulation.

AUGUSTIN, CARDINAL BEA

PART ONE

THE CHURCH'S MISSION

I

PREAMBLE[1]

THE CHURCH'S mission is, first and foremost, to make her gospel loved—the Gospel which is her way of life. The dominant notes of the apostolate are optimism and sympathy. The very name 'Gospel' means 'good news'. It is inaugurated by a song of angelic happiness on Christmas night: 'I bring you good news of a great joy which is to come to the whole people. Today a Saviour is born to you' (Luke 2, 11). The Christian message is not a prophecy of condemnation. It is a call to penance, because it is a call to salvation. It is not harsh or aggressive, not ironic, not pessimistic. It is a message of strong and cheerful generosity, full of beauty and poetry, full of life and splendour. At the same time, it does raise the cross; the cross of sorrow, sacrifice, death; but in order to bring comfort, redemption, and life.

[1] From *Radio Message for the Mission of Milan*, 1957.

2

THE REDEEMING AND SAVING MISSION OF CHRIST[1]

WHO DID the Saviour come for?

What are the evils from which he came to save us?

These questions call for answers not only about the unique Person who has entered the world's history, the tiny but tremendous Baby-King whom Isaiah the Prophet identifies beforehand as the 'Wonderful Counsellor, Mighty God, Everlasting Father, Prince of Peace' (9, 6), but about matters that concern us also, our condition, our true needs, our supreme destiny.

Seen from this point of view, Christmas is not merely the happy feast, idyllic and archaic, which we all more or less understand; it is also the day of dramatic fulfilment, which reveals to humanity its true state and its ultimate destiny.

Who did Christ come for, then?

First: Christ came for all men. The universality of the Redemption, one of the dogmas which the Catholic religion affirms most strongly and from which it draws its very definition, is among the greatest truths ever announced to humanity. It is at the heart of the modern world's search for unity, for equality among peoples, brotherhood among men. It is the urge behind the apostolic and missionary spirit of religion, the life-giving leaven for peace and collaboration. It is the dogma that undermines privilege, oppression, dictatorship, tyranny, imperialism, and colonialism. It arouses a respect for the human personality in every vital civilization. It sustains the supremacy of right over force, it promotes justice and liberty. It is the foundation of true democracy, which is positive and progressive about man's rights and his public and private relationships.

All human beings are loved by God and potentially saved by Christ; so all are equally worthy of consideration, of love, service, and protection. No discrimination can exist in face of the supreme criterion by which men should be valued: that is, their relationship

[1] Sermon given on Christmas Day, 1957.

4

with Christ and with God. When this relationship is forgotten or denied then discrimination, social and national competition, enmity, wars are always able to produce those justifications, superficially valid, which compromise the basis of human brotherhood. Christ the Saviour came for all![1]

The second point is this. Christ, when he came into the world, showed a preference for certain categories of human beings; or rather, he showed that some human conditions are an advantage in relation to the salvation he brought. Christ came as a saviour; his mission of salvation operates most closely wherever the need of salvation is greatest.

He said of himself: 'Those who are well have no need of a physician, but those who are sick' (Matt. 9, 12). He came as the doctor of the deepest human ills. And so our very sickness, whatever it may be, even sin, which is the worst sickness of all, becomes, in his overflowing mercy, a claim rather than an obstacle to the divine Saviour's help; 'But where sin increased, grace abounded all the more' (Rom. 5, 20–21). Our Lord brings this economy of salvation closer to our understanding, makes us more aware of it, by fixing his eyes on the human deficiencies that are most obvious. He shows us the innate sympathies of his heart for our suffering and desolation, by sending echoing round the world words which, though divine, are also the most human ever spoken: 'Blessed are you poor, for yours is the kingdom of God. Blessed are you that hunger now, for you shall be satisfied. Blessed are you that weep now, for you shall laugh. Blessed are you when men hate you . . . on account of the Son of Man . . . for behold, your reward is great in heaven' (Luke 6, 20–23).

These are the favoured ones: the needy, the suffering, the persecuted. So Christmas makes us think of human sorrows. We cannot forget them on this blessed day which reveals both the goodness of God and the suffering still in the world. Suffering due to injustice, to selfishness, oppression, malice, hypocrisy, or corruption; all sins that bring gloom to the lives of those who commit them, and misery to those on whom their consequences fall. Suffering due to poverty, to lack of food, homes, work, social security, to strident economic inequalities, from all of which millions still suffer. Suffering due also to physical illness, which holds innumerable sick chained to pain, weakness, or inertia. We

[1] Cf. I Tim. 2, 4–6. See also Pius XII, *Mystici Corporis Christi*.

cannot on this day be insensible to the sufferings of so many whom Christ has made our brethren. We cannot enjoy Christmas with minds at peace unless we consider them. For, more than any other day, Christmas awakens our human sensibilities; not just to an emotional response but to the need for charity, to our duty and capacity to recognize the needs of others and help them as if their needs were our own. The feast that we are celebrating today urges us to seek out the brethren close by who may be in distress.

Yes, close by—we must mention this now, however inopportune it may appear—there are brethren of ours in distress.

As we all know, at this very moment, out in our Cathedral square, there is a great public meeting of workers who have been out on strike for weeks.[1] We may regret that the sacredness of this time and place to prayer and peace has been left out of account; we may have reserves about the motives behind this meeting and the means by which it has been called. Yet we must warmly condole with the thousands of working families today who are in want and distress, bitter in heart, anxious about food and work. We had so much hoped that a peaceful and honourable agreement could have been reached before this feast-day. To all those workers we send our paternal greetings, exhorting all, employers and employees, to end this wretched quarrel as soon as possible, peacefully and according to law. May Christian values, rather than those based on material well-being, bring justice and peace.

May Christ grant us this blessing.

And now a third point. Christ, who came for all and opens the gates of his salvation to the less fortunate, will be reached only by those who want to reach him. Without our own co-operation we will not be granted his salvation. This salvation has nothing magical or automatic about it; there is nothing fatalistic about it; it is not a gift forced upon those who do not want to receive it. The economy of God's superabundant mercy offered to all does not dispense us from playing our own part by a free personal act of good will. Indeed, Christ's coming among us emphasizes the role that freedom plays in our own salvation: we are faced with a momentous personal decision, a fateful choice. Called as we are to a supernatural destiny, we are ourselves free and responsible in the choice of seizing it boldly or rejecting it. How magnificent, how tremendous is this 'morality play' of the world and of our souls!

[1] The reference is to a strike at Milan in December 1957 (translator).

3

THE CHURCH'S MISSION IS THE CONTINUATION OF CHRIST'S[1]

WHY, MY friends, do you ask me to speak to you about what you already know? The Church's mission is already known to you by faith, natural knowledge, and experience. What can I add to the words of Christ, who stated that mission once and for all in prophetic words: 'Go therefore and make disciples of all nations, baptizing them in the name of the Father and the Son and the Holy Spirit, teaching them to observe all that I have commanded you' (Matt. 28, 19–20).

Perhaps by hearing these well-loved words repeated you hope to catch their prophetic ring, to sense their historical reality, to admire their majestic simplicity, to feel them living still and working in you? Or perhaps you hope to hear them as if they had just been spoken, to glimpse that inner spark which turns a fisherman into an apostle, a disciple into a teacher, a timid follower into a heroic witness of Christ? Or still more: perhaps you wish to find those words addressed to you in particular; to find that, by the simplest and greatest of paradoxes, among the millions of human beings on this earth, the millions of Christ's followers, you yourself are in some measure called to take part in the same great mysterious mission? Do you wish to hear that the Church's mission is your mission too? Do you wish to turn these meetings of ours into momentary examinations of conscience, into meditations that reach into the depths of your soul, to comfort it and to give it a new inner conscience and energy, as if a voice, sweet but strong, firm but friendly, were echoing there?

'The Master is here; he is asking for you' (John 11, 28). Perhaps also you wish to hear a well-known doctrine repeated in order to honour the ministry, not the person, of the man repeating it.

[1] From *Discourses to the Second World Congress of the Lay Apostolate*, October 1957.

Perhaps you are hoping to gain a greater understanding of this teaching, its value and depth, its beauty and efficacy, by accepting it in loving humility, not as mere speculative knowledge but as a living message from one whose duty it is, by his divine mandate as priest and bishop, to hand it on as he himself received it.

Or again; perhaps in asking me to speak to you about the Church's mission you are recognizing your duty to give more thought to what she really is. You and I have been brought up in the Church, an education so much a part of us that we take it for granted. Now we must see to it that the Church becomes our science and our life. She has been our inheritance from the past; now instead she must enrich the present. She has been a tradition; now instead she must become for us an inward consciousness and power. Do you not feel that by deepening our knowledge of the Church's doctrine we discover more of its divine beauty and originality, the secret of its eternal youth, the principle of its inexhaustible fecundity? Do you not feel that such reflection on the Church's mystery becomes the main pivot not only for theological study but for the religious spirit of today? Is not such reflection the seal of its own orthodoxy, the fount of prayer, the hope for the spiritual conquest both of contemporary and future worlds?

If this is so, then listening to old but living truths about the Church's mission is no vain repetition. All can be contained in one simple statement: the Church's mission is the continuation of Christ.

The First Vatican Council declared: 'The eternal shepherd and Bishop of our souls, in order to establish for ever the work of redemption, arranged to build the Church; in this, as the house of the living God, all the faithful should be fellow-guests linked by faith and charity.'[1] And Pope Pius XII repeated in his encyclical on the Mystical Body: 'As the Word of God vouchsafed to use our nature to redeem men by his pains and torments, in a similar way he makes use of his Church throughout the ages to perpetuate the work he had begun.'[2]

The Church shows herself under two aspects at the same time. One is of coherence, conservation, community, loyalty, presence; and it is symbolized by the stability of rock. The second aspect is of movement, transmission, projection in time and space, expansion,

[1] Vatican Council I, Session 21.
[2] *Mystici Corporis Christi*, English translation, C.T.S., London, p. 12.

dynamism, hope which looks to a final end; and it is symbolized by the body which lives and moves and grows—the body of Christ.

To understand the Church's mission we are to consider this progress of Christ through the centuries, this trajectory which creates history, infusing the story of humanity with a sense and a value which it can seek and find nowhere else.

The word 'mission', while defining the vast areas covered by the Church's doctrine, also calls up the sense of movement which characterizes the life of the Church. She comes from Christ; she is sent by him. Her work is urged on, followed, watched over by him. The Church carries him within her, preaches him, communicates him, transmits him. Through her Christ reaches men, crosses the borders of nations, surveys the centuries, makes contact with human life, its forms, its institutions, its customs, its civilizations. The Church encounters obstacles, shocks, and persecutions; she finds loyalty, makes conquests, enjoys triumphs. And she carries on, suffering and growing, praying and working, teaching and blessing; on towards a prize which draws her as though it were within her reach. Through weariness and disappointment she is sustained by this prize, the hope of a last day, when the mysterious Christ whom she carries within her will reveal himself, absorb her entirely in himself and beatify her: the hope of eternal life.

This mission, then, is like a journey in the course of which the Church goes on living and developing, continuing the work of redemption. But although this journey has all the characteristics of a great event which is plain for all to see, this traveller, the Church, is not only human. She is a sure and continuous incarnation of Christ. She sets out and travels on, always in relation to a mystery— the presence of Christ within her.

The Church's mission comes into being and continues in virtue of the mystery which generates her, vivifies her, and prepares her for the final outcome, the second coming.

Jesus Christ thus described the pattern of his earthly life: 'I came from the Father and have come into the world. Again I am leaving the world and going to the Father' (John 16, 28). So too the Church can say of herself: 'I came out from Christ: in my journey through the world I receive my life from him; and then I return to him.' It is thus that she traces out the purpose and dimensions of her mysterious mission.

The Church's mission is the same as Christ's. He gave this mission to the Church, and invested the apostle Peter with its continuation, exercise, and guarantee. This twofold characteristic must always be remembered. It can be translated into two terms that are fundamental for an understanding of any participation in the Church's mission: orthodoxy and mandate.

Orthodoxy means the true derivation of the Church's mission from its source, the preservation of Christ's doctrinal and sacramental patrimony, of the '*depositum*' which St Paul said must be faithfully kept by a minister of the Gospel (1 Tim. 6, 20).

This may seem at first sight to hinder the Church's mission at its very start, to bind it to something static, inflexible, extrinsic, and obligatory, to deprive the missionary of his liberty of thought and action, to repress his personality. Modern individualism is restive to any formula fixed forever by authority. The modern religious sense would seem impoverished when modelled on immoveable doctrine. Fervour is apt to grow cold when impulses of feeling cannot be followed spontaneously, or free use made of personal experience. Indeed, the many efforts to give currency to a morality and a religion outside Catholic orthodoxy seem at times to achieve more and to use better arguments, simply because these efforts have no fixed starting-point, no obligation to accept definite dogmas, and are free of the sublime but heavy burden of divine truth. Such efforts depend on the personal whim and talent of their authors. These people are often generous and sincere when, fired by some precious fragment of natural morality, some memory of Bible or philosophy, some poetic or artistic impulse or some general Christian principle, they set out to preach the conversion of the world. But in reality they are apostles only of themselves. The only truth they have to announce is one that can be measured by their own human capacity. They do not possess the 'mystery' which must move and give shape to a true mission of salvation. They are without the true Christ. They lack the living God. Their mission is no longer religious but human, no longer a continuation of Christ but a human transaction.

We ourselves must be firmly convinced that Christ's mission requires a scrupulous orthodoxy. Orthodoxy is the link, the channel of communication, the guarantee of union with Christ, of his presence and authority. It is the indispensable condition for receiving the divine heritage, and also the guarantee that this heritage is being kept intact. Orthodoxy makes us realize that the Church's mission is to hand on transcendental values. So it demands an awareness of being disciples before being teachers, ministers before defenders; channels, in fact, not sources.

If Christ the Teacher said of himself: 'The word you hear is not mine but the Father's who sent me' (John 14, 24), what must be the credentials of those who wish to be his followers and missionaries? We must acquire a concept of orthodoxy different from that current at present. Nowadays it is thought of as a load on the backs of those who accept it, and a whip in the hands of those who exercise it. With us orthodoxy should mean a passion for the truth which Christ reveals and which the Church teaches. It should be a test of our wisdom and humility, of our capacity to welcome and transmit God's highest gifts. It should mean certainty, a certainty based not on the shifting sands of human opinion or on any arbitrary eclecticism, but on the rock of the Divine Word. It should stimulate us to investigation and to action, along paths which do not lose themselves in doubt or error. For us it can never be a pretext for argument. It must mean love for those whom we want to call to Christian salvation.

With orthodoxy goes the mandate.

Orthodoxy concerns the content of the heritage to be handed on; the mandate concerns the capacity to hand that content on. The first is the static, the second the dynamic element of the Church's mission.

The mission of the Church did not start up spontaneously, is not self-organizing. The Church needed to receive an initial command and power, which are then transmitted in definite forms through the sacrament of ordination and by ecclesiastical jurisdiction. Here we shall do no more than remark on this astounding doctrine, observing that no one, of himself, can qualify as an apostle; he must receive the mandate to exercise that sublime function. But the truth is that baptism has given to every Christian the capacity to participate in the divine gifts and in divine worship by that royal priesthood (1 Pet. 2, 9) which is conferred on all the faithful; so that every Christian can and should associate himself with the Church's apostolic action. At the same time, such action must have a discipline; and this demands a precise mandate from those who have themselves received it. They must guide and promote that action, whether it concerns the sanctification and direction of the ecclesiastical body or the faithful individually. This means, in practice, that anyone who would be an apostle must be dependent on the ecclesiastical authority, not break free from it. He must unite himself to it, not detach himself from it; he must offer his services, not demand his freedom; he must feel himself at one not only with the Church's interests but with her visible and actual structure. The apostolate is not a series of free exercises; it is an organized militia, a collaboration. And the more it is imbued with the spirit of community and hierarchy, the closer it will be to those whom the Holy Spirit has made guardians, to feed the Church of the Lord.

What are the specific and immediate purposes of the Church's mission?

Here again we must go back to Christ and recall how he defined his own mission. When Pilate was asking for a definition, Jesus said: 'For this I was born; for this I have come into the world, to bear witness to the truth' (John 18, 37). At another moment of his public life, he said: 'The Son of Man came to seek and to save the lost' (Luke 19, 10). As a boy, in the Temple, when Mary was looking for him, his answer was: 'How is it that you sought me? Did you not know that I must be in my Father's house?' (Luke 2, 49). All this is summed up in our profession of faith, the Nicene Creed: 'For us men and for our salvation, he came down from Heaven, and became incarnate by the action of the Holy Spirit, of the Virgin Mary, and was made man . . . suffered, was buried, and rose again from the dead.'

If the mission of the apostolate, that is of the Church, is the same as Christ's, we must pay the most scrupulous attention to the nature and purpose of Christ's mission as defined above. This is fundamental, both for theology and also for our Catholic conscience today. In modern times, as we all know, Christianity has been the object of very critical and usually destructive analysis. But since it cannot be denied that Christianity is a reality and one that still functions, various attempts have been made to deny its supernatural prerogatives, to challenge its originality and reduce its importance, while at the same time partial aspects of it have been emphasized for particular ends.

All admit that Christ's mission, and therefore that of the Church which is its continuation, is bound up with the idea of salvation, of a change for the better, that is, in man's condition.

But what salvation? What change? And how are these obtained?

We say that the salvation brought by Christ is the Kingdom of God; it is his religion; it is the relationship which he established between the Heavenly Father and humanity, with all the requisite conditions and consequences.

The Christian mission is essentially religious. It is not directly political, social, or economic. It looks at man in the perspective of his ultimate end; it explains and initiates the radical conversion of man to God and, by disposing him to receive that free gift which is at the same time most suitable to his nature, his supernatural elevation to a son of God. Thus it is that a word of divine truth enters human life and asks for acceptance because of the source from which it springs; the lips of God himself. It brings good news, this word. It interprets the world as seen by God, and invites humanity to judge itself and the world around it by this light at once blessed and searching. It is a free and marvellous meeting in the theatre of the world and of time between two utterly unequal wills; the will of God asking for love and the will of man staking his eternal destiny on his own reply. It is redemption effected by Christ, who is both priest and victim, by means of a sacrifice capable of absorbing and annulling all the debts of sinful humanity which it could never pay, and of bringing it to a new and innocent birth. Finally it is a communion of life and power which is handed on from Christ to his followers; it creates a special society called the Church, which prepares the final perfection of living union in Christ and his Mystical Body, beyond the confines of the world and history.

So the Christian mission is not a simple enunciation of a few principles which can then be taken over by human philosophy. Nor is it a vague spiritism for intoxicating the stirrings of conscience or for anaesthetizing its anguish. It is not a lyrical foreseeing of the future, a mysticism endowed with extraordinary forces from the inner regions of our imagination and instincts. It is not naturalist humanism which benefits the temporal order directly. Still less is it a revolution whose object is to bring justice to social disorders and to raise one class against another. But neither is it an apathy content to leave the world as it is, while awaiting a new order to come which is to restore all things.

The Christian mission is quite original. It is also very demanding. But it is easier to live than to define. The Church's mission consists in prolonging Christ's life in the world, and enabling humanity to share in the mysteries of the Incarnation and the Redemption, to establish a communion of life with him; so that humanity may become a community of brothers. The mission of the Church is to generate the Church, to make her live, to make her grow, to make her bear fruit by her own works of faith, by grace and the Gospel. Like a living tree, the Church extends herself, germinates her own branches, brings ripeness to her own fruit. 'I am the vine, you are the branches', says Jesus (John 15, 5).

If we have a right understanding of the nature of the Church's mission, we can draw consequences that are important in forming an attitude to the apostolate. The first is that the primary purpose of the Church's mission is within her. She is, in a sense, an end in herself. She serves no other end but that which is inherent in the affirmation of her own life. No purpose is higher than hers, and none more necessary. On this concept of the Church's mission is founded her independence, both from the State and from other human interests. The Church is free because by her very constitution she is self-sufficient. The Church is herself the Church's purpose. She must work directly for herself, not for a selfish autonomy or to set limits on man's goodness and activities, but because she contains a unique, superior, integral form of life from which the forms of human and temporal life can draw sustenance, not as means to their own service but as the principles from which their true advantage will derive. 'Seek first God's kingdom', the Divine Master teaches (Matt. 6, 33).

This pre-eminence in God's kingdom of evangelization, of the Church's mission, has given rise to lively polemics even among Catholics, polemics which, in recent times, have had their moments of spiritual drama. The attempt to put human and social redemption before moral and religious redemption has brought into the open certain attitudes which are as significant as they are unfortunate. These attitudes do not concern questions of practical method, which may prompt the Church to begin her missionary and pastoral work by exercising her gifts of human love, but questions of principle: the priority of temporal needs over spiritual needs, human means over supernatural means, economic redemption over religious redemption, social reform over moral reform. As you all know, the Church's first aim is to spread the faith, though she may use practical charity as a means to achieve this. But some consider the preaching of a definitive and demanding faith to be secondary, and give priority to the diffusion either of a few moral precepts, for some unknown reason called 'absolute', or of works of philanthropy or culture. Some among us, too, sad to say, have wandered from the right road through anguish of spirit and excess of zeal. This is the sort of thing they say:

'The present conditions of the working class make it very difficult to christianize the workers. We suggest that Christians try two successive phases of action; first give the workers freedom, and only then the Gospel. The first of these two phases has nothing to do with Christian principles. There is only one course open to us, to remain silent for a long time, perhaps for years, and in the meanwhile to play our part, perhaps share completely in the struggles and the latent culture of our working class, the class which we have often unintentionally deceived. We even renounce any intention of converting them. . . .'[1]

Such can never be the Church's mission.

Like every living organism, then, the Church develops from within; but along with this, it belongs to the nature of her mission that she should spread her teaching. This is because she herself is the prolongation, the projection of Christ's mission. She communicates his grace and power. She participates in his priesthood. She is the result of his love. She is the vehicle of the Holy Spirit. She is the executor of God's design. She is the object of Christ's prayer.

The work of salvation conceived by God is unifying and universal. Christ is at the very centre of God's plan of unity, and the Church develops according to this design. Unity has already been given, it already exists in the world, in the one true Church, in the one vicar by legitimate succession of Christ's fullness, the pope. But though the divine plan embraces all humanity, its catholicity and universality is not complete in fact. To bring about this completion God willed to make use of Christ's humanity and of the ministry which derives from him; he has willed to use men both as direct instruments of sacramental power, and as secondary instruments of his jurisdiction, men who are freely supported by others faithful to him. God has willed that mankind should be associated in the work of salvation. 'We are fellow-workers for God,' says St Paul (1 Cor. 3, 9). In this sense one can say that 'God

[1] Montuclard. Cf. Suenens, *L'Église en état de Mission* (English translation, *The Gospel to Every Creature*, Burns Oates, 1956).

needs men'. Unity expands into universality by means of the
apostolate, and through the same apostolate universality flows
together into unity. This is the dynamism of the Church's mission.

What does the Church take with her on her mission? Where is
this mission bound for? Who takes part in it? These are all questions
bearing on our theme, and they bring up as many others. But we
can now see all these questions as a whole, rather like a landscape
seen from a height.

We know now that if the Church is a continuation of Christ,
then her mission is to take Christ with her. She is to generate Christ
in the life of the world. She is the world's mother: its Mother
Church. She incorporates us in Christ. This is a doctrine we have
from St Paul; and it requires a new terminology, 'most of which
can be translated into another language only by an uncouth expression, or by a circumlocution. The Apostle has invented them or
revived them in order to give a graphic expression to the ineffable
union of Christians with Christ.'[1] The phrases 'incorporated into
Christ', 'union with Christ', mean that we are to be born, live,
suffer, die, rise again in Christ and with Christ through the ministry
and mystery of the Church, Christ's Mystical Body; she herself is
in fact 'the fullness of Christ'.[2]

Christ has spoken. He is the Word of God made flesh. Christ
is the master. The Church is to utter, to repeat his very words.
The Church is to teach, guard, interpret and spread God's
doctrine. Her mission is to be a school, her missionaries are to be the
catechists, the teachers, the preachers, the doctors, the bishops, the
pope.

Christ has dwelt among men. He has become the prototype, the
model, the example of the art of living. The imitation of Christ is
to be the pattern of the new ethic, the structure of restored human
virtues, the ladder of asceticism and heroism.

Christ ended his temporal life by the sacrifice of the cross, and
he redeemed the world by his passion and resurrection; he is therefore a priest. His priesthood is to be communicated to the Church
which is to prolong it until the end of history. The sacramental life
of the Church constitutes her vital mission; this is the treasure she
carries with her, which she continually renews and dispenses as
widely as she can.

[1] Prat, *Theology of St Paul*, London, 1942, p. 14.
[2] *Ibid.*, pp. 242–3.

To whom does she dispense it? To her children. And where does she find her children? In the world. And so the Church comes into contact, into converse with the world. If we look closely, we shall find that the aspect of our theme which most interests us is here: the object of the Church's mission, the field of the apostolate.

So now our theme becomes up to date. We can try it out for ourselves, make it our own. It becomes a drama; the Church's meeting with the contemporary world is a drama as fascinating and complex as it is mysterious and yet real. It is the true drama of history. Our picture broadens; in the trenches of humanity, powers of heaven and hell are locked in a transcendental battle (Eph. 6, 12) which providence will eventually bring to its final phase. Now the apostolate becomes a militia. It becomes an art. It acquires methods and theories. It gathers equipment, becomes practical. Now its participants range from those who enter into it little by little to those who hold official positions and responsibility. Now it takes on a hundred different forms; from the spiritual—prayer and reparation—to the subtlest and most imponderable—a good word, a good example. These forms can be classified by their varying efficacy; in terms of presence, testimony, action. They can be studied against the particular background in which the Church's mission is to develop: according to sex, age, social condition, capacity to receive or reject the Christian message, whether hostile, refractory, difficult, docile, or frank. And much more.

The apostolate and the contemporary world

Pope Pius XII, at the audience granted on 14 October 1951 to the First World Congress of the Lay Apostolate, gave an admirable summary of this aspect of the Church's mission. He said:

'As far as the Church is concerned, she has, towards all, *a threefold mission to fulfil*; to raise up the fervent believers to the level of the needs of the present day; to introduce those who hesitate on the threshold into the warm and salutary intimacy of the hearth; to lead back those who have separated themselves from religion, and whom she cannot, for all that, abandon to their miserable fate.'[1]

Here I will limit myself to a few simple observations intended to stimulate, rather than to satisfy, interest in this aspect of our theme:

[1] English version in *Pius XII speaks on the Lay Apostolate*, Rome, 1956, p. 10.

the relationship between the Church's mission and the contemporary world.

This aspect directly concerns the apostolate of the laity, because they live in that world to which the Church is sent. The laity have more experience of the world than the clergy, and they are the closest witnesses of its contact with the Church. They live in it and see what happens in it. This is where collaboration between the laity and the hierarchy begins. The laity study the world around them and present their findings to the Church. The study of religious statistics and sociology, carried out under the guidance of expert ecclesiastics, can be extremely helpful, and is already beginning to produce useful information for the pastoral ministry. Studies by the laity of their environment, giving psychological diagnoses and accurate reflections of local conditions, investigations into existing laws, modern theories on pedagogy, public relations, all this can be an invaluable help to those responsible for guiding the Church's mission.

Contact between the Church's mission and the world is a constant problem. This is because the world, particularly now, is going through a phase of rapid and far-reaching evolution, and because the application and enunciation of the Christian message can vary in form according to the times. But it is for the government of the Church to decide when the times are ripe for particular reforms. This is a rule which the laity in particular need to bear in mind. For they are apt to be impressed by direct experience and to be less aware of the general norms which govern the Church's life. Their very fervour often makes them impatient for the introduction of arbitrary changes or the hastening of reforms in ecclesiastical law and custom, without the necessary authority, the over-all vision, or the help of the Holy Spirit for such innovations. If in the actual experience of the apostolate, innovations suggest themselves as useful and entirely suitable, experiments in such matters must always be carried out with the help and approval of the ecclesiastical authority. Nor is this a negative rule; it is the secret of Catholic strength. As St Ignatius of Antioch wrote: 'Let no-one act in matters regarding the Church without the bishop.'[1]

For the rest, we must have confidence; Rome is under way, with the pope at the helm.

The distinction between the sacred and the profane should be

[1] *Ad. Smyr.*, VIII.

studied with particular care. It is a problem which readily lends itself to serious and harmful misunderstandings and can easily give rise to wrong solutions. Obviously a complete separation between the sacred and the profane would paralyse or altogether neutralize the Church's mission. Modern secularists recognize this; they profess an apparent respect for the sacred, but in order to exclude it from real life. And confusion between the sacred and the profane with regard to their respective interests and conduct will lead to the denial of the transcendent character of religion and the purity of the Christian message. The Church's mission is to carry the sacred into a relationship with the profane in such a way that the sacred is communicated without being contaminated, and the profane is sanctified without being falsified. This is the continuation of the mystery of the Incarnation, of God made man. It is easy enough to say this, but difficult to achieve. Here too the governing body of the Church must help us to act clearly. The studies in Christian humanism now being made by Catholic philosophers and scholars can make a real contribution [here both to our thinking and our action. It is an essentially delicate problem, complex and fluid; it should be studied with competence and care.

There is another question which I also leave unsolved but which it is useful to mention here. As apostolic action, particularly of the laity, gradually spreads outwards from the inner life of the Church and the purely religious order into the temporal and earthly order, it is apt to lose its power of representing the Church and of exercising her direct mission. The activity of the lay apostolate becomes gradually more remote from its central point of departure and responsibility. Religious action then turns into action that can be social, economic, artistic, political, private, and so on. At a certain point it ceases to represent the Church's mission in any true sense. It becomes, as we might say, non-confessional. This change in scale is also something that ecclesiastical authority must examine and determine. It should always be remembered that religious and moral principles are to be applied in every field, even in matters purely temporal. A Catholic can never leave the law of God out of consideration, no matter how secular his activity may be. He must always, and in all his activities, preserve an apostolic spirit, and at the very least reflect the Christian faith by his manner of life.

The Christian witness: love

The first duty of the apostolate, for laymen in particular, is to show the world a Christianity that can be admired and loved.

We do so firstly by our own unity and mutual love, by an inner cohesion that makes us cordial and sociable. 'Love one another,' the Master teaches us, 'even as I have loved you, that you also love one another. By this all men will know that you are my disciples, if you have love for one another' (John 13, 34–35). The first Christian apologetic is to be found in what Tertullian puts on record about the primitive Christian community: 'See how these Christians love each other, people say.'[1]

Secondly, we show this by loving those whom we want to evangelize. That is our main instrument of policy, as it were, in the apostolate. Yet it is one we should use not in our own interests but in those of others. Its aim is not to conquer but to serve. It is intransigent to error, not in order to condemn but to redeem.

This raises another great practical problem. Apostolic love entails a close contact with the world to be converted, and this can be full of dangers. St Paul authorizes us to become Jews with the Jews and weak with the weak. 'I have become all things to all men, that I might by all means save some' (1 Cor. 9, 23). How far is apostolic relativism to go? How far our intransigence? How tolerant should Catholics be? Such questions will he answer who guides the Church; and the matter is an extremely delicate one. We must be careful that our attitude of love and respect towards non-Catholics does not degenerate into indifferentism, ecleticism, or complicity and so to defection. These are the dangers for those who immerse themselves in the ideas of others, or who frequent pagan society or put on the world's clothes to draw closer to it, who exchange their priest's cassock for a workman's overall. Some may become so tolerant with dissidents that they find themselves justifying these dissidents' position, or may pay so much attention to those away from the Church that they offend those in it, and when they say 'open wide the house' it is rather to leave it themselves than to invite strangers to enter. We must be watchful, I say. But we must never forget that the fundamental attitude of Catholics who want to convert the world is that of love. This is the genius of the apostolate, to know how to love.

[1] *Ap.*, 39.

Here in Rome, centre of the Catholic apostolate, let us make this Christian precept both our goal and our programme. Let us love those near by and those afar; love our own country and those of others; love our friends and our enemies; love Catholics, schismatics, Protestants, Anglicans, the indifferent; love Moslems, pagans, atheists; love members of all social classes, particularly those most in need of help and support; love children; love the old, the poor, and the sick; love those who deride or despise us, obstruct or persecute us; love those who deserve love and those who do not; love our adversaries—we want no man as our enemy; love our own times, our modern civilization, techniques, art, sport, our world. Let us love it and try to understand, appreciate, esteem, serve it, and suffer for it. Let us love with the heart of Christ. 'Come to me, all . . .' (Matt. 11, 28). Let us love with the breadth of God. 'God so loved the world . . .' (John 3, 16).

Is it expecting too much to say, 'Let us love our world'? Has enthusiasm run away with us, made us presumptuous and over-emphatic? Have we forgotten humility? No, humility is still with us, and so is our sense of reality. But the Church's mission opens up these vast horizons. To raise our eyes to heaven is not pride or folly. It is hope; and prayer. Yet already the Kingdom of God is potentially with us. It is within our view. Listen to the voice of Christ: 'I tell you, lift up your eyes and see how the fields are already white for harvest' (John 4, 35).

When I look around I see you, my brothers, my sons, my dear friends, come from the four corners of the earth; come to Rome in unity and ready to spread over the world in universality. So do not ask me now who is to carry out the Church's mission. The apostles are to do so, as we all know. Yes, we all know that it is you, the laity, Catholics from all countries, who are called upon to assume that mission; as collaborators, yes, but in a mission that is your very own.

4

THE CHURCH'S LOVE FOR THOSE ESTRANGED FROM HER[1]

JESUS CHRIST, light of the world, arose in the midst of human history and became its pivot. He divides history into two great parts, the Old Testament and the New. He gives a unifying and transcendental meaning to the contrasting events of civilization. The fate of civilizations and, more directly, of every individual human being, is influenced by him. He reveals himself as Teacher, Saviour, Father, Judge, Archetype, Leader of humanity. The whole doctrine of St Paul, first apostle to the Gentiles (that is, those outside the chosen people), first to explain Christ's significance in theological terms, can be summed up in his twofold affirmation of our Lord Jesus Christ's sufficiency and his necessity.

So Christianity, from its very birth, proclaims itself as universal and until this universality is an established fact we have a set plan of action—the apostolate—and an organization—the hierarchy—working to draw the Church closer to human beings of all times and all places, to attract and instruct and link them into a vast, new, sovereign, visible but also supernatural society.

There is no limit set to this programme, but there is no longer any option about it. However little it is realized, it always represents the world's highest destiny. It is a programme quite unlike any other. It profits from the unifying processes that emerge from time to time in secular history; it arouses these processes, it encourages and enlarges them, stimulating in humanity its desire for peace, unity, and universality. When they reveal their limitations it looks beyond them, if need be condemns their limitations—if, for instance, some anti-human principle is at work as in tyranny, imperialism, self-centred capitalism, communism or any other fallacious system of fraternity. It is ever active, its driving-force an

[1] From *Discourses to the Eighth National Week of Pastoral Renewal*, September 1958.

implacable sense of responsibility urging on that portion of humanity which is already part of Christ's Church. This sense of responsibility lends a superhuman boldness to feeble human hearts, fills them with heroic energy, fires them with conquering missionary plans, makes them capable of incredible sacrifices, of magnanimous hopes that are never disappointed. From Christ's redemption the Church's universal programme draws the charge of love necessary if she is to become in reality what she already is in name and origin: the Catholic Church.

The beauty, majesty, and dramatic power of this word 'Catholic' should fill anyone who has a sense and vision of human grandeur with admiration and respect. The very word should show the folly of those secularists who endeavour to ignore it and banish it from our living language. Today many young people, scholars, idealists, are trying to turn the word into reality among the seductive expressions of a threatening materialistic universalism. Nor should would-be reformers in material or spiritual fields ever consider that the word 'Catholic' is in any way different or detached from the word 'Christian', whence the word 'Catholic' draws its reason for existence. For us, whose fortune and responsibility it is to use the word as an attribute and definition of ourselves, it should always be a living spark in our religious and human conscience, always alight, urging us to forge links of faith and charity with others.

A Catholic should regard all men as belonging to him. That is the argument. But since in fact there are people outside the Church (How many they are! How their numbers increase! How they oppose us!)—the subject poses colossal problems.

To get a brief general idea of the question, we can group it into three parts: the first, the basis, is the Church's love for those outside her, which is why she must interest herself in them and engage in this unwearying mission of hers.

The second covers the means and methods of the apostolate, the various manners in which the Christian message has been presented from the time it was first handed on by men to other men—i.e. by a definite ministry, acting in society, with which Christ willed his Gospel to be linked. This Gospel is not a simple doctrine that is self-diffusing, not a book which is sufficient unto itself. It is a religion, needing a human vehicle, and realized through a visible organization. And here arise innumerable questions about the means

and channels of communication between the source and those who
are separated from it.

The third part deals with the actual ones who are estranged from
the Church. These are split into individual cases so varied and
complex that they call for the examination of entire civilizations,
as well as analysis of the most intimate and fleeting movements of
each human heart.

Let us now dwell briefly on our first division, the 'terminus a quo'
of this wonderful and mysterious drama, which is concerned not
with the conquest of men but with calling them to the Gospel, to
their salvation.

We do not intend to deal with the doctrinal aspect of our subject,
such as the revelation of God's mercy or the scope of ascetic penance,
the basic theories of missionary evangelism, the relationship between
truth and love, the presentation of dogma through preaching, and
so on.

We will limit ourselves to a review of the present-day conditions
in which the Church must exercise her charity by holding out to
those separated from her the benefits of her Word and her charisms.

Seen as part of the Church's great apostolic plan, one might say
that this practical concern is now very active, and held in high
esteem. Indeed, there is much to admire in the Church's present
efforts at evangelism. This apostolic vitality is proof of her perennial
youth and of the support of the Holy Spirit. No religion is as aware
of its universality as the Catholic; and never before has this awareness released such apostolic energies as in the present age. Yes, this
age, characterized by indifference and enmity to all religion, by
apostasy even amid nations that were once part of Christendom
and gloried in their faith, is characterized also by an apostolic reawakening within the Church. Only two complementary aspects of
this reawakening need be mentioned here: missionary work, which
has assumed world-wide proportions, though it is still quite inadequate to the vast fields to be covered, and oppressed and
obstructed in many areas where it has shown signs of development;
and the organization of the Catholic laity, particularly in Catholic
Action, which has come to collaborate with and complement the
hierarchy in its religious and civic mission, and has extended its
apostolic range.

To these great movements of apostolic love in the Church today we should add a glancing reference to others; the diffusion of Catholic thought by many and varied means such as science, apologetics, doctrine, literature, the press, art, and the like, and through our universities and schools, our books, newspapers, magazines, and theatres. Catholic thought is not dormant, is not buried in the codes of the past, has not lost its capacity to engage in lively discussion with the culture of the day. Volumes of papal pronouncements are there to show the Holy See in frequent, enlightening, almost daily contact with the authoritative representatives of modern science and contemporary life.

Another sign of the Church's eagerness to let others share the benefits of her faith and culture is the development of her social teaching. This is humane, receptive, aware of the necessary and proper changes in social structure inevitably brought about by modern progress. Thus the new systems coming into being can find the paths to justice and human goodness already laid. This could avoid much confusion and harm to the working classes and to the economic and social order for which these systems are mainly conceived.

The adaptability of the Church

There is another aspect to be remembered, broader, more complex, but no less significant of the Church's concern to smooth the ways towards her fold for those separated from her. This is her spirit of adaptability to the thought, customs, currents, idioms of our time, a time when men are absorbed in the processes of quick and complicated social evolution, and demanding in regard to their individual tastes and personalities. This adaptability of the Church, which is part of her catholicity, reveals almost day by day new attitudes towards the admission, absorption, purification, even sanctification, of varied forms of human life. Here for example is Pope Pius XII on ways of teaching the immutable truths of Catholic doctrine. He was speaking to the General Congregation of the Jesuits, whose sodalities, he said:

' while venerating above all the truths of faith, should also acquire as perfect a technique as possible in diffusing them. They should follow the latest developments of these techniques, however difficult, convinced that in this they give glory to God and edification to the Church. They should be in contact with men

of their time by a spoken and written word that can be clearly
and easily understood. It follows that in choice of subjects and
arguments, as well as in manner of treatment, they should tactfully adapt themselves to the temper and tendencies of their own
century.'[1]

In the encyclical *Humani generis* (which also sets necessary barriers
to the spread of theories subversive to Christian dogma), we find
advice for the encouragement of positive studies, both in the fields
of scripture and of science.[2]

We might also mention the boundless possibilities Pius XII
opened up for discussion between dissident Christians and Catholics
with the aim of favouring the return of the former to the unity of
the Church.[3]

Another straw in the wind is the incipient use of the vernacular
in the liturgy. A good deal might also be said about official contacts
between the Holy See and non-Catholic countries; and about the
appeal, often repeated by recent popes, to all those who believe in
God—of whatever religion they may be—to oppose by mutual
agreement the onslaught of atheism; about the Holy Father's warm
greetings, in his audiences, to people of all classes and professions;
and much else.

This is not the moment to go into the outcome of these and
similar gestures by the Church towards those separated from her.
Others can tell you of these. Here I want simply to call your
attention to the Church's proven desire to help the world accept
the Gospel. She is the first to remove obstacles, to smooth the
way. She is ready to discuss. She awaits, vigilant and maternal,
to dispense as widely as possible the salvation which she holds.
She maintains no closed and impenetrable positions, breathes no
threats or anathemas, shows no indifference to those who neither
understand nor want her. She is ruled by the law of apostolic love.

But we should draw attention to one fundamental point which
distinguishes the Catholic Church from all forms of ecumenism that
are flexible in matters of faith and contrary to the Church's
unifying and hierarchic constitution. The Church, in order to come
to an agreement with sects of dissident Christians, cannot deny or

[1] *A.A.S.*, 1946, p. 384.
[2] *A.A.S.*, 1950, pp. 575 ff., English translation, C.T.S., pp. 21 ff.
[3] *A.A.S.*, 1948, p. 257; 1950, p. 142 ff.

minimize the truth whose inviolable deposit she is charged to guard and spread. She cannot betray the faith. She cannot trifle with any equivocation, reticences, and ambiguities which would radically deny her mission of loyalty to divine revelation and of testimony to divine light. Without betraying Christ and denying herself she cannot be content with vague formulas and eclectisms. So, too, she is bound to denounce errors which, both within and outside her orbit, may draw people's minds away from the path of religious truth—that truth, which, projected over human thought and life, can illuminate even dubious philosophies and set irrefutable canons for an accurate conception of human life.

We moderns, used to the prevalent confusions in philosophy and to the tolerant contradictions of our social life, may find it difficult to appreciate the firmness of the Church in matters of dogma. But we must remember that this is the law of her life, and for the world to which she offers her mission it is the law of salvation. Truth is salvation. Truth is good. Truth is being, is life, is God. So truth is the gift which the Church makes to the world. That is her way of love; the highest way and the most indispensable.

The necessity for skill in pastoral work

When the Church affirms a truth it is an act of love. If men reject her because of that affirmation, she cannot silence or attenuate or deform the truth. '*Est, est: non, non.*' Rather than that she teaches by her blood what she has been unable to teach by her words. Her love can then take the form of suffering opposition, hatred, division, persecution, martyrdom. This is the drama, and often the tragedy, of the Word made flesh, '*his own received him not*'. The necessity for orthodoxy means that some will reject it and seem to be precluded from access to Christ's fold.

But many paths weave around that sheepfold, and the good shepherd is not content to remain inside it. When he sees that a sheep is lost, he takes to these paths and goes in search of it. Orthodoxy does not satisfy his spirit unless it is shared by all. Orthodoxy must of necessity mean separation from and reproval of those who do not accept it, but it does not authorize the abandonment of those who have themselves abandoned it. Orthodoxy does not justify inertia, create self-sufficiency and pride, abolish the pain of separation, or the anxiety of waiting and searching. Pastoral love is not limited to the confines of orthodoxy.

And so from the apostolic plane we come to the pastoral one, which we want to study here.

We can, I think, describe in one word the Church's duty to those away from her: approach. This simple word holds many pastoral implications. The initiative is always one of love and prayer. And, when no other approach is possible, we must always gladly watch and endure.

This supposes a basic attitude of the spirit on our part, a constant looking beyond our own fold. It means knowing those outside it. Italy, for instance, is still usually called a Catholic country because the great majority of its inhabitants are still lucky enough to be baptized. But we do not realize how few Italians conform in their personal lives to the dignity and moral obligations brought to them by baptism. Many Italian parish priests, particularly in the cities, are resigned to ministering only to those who frequent their particular church; and this often satisfies their pastoral zeal. But what about people who never go near a church? How many of those are there? We still lack a reliable and uniform system of religious statistics. Our study of religious and pastoral sociology is rudimentary. Yet we must recognize that the greater part of our so-called faithful are actually not faithful at all; that the number of those not practising far exceeds those who do practise, and that in many areas there is a gradual restriction of the range of pastoral work.

Pastoral awareness

Love is always looking beyond itself, counting empty places in the home, thinking of children no longer there, of children not yet born. This attitude is characteristic of the good shepherd; he thinks of those afar, counts them, looks for them, finds them, identifies them, wants to know them.

So the pastor finds growing in him a particular attitude towards those outside the Church. Others may think of them as strangers. But he still regards them as his own. It depends on them, not on the pastor, whether they are strangers or enemies. But he will always try to behave towards them with a dignity that is clearly consonant with his ideas and way of life. In dealing with them he will have an inner sense of freedom and strength: he will use language that is frank and sincere, and at times heartfelt and firm. Moral weakness has never served the cause of Christ nor brought about real conversions. But the pastor will also take great care never to offend,

never to fail in the respect owed to every human being. This respect
we Christians owe to the freedom of the human personality. We
pastors must strive to maintain it towards those whom we must
always consider as possible members of the family circle, possible
future children and friends. This may be a vain hope, an unjustified
and ingenuous optimism, on which we should keep a careful watch,
lest it become weakness and connivance or turn into crass insensi-
bility; people may play upon it and ridicule it, for these adversaries
of ours can get up to some very mean tricks. But respect is an indispensable attitude if we are to be able to pray for them, wait for
them, talk to them. The clergy, when dealing with those outside
the Church, must avoid polemics that are bitter and long-drawn-
out, unless justified by serious provocation. An acid or aggressive
tone in preaching is both inopportune and unproductive, particularly if repeated and not accompanied by arguments designed to
convince rather than wound. How carefully studied should be our
preaching in reference to those outside the Church! Whatever we
say should be said with evident and sincere good-will. Given that,
we may reprove if need be, even accuse and shout aloud (those
'Woe to thee' in the Gospel came from Christ's lips also). But, above
all, given that, we can sorrow for them, call to them, invite them.

This brings us to one of the most important and delicate aspects
of our subject. The use of authority, and particularly its manner of
exercise, seems a factor that greatly affects people today. Authority
attracts if expressed in a kindly, polite, and considerate manner. It
repels if it is at all exigent, hectoring, or rude. Lack of courtesy and
moderation is, alas, one of the most frequent and pernicious causes
for estrangement of the faithful from their pastors; it also shows
little understanding of the effects of modern education, which no
longer tolerates abuses of authority, rough treatment, disrespect, or
bad manners. It shows serious failure to remember that the Church's
authority is paternal, based on service and love.

Love, not criticism

There is another aspect of interest in connection with respect to
those outside the Church: those who search out and denounce with
penetrating and often bitter irony the defects of brethren in faith,
of other Catholics (in particular deriding those whose zeal in dubious
devotions makes their defects the more obvious), are the very ones
who insist with generosity and sympathy on the many virtuous and

praiseworthy attributes of those outside the fold. They criticize their neighbours and recognize the merits and talents of those at a distance from them.

It should be said at once that this transposition of moral judgment, which finds evil in the so-called good and good in the so-called evil, actually originates in the Gospel, where the Pharisees are set below the publicans and sinners. So there is a Christian axiom behind it, and one which we should follow humbly; it can give sincerity and inward value to virtue and prevent its dispersal in conventional forms whose human content and divine grace are both slight. We should also follow it humbly lest we lose our esteem for and trust in any human being, all of whom are capable of inner regeneration and open to divine mercy.

But this evangelic process presupposes divine sanction; and even where moral analysis makes it our plain duty to pursue this process, it must never become a method, never authorize us to insult our brethren in order to exalt our enemies. To condemn good people on hasty presumptions as a way of glossing over blameworthy thought and actions only impairs the moral order which we are trying to re-establish.

It is uncertain, too, if the Catholics criticized on these grounds really are pharisaical, and if the others, treated with such generous indulgence, really do have the same repentance for their sins as those mentioned in the Gospel. This is a widespread modern habit of mind. It has had great success in literature (Dostoyevsky, Mauriac) and given credit to many eminent and admirable preachers. But its followers include some who, in their efforts to draw closer to those estranged from the Church, seem bent on rejecting their own brethren.

The moral austerity of such critics deserves respect. But I have doubts about the worth of their method when it becomes habitual— I wonder if it may not lack humility and charity; if it may not engender disquiet, hinder unity, and present a bitter, one-sided view of Christianity. Carried to extremes, such a method could eventually destroy any sense of brotherly love and insinuate instead a taste for dangerous and dubious friendships. Those who grow intolerant at living under the Church's paternal roof lose their capacity to invite anyone in, and expose themselves to the danger of leaving the Church through drawing upon themselves the disapproval of their brethren.

Pastoral action

What, then, should be the effect of pastoral love? It will alter and give a new shape to the pastor's own interior life. But that is not enough. Love cannot mean only a change of mental attitude, or mere inward emotion. It must pass over into action.

We have said, and we repeat, that the true pastor, that is the seeker of estranged souls, must never forget, much less minimize, the jealously guarded and vital inheritance of truth in his keeping, which it is his duty to bring to those outside the Church. We may add that he must preserve intact not only that truth but his own moral principles too; this is obvious. But we would go on to say that he should never falsify the authenticity and purity of his priestly character. It is true that in order to draw closer to others he must make himself like them, '*gaudere cum gaudentibus, flere cum flentibus*', 'rejoice with those who rejoice, and mourn with the mourner' (Rom. 12, 15). But that must in no way prejudice either his interior life or his outward behaviour as a minister of Christ. Those who try to camouflage themselves by taking on the forms of the world in which they intend to exercise their ministry weaken their own moral force, and expose themselves to the danger of being influenced by others rather than influencing others themselves. Sometimes they may even arouse suspicions of their own virtue and sincerity. The worker-priest movement was an example of the priest's excessive assimilation to his secular surroundings; though the worker-priest first went in under the impulse of apostolic love, in the end they became not only a physical prison to him but very often a spiritual one as well.

A more usual example is the priest who becomes inveigled by the charm and ease of the social world in which he is called upon to act, and is eventually enslaved by it, thereby losing both his independence and his spiritual efficacy. A case of this sort is difficult to analyse. It usually involves a question not of principle but of discipline, often only of behaviour. Doctrine does not come into the question, only a particular method devised by a pastor, guided by his own apostolic instinct. He has followed and applied laws of human psychology and not of theology. He wants to learn the ways of the world, not so as to remain in the world, but in order to find by what paths he can return to the fold together with the souls he has met outside. Such a course is certainly full of dangers. But we must not make the way too impenetrable or difficult for our confrères who are feeling their way along these unexplored paths: venturing on to the fields of culture, for example, or the press, film-criticism, art, sport, or aid for workers, servicemen, emigrants, prisoners, etc., when they are authorized by a superior and guided by love and prudence.

Perhaps too often in the past there has been an outcry whenever some venturesome pastor has tried out a new method which calls for courage. To take risks is part of a pastor's duties. And if we do not want pastoral work and methods to be static, we must take the large view of zealous pastoral endeavours and help and direct them until we have sufficient evidence whether or not the methods are valid. The really important thing for us priests is to foster in ourselves a spirit of love towards souls estranged from the Church. This is not easy, particularly in a period like ours of such deep-rooted aversion to religion and the Church. It is not easy, when our every gesture of goodwill is at once interpreted as a sign of weakness or even of complicity. It is not easy, when the striking proofs of the Church's bountiful and humane generosity, such as those given during the terrible years of the last war to so many people in such varied categories outside the fold, are now all ignored.

No, it is not easy when so many of our attempts at approach have borne so little positive fruit, though we have made wide concessions to the modern spirit of liberty, tolerance, and democracy. It is not easy, when overtures are made to us which are dangerous, as they might advance the errors of others more than they do our own principles.

But we must go on showing love. Here in Italy we must avoid adding fuel to the fire of anti-clericalism, which so many are apt to treat as if it were an integral part of this country's historical dialectic. But Catholics in Italy, now the Roman question is solved, are not hostile to our own country in any way at all. We nurture no secret temporalist or theocratic aims, but want only to be loyal servants of our country, of its institutions, and of our fellow citizens.

Nor must we ever submit in silence to calumnious assertions that because the Church has condemned Communist atheism, as was her duty, she is an enemy of the working-classes and supports any regime whose laws and social organization aim to prevent the bettering of these classes. What we must do is, coherently and with vigour, put into practice Christian social doctrine and the popes' repeated directives about it. On this very important matter we must show that the Church, after proving her firmness and courage in defence of truth, gives even greater proofs of her inexhaustible love. '*Veritatem facientes in caritate*', 'Speaking the truth in love', as St Paul teaches us (Eph. 4, 15). Pastoral love and the defence of doctrine must fuse into one.

Yes, we must go on showing love. And perhaps the main fruit of our discussions here will not be to reach decisions about programmes or any great practical results, but to foster our pastoral and priestly spirit of love for souls estranged from the Church. The gain will not be slight if we become more faithful disciples of the Master who came not to 'call the righteous, but sinners to repentance' (Luke 5, 32). He who warns us that 'those who are well have no need of a physician, but those who are sick' (Luke 5, 31) and that there is no merit in loving only those who love us (cf. Luke 6, 32). He reproved his apostles when, indignant because the Samaritans had refused their tired Master hospitality, they wanted to call down the fires of heaven on that village. 'He turned and rebuked them' (cf. Luke 9, 55). When the apostle Peter asked, 'How often am I to forgive my brother if he goes on wronging me? As many as seven times?' Jesus replied, 'I do not say to you seven times but seventy times seven' (Matt. 18, 22). So it is both consoling and helpful to recall that Our Lord 'gave us the ministry of reconciliation' (2 Cor. 5, 18), and that it is the mission of the priesthood to be called to 'feel for others', to share misfortune. '*Condolere eis qui ignorant et errant, quoniam et ipse circumdatus est infirmitate*', 'he can deal gently with the ignorant and wayward, since he himself is beset by weakness' (Heb. 5, 2).

Yes, that would be a great gain, venerated brethren. We shall have learnt to understand better the meaning of our own mission. We shall have learnt to turn our devotion to the heart of Christ into a source of pastoral strength: and to prefer, above all, two other ways of helping our brethren estranged from the Church, which are rooted in the Church's love and in our own souls: to present the authentic religion of Christ, and to make a personal approach with diligence, zeal, and patience.

5

WHAT THE CHURCH IS AND WHAT SHE IS NOT[1]

A POPULAR current conception is that the Church is inconsistent, belligerent, and vague. Like Christ she is a target for contradictory opinions: '*signum cui contradicetur*', 'A sign that is spoken against' (Luke 2, 34). She is an enigma. A strange thing this: that the Church, who should be (and in fact is) the '*signum elevatum in nationes*,' 'an ensign raised for the nations' (cf. Isaiah 11, 12) the lamp raised amid the peoples to show them the place of salvation, she who is defined as 'the pillar and bulwark of the truth' (1 Tim. 3, 15), she who by her four marks demonstrates the authenticity of the Catholic religion, should herself be an obstacle to faith, a scandal to the religious world of our day wherever there is a sincere if somewhat superficial grasp of spiritual values. Why this difficulty, this ambiguity?

Before answering, let us glance at the most common ideas current about the Church, which present her as she is not.

As she is not; in her essence, her function, and her final purpose, by which I mean in her profound and in great part invisible reality. For there are certain less estimable aspects which are, alas, none the less realities too, or at least give the appearance of being so, though they do not comprise her true and complete reality.

St Paul, reading Christ's thoughts, describes the Church, in an image of sovereign beauty, as humanity transfigured 'in splendour, without spot or wrinkle or any such thing, that she might be holy and without blemish' (Eph. 5, 27), worthy of Christ's love.

Where, an observer not initiated in the Church's deep truth might ask, is this beauty, this splendour of the Church, which the facts of history do not confirm?

The people of Florence, for instance, can recall from their literature stories in which certain types of religious, infamous still, are

[1] From *Introductory Speech to the Mission of Florence*, 1960.

lashed with bitter jest and invective; we need remember only the satire of the great Dante. For the commonest stains on the Church's splendour and regality are due to many of the very men who are part of her and sometimes, alas, are even her representatives.

A common theme in the literature of the last century was the priest who lacked the requisite qualifications for his mission; one who, perhaps without failing in his vocation through his own neglect, yet fulfilled it so badly that he brought it into ridicule, which is one of the wounds most difficult to heal.

Modern literature tends entirely to reverse this, and to present priest or faithful as a perfect member of the Church, as the ideal; so that, once again, it shows the reality to be less than the ideal and unwittingly creates a lack of confidence in the member of the Church as he actually is: he proves to be a disappointment, lacking in the very qualities he ought to possess: an inner life, magnanimity, heroism, humility, disinterest, love. And also when the modern writer or artist does bring out some particular merit in these characters of his he seems to hint that this is not actually a religious quality and is not characteristic of Catholic or, as he calls it, 'clerical' life.

Literature and the theatre apart, an 'anti-clerical' attitude towards persons and institutions connected with the Church is so widespread (in a country officially Catholic like Italy) that it is hardening into general prejudice.

The great and tragic events of two wars shook this prejudice, but there were areas in which it was at once strengthened and re-affirmed. So we still find our public life impregnated with an instinctive distrust of the Church, with a collective and sometimes even official attitude towards her of mere human politeness. Around us we find an antipathy for all that is religious and ecclesiastical; or at best an indulgence due more to good manners than to balanced and friendly recognition of any right or merit in the Church, of anything to be esteemed or trusted.

I am not saying that the churchmen and the things of the Church are blameless; in fact I myself feel tempted to deplore the failings, blameworthy or not, of the ecclesiastical world.

This disproportion between the Church as she appears in her human guise, and as she should be, is a constant and deep sorrow for anyone who loves the Church and holds any position of responsibility in it. I am often worried by the thought that it is we churchmen who sometimes offer the pretext and reason for aversion to the Church and to religion among, maybe, the ill-educated, who are apt to make summary judgments about spiritual values from the way in which such values are personified in the clergy.

Sometimes this aversion is also to be found in the educated, among people who instinctively expect to find religious ideals truly and worthily represented in men and circumstances normally called religious. Such people are often scandalized when faced with a reality wretchedly inferior to the Christian ideal.

Here I feel it my duty to apologize to all those who have been scandalized and are unbelieving, those far from God and from Christ and hostile to the Church, because we have not shown ourselves worthy of the ideal that marks us out as men of the Church, have not deserved their esteem and trust.

Perhaps I myself may have become a barrier instead of a channel for the truth of the faith, a dirty mirror instead of one which reflects Christian virtues.

Mea culpa!

Contemporary thinkers have noted as a general fact that one of the causes of modern apostasy is a deep resentment against a Christian world which falls short of its own principles, resentment 'not only against the Christian world but—and here is the tragedy— against Christianity itself' (cf. Maritain, Berdayev, etc.). As a priest the Church has made me keeper of her treasury of truth and minister of her power and grace. I must reflect on this responsibility humbly and seriously and should not be ashamed to ask pardon from my contemporaries if I fail to give them a bright and living image of the Church as she truly is, of her truth, and some proof of her power and her grace.

But I in my turn say to my contemporaries that they themselves, by assuming this critical and hostile attitude of theirs, are not being as intelligent as they claim to be. For very often those who are scandalized are just not being intelligent. The time-honoured reply to the formidable and recurring objections against the Church which we have mentioned is still valid and worthy of intelligent attention; that we must be careful to distinguish the person from the office he exercises, the minister from his ministry.

It is not so difficult to distinguish a man from his function, and we all have to do so constantly in any advanced form of organized social life. It is more difficult to apply this distinction in the religious field because whoever preaches sanctity should be a saint, and whoever preaches Christ should be truly Christian by an inner compulsion of loyalty and integrity and also of action. The distinction is not improper and conforms to the essential divine economy of Christianity. We might recall St Augustine's great polemic about this and all the controversies which followed on his teaching. The validity of supernatural gifts in the Church does not depend on the person who dispenses them, but on Christ alone. This is a distinction which is especially suited to the intellectual maturity of our day. People today are aware of the grandeur of religion, a grandeur that is permanent, both when it suffers humiliation and when it demands humility from those who would have contact with it.

But that is not the only cloud across the face of the sun. There are many others which obscure the reality of the Church and show her as she is not.

We must make brief mention of these.

One main cause of antipathy towards the Church in the mind of the modern man is revealed when he accuses her of being out-of-date, an institution belonging to the past. She has had her day, he says. And she is also appallingly conservative. Her scrupulous loyalty to the past certainly binds her with fetters heavy enough for her own members, but heavier still for those who are attracted to her.

Tradition has almost no meaning in a period born from revolutions, a period which has repudiated as useless the past and its heritage. Modern man looks to the present and the future, he says, not to the past, as the Church does, and is bound to do; the continuance of such an institution in our time is obscurantism, immobilism. The modern mind is constrained to declare flatly that positive and natural sciences, technical and industrial developments, the anti-religious upsurge of contemporary social and political movements, the overshadowing of speculative thought, a repugnance for metaphysical reality, and a mistrust of logical certainty, all these have rendered the Church obsolete. It is impossible, one hears people say, for a modern person to understand the Church.

Such people, if they have any respect left for human expressions of the past, reduce the Church to a simple historical phenomenon, a phase in the evolution of civilization, an interesting relic fit for treatises of mythology and archaeology, for museums.

Then at least treat her with the benevolence with which people treat the dead. As for herself, the Church lives!

We will make only two observations about this way of judging the Church, as though her face bore the lines of inexorable old age or even the corpse-like pallor of an importunate ghost.

Firstly, people would not judge the Church so if they had a more perceptive knowledge of history. But the irresponsible revolutionary mentality of so many in our time has become one of the permanent attitudes of modern thought; hence these fanciful ideas about the Church as old and obsolete, a useless presence in the contemporary world. To regard the tradition of which the Church is the perennial representative and custodian as a dead weight on the modern spirit both dishonours our own culture and prevents us from making anything stable, coherent, or congenial out of a new civilization.

Secondly, the opinion that the Church is merely a relic of the past, a creation of time, an organization forever looking backwards and counting the centuries of its history as its only glory, this opinion has no foundation whatsoever.

For the Church not only bears within her the present moment which is eternity, an eternal youth, a vitality not of this earth, but she is certainly not turned only to the past.

Her gaze is fixed on her source, on Christ and the Gospels. She belongs firmly to time and history. She bears within her that fact of history, that moment which was the redemptive mission of the God–Man in the world. But at the same time she is turned towards the future, to the coming of Christ in glory. That is, she is bent on her eschatological destiny. She draws vitality from the past but lives in the present; she lives also for the future, because hope is her strength.

This nature and structure of hers means that she always retains her identity yet is always susceptible to the present and capable of adaptation, always old and always modern.

This does not, of course, happen without the strain or stress proper to human things, even when they are guided by superhuman principles.

But what we want to emphasize here is the Church's prerogative to remain both always faithful and always young; that being made up of human beings and for human beings, no one is by nature a stranger to her, no one is her enemy; and that potentially she belongs to everyone, and can adapt herself to all those united to her in the faith.

But we are faced with another, graver difficulty, that of bringing modern men to understand and love the Church as a mother, when what they see in her is not life and love but a stony, corpse-like rigidity incapable of speech or motion. This, they say, is the aspect she gives herself by setting up as teacher of a doctrine which in our day people consider incomprehensible, intransigent, and based on invalid assumptions.

They see the Church as tyrannous, sinister; that is what she really is, say those who claim to have penetrated to her true nature. And that, they go on to say, is why they cannot accept the Church, sons of liberty that they are, sowers of systematic doubt, wandering seekers for truth, eternally restless and unsatisfied.

This repugnance for ecclesiastic dogmatism sets secular thought at opposite poles from the Church. Her doctrinal intransigence will, they say, eventually exclude her from the world of modern thought, education, science, and progress. Here the abyss seems unbridgeable, the opposition irreduceable.

Yet this false vision of the Church is, theoretically at least, more easy to correct than any other.

Because he who loves the truth will see that error, coming from the dogmatism of the Church, simply cannot exist.

If the Church's doctrines are the truth, if they really belong to a body of ideas thoroughly sifted and formulae carefully studied so as neither to deny what is certain nor to affirm what is uncertain, why should these doctrines be rejected?

It may be difficult to prove that these doctrines are the truth, but if they are why should they be rejected by the man of culture, the man of thought? In doing so, would he be basing himself on unproven assumptions? And suppose these truths had not the seal of logical evidence, but only that of an honest authoritative body, would that be sufficient reason to reject categorically, out of hand?

Here too it may not be easy to prove that this authoritative body really is guaranteed by divine institution. But if it were, as in fact it is, then why reject it? If it brings us good news, a revelation which we cannot reach by ourselves, are we to deprive ourselves of this new knowledge and new light?

Then are we ourselves the obscurantists?

This question is age-old and much debated, complex and delicate, but not without positive solution. Leaving aside the most important point, that dogmas are not dead and arbitrary concepts but living truths, we might ask ourselves sincerely if our Mother Church really is an obstacle to culture, thought, scholarship, and science. Facts say quite the contrary. Today, indeed, defence of the validity of thought, fervour for humanistic knowledge and even major homage to scientific research actually comes from Catholics who are trying to sustain within modern culture itself an awareness, an enthusiasm, and a confidence which is threatened, we believe, by the contemporary currents of materialism and existentialism.

Who today maintains a trust in truth? Who protects truth from the dizzy heights of the absurd to which some would lead human thought? Who rescues us from Utopian illusion, that opium which would deaden the very principles of thought itself?

And who, amid the mental and moral apathy, the boredom of the modern spirit, the satiated sensuality of today, suggests a hidden endurance, a sigh, a desperate hope of redemption and love?

The pure countenance of Mother Church still bends over the dimmed and red-rimmed eyes of humanity, suffusing it with light and a hope of vistas yet undreamt of.

We have not exhausted the images of what the Church is not. There are innumerable others. Here we can consider only one more, perhaps the most disconcerting.

The Church, it is said, is nothing less than a distortion of Christ.

The idea that the Church is the direct opposite of the figure of her Founder has had much success in anti-clerical controversy. It originates in a kind of puritanism or false enthusiasm for primitive Christianity, in impatience with certain outward expressions of the Church's life.

These objections take two lines, doctrinal and moral. The first accuses the Church of having altered the true message of the Gospel by theological speculations, an objection still levelled against scholastic philosophy and theology; the other denounces the Church's moral failings and political mistakes.

The comparison between certain churchmen and Christ our Lord sometimes seems to give justification to the theory that the Church is a distortion of Christ.

We remember for example those friars denounced by Pope John XXII in the fourteenth century.[1] The decadence of Christian living at that time, in comparison with the Gospel ideal, gave much fuel to the critics of the Church. The Protestant reformers accused the Church of a breach of trust and made this a keystone of their system. Then came men of letters. Tolstoy was a prime example in attacking all churches as anti-Christian institutions, representing, according to him, 'Satan's revenge'.

This is certainly false and paradoxical. But what are we to say of all the evils there undoubtedly have been in the Church? Can we deny them, quibble about their gravity? Justify them? No, we must be sincere and look reality in the face, particularly the historical reality which can be valued most frankly and objectively. And we must not alter our evaluation for love of our cause.

We should also reflect, particularly when dealing with the contemporary scene, that the Gospel forbids us to judge the final responsibility of men, to judge what makes them good or bad before God. We are not competent to judge. Even in purely historical terms we would need a complete knowledge of background and conditions in order to give a true, unprejudiced opinion.

Then we must remember that in our time criticism of the Church, particularly of the historical and doctrinal development of her prerogatives, has grown in emphasis.

'A church [writes Fr Congar] is more severely criticised the more it develops the theory of its own powers (some would say of its own pretensions). . . . This is the basis of the famous anti-Roman complex, which is one of the strongest and most carefully maintained feelings in non-Catholic countries.'

But Catholics themselves have become more intolerant of the weaknesses which they find in the Church; they are no longer willing to assume the task of defending her on this point. In fact the self-criticism of Catholics sometimes goes too far; today they tend to blame the Church herself for many evils inflicted on her by powerful enemies.

But, I repeat, what should we say in reply? We will say, before all else, that the first to recognize and condemn her own failings is the Catholic Church herself. She has never pretended to be perfect

[1] Denz, 485.

in this world. She blames herself for her own failings. She preaches penance to herself. She recognizes the weaknesses of her members. She promotes a continuous reform in herself.

None can possibly affirm that by these efforts the Church is betraying her divine, crucified model.

Secondly we can say that anyone who wants to discover the Church's true features must take a longer look at her face, dirtied and wounded as it often is.

6

CHRISTMAS: CALL TO UNITY[1]

To FIND the root cause of the unity brought by Christ into the world, we must fix our eyes on the person of the Redeemer himself, the person of the Word of God who, becoming man, unites his divine nature with his human nature. God and man live in Christ by the same vital principle, the Word; *non duo tandem, sed unita est Christus*; Christ is not two, but one; so we are taught by the Athanasian Creed. In this unity—the fusion of the divine with the human—consists the mystery of the Incarnation, source of the whole Christian religion, principle of the unifying urge that derives from Christianity. Not in vain did the Fathers, when celebrating Christmas, refer so often to this essential aspect of the Incarnation, of the union which God deigned to bring about in such a way that the Son of God and the Son of Man live in a single person. As St Ambrose wrote: '*Deus erat qui novabat naturam; et homo erat qui secondum naturam nascebatur ex homine*',[2] 'God renewed nature; and as a man according to nature he was born of men'. So also St Leo: '*Unum manet ab aeternitate, aliud coepit a tempore; quae tamen in unitatem convenerunt nec seperationem possunt habere, nec finem*',[3] 'one remains in eternity, the other in time; and both are together in unity, and can have neither separation nor end.' This unity, this alliance in substance between God and man in the personal unity of the Word, is a subject for endless meditation.

Then we should remind ourselves that the appearance of Christ in the world fixes its centre; the centre of history, the centre of human problems, the centre of our destinies. All draw their light and meaning from Christ. As St Paul solemnly declared in the prologue to his Letter to the Ephesians, in Christ God 'has made

[1] Sermon given on Christmas Day, 1958.
[2] St Ambrose, *De Incar. dom. sacr.*
[3] *P.L.*, 54, 233.

43

known to us in all wisdom and insight the mystery of his will according to his purpose which he set forth in Christ as a plan for the fullness of time, to unite all things in him, things in heaven and things on earth' (Eph. 9, 10).

Catholic unity

Hence it follows that Christmas offers everyone a unique point of reference, an invitation to us all to come together, turned towards him as our only Saviour and master. He is thus the sole beginning of human communion, sole source of his mission of salvation. This communion, derived from Christ, is the Church. Today, in celebrating Christ's birth she also celebrates this essential quality of hers, the quality of one-ness, of being intrinsically animated by the same faith, the same hope, and the same charity, that is by the same Holy Spirit, with an extrinsic framework under one consistent authority, headed by the Vicar of Christ, which makes up Christ's Mystical Body. That part of humanity which accepts God made man in Jesus Christ is today pervaded by a sense of fraternity, of belonging universally and spiritually to the same family.

It is indeed a great thing that the invitation to Christmas, the vocation, that is, to participate in the benefits of the Incarnation, to belong to Christ's family, is not reserved to any privileged nation or restricted to any particular category of persons. It is open to all. Christ's salvation tends towards universality. The unity brought by him is intended to be reciprocal in its universality. Christmas arouses, in us who celebrate it in this way, an awareness of Catholic unity, and makes it our duty to increase our awareness of the truth from which this unity derives and of the virtues in which it is manifest.

This awareness deepens as we examine our own minds about it. Is our conception of that vast divine plan which, while respecting and in fact encouraging each of our personalities, yet absorbs us in a common destiny, in any way adequate? Are we aware of the true, deep-seated unity of humanity? Not only of the unity of the human race (there being already a natural basis for fraternity between men, due to their common origin), but of humanity's unity in destiny, a unity already conceived by God's love and always to be promoted by man's love? A unity that must therefore be expressed in missionary fervour, as well as in fostering efforts at fraternal, peaceful, fruitful relations between peoples? A unity that, when promoted between us, brings us closer in Christ to our one Father in Heaven? Of a unity whose fracture rends the plan of God's love for humanity?

Call to the unity of the Church and of peoples

For there is an anguish in our awareness. We are not yet brothers, not all docile to the divine plan of unity in adherence to Christ. Looking out over the world one sees with sorrow two characteristic fractures in Christian unity: one, heresy, breaks this unity's inner communion; the other, schism, breaks its exterior communion. Here arise a number of questions which we will try to answer another time. Now, with the prospect of Christian Unity Week before us,[1] we can only wonder if we, who have the inestimable gift of the true unity which comes from Christ, can rest content. What should we do so that our separated brethren may enjoy with us this supreme gift of the Redeemer? Not for nothing did the Holy Father launch a call to dissidents at the end of his radio message this Christmas. Is it not a duty for each and every one of us to follow this call in spirit and practice, and see that it bears good fruit in our history now or in the future?

Eager for signs of unity throughout the world, let us look from the Christian horizon to the temporal life of humanity. Here too there is much of interest, but it varies and is, at first sight, contradictory. On one hand the world is obviously unifying; distances are annulled, barriers fall, contacts multiply and relationships become more and more interdependent. Unification proceeds. But on the other hand one can observe that this unity is weak and equivocal and maybe even dangerous, because it lacks any formulated higher principles. Such unity could turn into monopolist or imperialist or totalitarian systems, as it could also induce a flat uniformity governed by politics, economics, or propaganda. These are dangerous both to the dignity of the human personality and to mankind's orientation towards its supernatural destiny. Often too we find that people, though close, are not united. They lack a common spiritual principle to make them work harmoniously and with mutual advantage towards higher aims, within which ephemeral and inferior aims would find their proper proportion and surer stability. To us it is clear that Christ is lacking.

Will ever a day come in which those who form Christendom will

[1] Octave of prayer for Christian Unity, held every year from 18–25 January.

solve the gigantic problems of universal living together? We cannot know; but we can always hope. For we are celebrating Christmas, source of unity between men of goodwill.

The first foundations of unity: the family

There is a life in common close to us all, which commits each one of us to put heart and soul into bringing about the unity whose principle is Christ. This is the primary and natural community of the family. Not for nothing is Christmas the family feast. The reunion of the family in the intimacy of the home is among the loveliest and most moving of Christian customs. Family relationships are then at their most serene and genuine. At Christmas joy and peace are in the air we breathe. Talk is unconstrained, yet says more by allusion and asides than by flow of words. Then there are memories of dear ones that bring up reassuring stories or cautionary tales. And there are Christmas greetings to renew bonds of love, esteem, and loyalty. Each member of the family is in the right place, receptacles, as it were, of reverence and affection. What dignity the father and mother have! Then there are the grandparents, treated with affectionate deference, and friends, welcomed as honoured guests. And if there are servants, they too form a real part of the family circle. But above all the children are the family's living glory; the little ones enjoying their feast most of all—for Christmas is *their* feast. They have prepared for it with prayers and little carols, have given presents to the poor, promised to be especially good. How they enjoy their party with its wonderful surprises! They sense, as children do, that all there are happy together. Such is family unity; the most heartfelt joy in human life.

All this is on the natural plane, of course; but it is life lived as sacred, with true dignity, purity, and peace. And when Christ is not there, can we say that this dignity, this joy, is ever achieved? And why do those who see only natural values in the family strive so hard to debase them? Do they not see that the mere suggestion that it could be right to break up the family casts a shadow over the security of the home? Who but Christ can guarantee the lasting and inviolate unity of the family? Christ, in his infinite love for redeemed humanity, for his mystical bride the Church, himself gives the family the supreme example of its unity and loving permanence.

In a home that is well-ordered and good the Christmas crib is not a toy. It has something new to say, something that can scarcely be put in words. It says that Christ is blessing and watching over human life at its natural source. Showing its way, pointing out its goal. It says that family unity is his law, his gift.

And so I end by offering my blessing and my Christmas wishes to those cribs which are your homes. And I extend my wishes to each one of you. A happy and a holy Christmas.

7

EPIPHANY'S CALL TO UNIVERSALITY[1]

As CHRISTMAS recalled to us the divine plan of unity centred in the Incarnation, so Epiphany, which we celebrate today, makes us think of the divine plan of universality which also derives from the Incarnation. Unity and universality are correlated aspects of one mystery of salvation, the coming of the Son of God on earth, of one Saviour for all mankind. '*Omnes unum*' (John 7, 21). One and all; these two words announce the divine plan for the world, the plan overlying the story of the Redemption, the plan still in progress for humanity. Every year Christmas recalls these supreme thoughts; but every year their very greatness leads us on to others that are new and fruitful.

As we already know, the Feast of Christmas draws the soul to gaze upon the Divine Infant, to dwell on the central mystery of him who came among us, on the Word Incarnate. And we know that the feast of Epiphany on the other hand urges the soul to look around it, over the boundless vista of humanity which, aware or not, converges around the Christ just born. Christmas invites us to think of unity, Epiphany to reflect on universality. We do so now with a few brief and modest observations which certainly do not exhaust the immensity of this subject, but which may help to connect it with certain ideas and states of mind to be found in contemporary life.

The Epiphany leads to the idea of human unity

Nowadays, for instance, there is much talk of humanity. The mystery of the Epiphany has educated and continues still to educate man to a true concept of humanity; to the irrefutable concept, that is, that all men, however different and separated, can and should be thought of as part of one single, mutually responsible whole, all coming from the same origin and going towards the same destiny,

[1] Sermon given on the Feast of the Epiphany, 1959.

48

all marked with the same dignity, all defended by the same right which makes life sacred. When the idea of this human unity really forms the basis of men's values and relations, then we can use with sincerity and efficacy such terms as equality, brotherhood, solidarity, rights of man, and, if you like, democracy, United Nations, internationalism, and world peace. Then we may use them without fear of mere verbiage or of distorting such concepts into those of either imperialism or communism, both degenerate forms of universality; without danger too of falling into uniformity, the levelling out of all human expression.

Universality derives from the mystery of the Incarnation. It bases the relationships between men on their relationship with Christ and God. It is utterly contrary to totalitarianism, to the negation, that is, of the human personality and the suppression of the legitimate expansion of individual liberty. So, too, in the religious sphere where it has its source and first affirmation, Christian universality or catholicity is not opposed to this world's many kingdoms and varieties of temporal sovereignties and authorities.

'My Kingship,' Christ said, 'is not of this world' (John 18, 36). And Sedulius, the Christian poet of the fifth century who gave the Hymn of the Epiphany to the Roman liturgy, solemnly sang: '*Non eripit mortalia, qui regna dat caelestia*', 'He who has come to give us a celestial kingdom does not take temporal kingdoms from us.'

What we have just said seems worth mentioning, because we live in a period when universal concepts are daily applied to human progress. Modern life moves around ideological, political, cultural, economic concepts which are ever broadening and tending towards the universal. Even the general public is now in the habit of arguing passionately about international problems or abstract ideologies. They often seem, indeed, to draw more spiritual energy from some universal concept than do we, who are Catholics, universal that is by definition and education.

Here it is worth observing once again that our Catholic formation should predispose us to understand and foster the significant currents of modern civilization and progress, such as the seeking for unity in various advanced expressions of man's life today. Pius XII warned us:

'International unification is making notable progress in spite of mental obstacles that are difficult to overcome. Technical

progress, politics, need for common defence are urgent problems
which seem about to achieve solution. To the Church and to
Catholics of different countries these problems create duties
requiring serious attention and care. Catholics are, in the first
place, particularly well-placed to help create an atmosphere
without which common international action can have neither
consistency nor useful increase. . . . Catholics throughout the
world should always be living in this atmosphere. They themselves are united in the riches of their faith, and so in what is
highest, most intimate, and most dominant in man, no less than
in the irradiation of their faith throughout social and cultural life.
Catholics are also educated from childhood to consider all men of
whatever place, nation, or colour as creatures and images of God,
redeemed by Christ and called to eternal destinies, and to pray
for them and love them. No other human grouping has premises
so favourable, both in breadth and depth, for international
understanding.'[1]

The call to the faithful to understand the true meaning of the word 'Catholic'

We may also observe that an education in Catholicism offers us
Christians a universality whose content is original and sure, a content which searchers for universality outside Catholicism have to do
without. Their form of universality becomes very generic indeed,
and often equivocal and insignificant too; at times it makes do
with mere symbols, at others with expressions of humanitarianism
that are eirenic and ingenuous. Pan-Christian ecumenical movements, too, create a semblance of universality that prejudices truth
and allegiance to the Christian doctrines and moral pledges that
these movements are trying to promote.

A contemporary writer, Giordani, observes:

'Some years ago there appeared in France, where it caused
much comment, a book called *Catholics, are we Christians?*
That, at first sight, seems the most serious question of all. But the
really important one now is, if, while being Christians, we are
Catholics too; that is if we are Christians in a Catholic way.
For to adhere nominally or partially to Christ is no effort; even
Proudhon could pay homage to the carpenter's Son and Tolstoy

[1] *Discorsi*, XIV, 257, 258.

put the Gospel before the manual of the Russian corporal. One may immerse oneself in the Gospel, and let oneself quiver with emotion at sacred music. . . . That is not difficult emotionally . . . the difficulty comes when one is asked not to trifle with Christianity. . . . It is not difficult to be a Christian. . . . It is difficult to be a Catholic. For Catholicism is the very fullness of Christianity.'

All this has not only a speculative but also a practical value for us, a value very close to our immediate experience. Think for example how our Catholic, that is universal, formation, makes us understand the problem of the missions as if it were our own direct responsibility. This is the root cause of the wonderful flourishing of missions in our era and, we can also say, even in our diocese. Humble believers, who have never travelled, who know nothing of distant countries, of other peoples' customs, who have no idea even where and how their coin will be used, impose touching sacrifices on themselves to help the missions. These good souls have understood a vast idea, that Christ came for all men and that the charity taught by him is the more genuine the more universal it is.

Another idea understood by those faithful who want to live in a Catholic way is that this essential attribute of Christ's Church (universality, catholicity), though a prerogative intrinsic to its nature, because it holds out a permanent goal for all humanity to reach, is yet in its historical and practical application in process of evolving and hence imperfect and incomplete. It calls therefore for a constant effort at perfection, a dynamism, an attempt to adapt to God's plan, 'Qui vult omnes homines salvas fieri', 'Who desires all men to be saved' (1 Tim. 2, 4) and to its human realization. It calls, that is, for human collaboration. This begins with Catholics who have an awareness not only of what they are—we may call this the 'Catholic sense'—but also of what they should be—and this we may call the 'sense of Catholicity'.

Catholics must feel themselves universal. A clear univocal adherence to Christ preserves them from an eclectic, doctrinally soft and equivocal eirenicism. But an inward urge impels them to try and understand other human circumstances, whether distant or close at hand. They try, with affection and respect, to offer to others their treasure of charity and truth.

Catholics should not be closed in upon themselves, not egoists, or class conscious, or sectarian. They should not consider everything—Church, state, or party—in terms of their own advantage, but offer their own services to all. They are trying to build the Church and not a private chapel. And when they put their hearts into the service of some particular work for the Church, spiritual or social, they must not forget the common good, in fact they should want nothing better than to serve it and promote the 'communion of saints', even when limitations oblige them to choose one particular form of service.

All this is understood, when they have the right spirit, by our Catholic associations. These are like little sheepfolds, each distinct but open to all who want to enter, organized not only for the good of their own members but of others too. It is certainly understood by the religious bodies, so many of which flourish in the world today, whose reason for existence is not so much their relative autonomy in special circumstances as their intention and capacity to serve God's church in a universal way.

Springing from this awareness of the universality of the Christian message, Catholics feel urged to bear testimony to that message, to help spread it in society and history. This is the apostolate.

On this thought, this aim, we can focus our celebration of Epiphany. The Epiphany shows us the primacy of the Gentiles called to the Kingdom of God. It reveals the capacity of Christ's message to spread out over all humanity, and awakens in us the vocation to the Catholic apostolate. Unity concerns the soul of the Church. It already exists, and has triumphed over innumerable and dramatic difficulties in the course of history. Catholicity or universality on the other hand concerns more the body of the Church, that is, the men who compose it. Virtually, this universality has already, since the days of the three Wise Men and of St Paul, been glowing in the true Church of Christ (as it did eventually in the anxious spirit of Newman). Yet from Epiphany and Pentecost it still awaits an effective extension throughout the kingdom of souls and the world.

8

THE CHRISTIAN APOSTOLATE AND THE UNIVERSALITY OF CHRIST'S REDEMPTION[1]

THE CENTRAL fact of the Epiphany is the manifestation of Jesus Christ to humanity.

The word 'epiphany' means the appearance, the publicizing, the revealing to the world of God's Word made man, whose arrival has been celebrated at Christmas. Now we celebrate his showing forth to men. We see the light lit at Bethlehem spreading over the dark earth and its history. This is the first result of the Incarnation, the first projection on the human screen of the divine intention to communicate with men through Christ. We find the idea in the first page of St John's Gospel, 'the light shines in the darkness' (1, 5) and at once it brings drama into the world's fate. 'He came to his own home, and his own people received him not' (1, 11). This is the theme of the very first synthesis ever traced of Christianity, of what St Paul called the 'great ... mystery of our religion':

> 'He was manifested in the flesh,
> vindicated in the spirit,
> seen by angels;
> preached among the nations,
> believed on in the world,
> taken up in glory.'
> (1 Tim. 3, 16)

Just as Christmas is the feast of the birth of Christ, so Epiphany can be called the feast of the birth of Christianity, the celebration, that is, of the spreading of the Gospel, its first penetration into the ranks of mankind, its universality.

Now let us think about this under two different aspects. Firstly

[1] Sermon given on the Feast of the Epiphany, 1960.

the interior one. We can introduce this by a question: how does Christ manifest himself? How does it happen, this illumination by his truth, usually called revelation, and its acceptance, called faith? This question leads to a study of the stupendous and mysterious ways of God which are open to the human spirit, as well as of the complex and in a sense no less mysterious ways with which the human spirit greets the light and lives by it.

The Epiphany's other aspect, which we might call external, can be introduced by the question: for whom did Christ manifest himself? How far does this manifestation extend, at least in potential? Is it limited? Is it a mystery for the initiated, or a beacon for all? Is it restricted to only one people, the Jews, in whom it took historical shape, or is it announced to all? This is the catholic or universal aspect of Christianity. And it is on this second aspect of the Epiphany that I ask you to meditate for a few moments.

Christ is for all human beings, all times, all nations. He has come on to the earth. So the earth is for him. History is for him. This truth, to which our minds have grown stale, is very wonderful, marvellously up to date and rich in potential. We should try to realize its capital importance. For it shows us God's extreme mercy, which excludes no one from his plan of salvation. We recognize God by this universal compassion even more than by his other work in the world. 'Oh God,' exclaims the liturgy in one of its lovely prayers, 'Oh God, who manifests thy omnipotence most by thy pardon and thy mercy' (Collect of Twelfth Sunday after Pentecost, Roman rite). For this really is true, if we remember St Paul's teaching. God 'desires all men to be saved and to come to the knowledge of the truth' (1 Tim. 2, 4). The universality of Christianity reveals the dimensions of God's love, the breadth of Christ's heart.

It shows how a unifying destiny entered into human history to bring humanity together in brotherhood; to break down the barriers of human antagonism, to inaugurate a peaceful future, to call all human expression, racial, ethnic, national, cultural, each with its own dignity, to a great concert of spiritual and civic harmony in Christianity. The world, which at this very time, in these very days, is working to achieve peace between peoples, does not realize, or perhaps does not wish to recognize, that it is following a Christian path. May God grant it follow it with sincerity of purpose and with success.

The universality of Christianity shows also that it is not fanciful to think of future changes in the world's spiritual panorama. We have the habit of regarding the world as divided into fixed religious, cultural, social, and political zones; zones impenetrable to Christianity, refractory to the Catholic call, unyielding to the Church. But if Christianity is not a privilege for some but a gift for all, if Catholicism is God's programme for the world, if the Church is not a particular sect but the spiritual family of humanity, we must always hope that one day at the feast of Epiphany other peoples, all mankind perhaps, will participate in singing the Christmas hymn of glory and peace. That is our hope, our hope for the world.

But to prophesy like this forces us to consider the enormous contrast between the universality of Christianity as it should be and as it actually is: the one seems in sad contradiction to the other. There is a universality in Christianity begun by Christ's coming for all, but for the majority of the human race it exists still only in potential. But this universality is being realized, is expanding, and tending, with great effort and many delays, to spread over the whole earth.

Leaving aside for the moment any attempt to trace God's inscrutable reasons why the Gospel's universal message is still in actual fact circumscribed and almost inoperative (cf. Luke 4, 25–27; Matt. 13, 14) we may note that the message of salvation is not usually spread (as it might have been) by virtue of the message itself, in the manner of human ideas and scientific truths; it is spread by means of a human ministry, of precept, that is, and example, tradition, propaganda—in short, an apostolate. The Christian economy of salvation is linked with a human work which associates man to God, the minister to Christ, the apostle to the Saviour. In a sense human charity conditions divine charity. 'Everyone who calls upon the name of the Lord will be saved', St Paul teaches us, following the prophets. But he adds at once: 'But how are men to call upon him in whom they have not believed? And how are they to believe in him of whom they have never heard? And how are they to hear without a preacher?' (Rom. 10, 13–14).

This dependence of the divine plan on human collaboration is the mystery of the Christian apostolate. Christianity becomes universal in fact through the apostolate. Universality is achieved by apostolic effort, by missionary dynamism. This is what a consideration of the Epiphany leads us to: if this is the feast of mankind's vocation to Christ the Saviour then who is to herald this vocation? Surely we see here the birth of our responsibility to spread the light of Christ? The mystery of the Epiphany is linked with the mystery of Pentecost. Now the lamp of faith is lit; is it to stay under a bushel?

That is why we are led today to reflect not only on our duties to welcome the revelation, that is towards the faith within us, but also on our duty to spread the revelation, that is, towards the faith in others. Each of us, if we are Christians, becomes a child of light (Eph. 5, 8). We must burn, we must glow.

Granted, the work of spreading the Gospel is specifically reserved to the Church's hierarchy, and to be properly exercised it requires a mandate. But, as we all know, nowadays the concept of the apostolate has broadened the application. It extends to each of the faithful who feels his honour and fortune in being such; who senses the impetus of truth seeking every mind capable of accepting it; it has compassion on his brethren in need of light and listens to the Church's call to be an active and generous, not an indolent or passive, son; and who accepts the rules established by the Church for ordered and loyal collaboration. To the intrinsic reasons, which oblige every one of the faithful to share in the world's salvation according to his capabilities, are added contingent reasons peculiar to our own times.

Today, in fact, we are all called to be apostles and missionaries. The spiritual and social crisis on the one hand, together with the maturing in the world of certain conditions which seem to augur its conscious pacification and unification, call the Christian to active witness of his faith.

This is a more or less daily topic for us these days. But I feel bound to repeat it on this luminous and spiritually vitalizing feast. It summons to a full Christian life those still hesitant, those who think that passive adherence to religion is sufficient, who measure out this adherence so that it brings them no disadvantage, constitutes no danger, demands no real sacrifices, and is not too exigent in its observance. Contented Christianity, comfortable Christianity, possibly self-advantageous Christianity—this is still the concept many have of our religion, reducing the profession of faith to intermittent and almost meaningless habit. Such Christians, if they are still Christians, certainly never think of professing their faith in a way that could give example and comfort to others. Having weakened in themselves the burning lamp of knowledge and consistency which is the faith, they do not notice they are casting a dark shadow over anyone who might get from them some gleam of consolation. That inner light must flame up again and shine out again for others.

These remarks are also addressed to those dear sons and daughters of Mother Church who, one significant day in their lives, listened to the call for an active profession of Catholic principles, and have given their names and work to some form of action aimed at diffusing a vivifying Christian spirit in our world today. I hope they will feel the special encouragement that today's feast gives to their wish, their longing rather, for the spreading of Christ's Kingdom. They long to pass on to others the treasures of faith and love which have been so generously given to us, to awaken in others a sense of the Church's ideal and a yearning to bring a loyal, unselfish contribution to the Catholic cause. The apostolate presupposes great idealism, great faith, principles which can never be put aside but are ever present and operative like light over a desk. They must never restrict the action of the apostolate between narrow or puritan limits, but stimulate its activity towards ever wider circles of influence and conquest.

The subject of the apostolate in the modern world merits careful study, embracing as it does the functions now being assumed by the Catholic laity both in the Church and in society.

These functions are constantly developing new applications. They also create unforeseen problems and open up dangers which the promoters and followers of this modern Catholic activism should be careful to watch, lest the great experiment of the laity's vocation for the apostolate run into crises and useless delays.

It is understandable, even desirable, for example, that the style of Catholic contact with modern society, of our dialogue with particular classes or single individuals should change and be brought up to date, its forms and language coming into line with the modern mind. Such contacts should certainly be varied and open to a broad variety of religious professions, involving more or less obligation according to the times and the fields of action.

But we would like to ask these dear militants of ours to avoid two dangers to which their very zeal seems to expose them. Firstly that of thinking it ingenuous to refer continuously to the motives generating and still justifying their activity—loyalty to Christ and the Church, firmness in morals, reasons for Christian love. This is a spiritual patrimony to which we must not only adhere ideologically, but from which we should always draw food for thought and vigour for action. Then there is the danger that our approach to those who are indifferent or estranged from the Church may turn into an assimilation with their ways of thinking and behaving. In this case we would no longer be conquerors but conquered.

Dialogue, a method necessary for the apostolate, should not end with the denial or disregard of truth to the advantage of error or of the partial truth which we were trying to redeem. Equivocation about this is tempting today. It could weaken the affirmation of the faith, diluting it in a hybrid syncretism of ideas and methods, and accustom the militant Catholic to an opportunist and servile conformism. Salt is no use without its savour.

Epiphany not only makes us think of this apostolate at home, but of another beyond the confines of the home; the missionary apostolate, the world apostolate. Luckily the missions are well supported in our diocese. But we cannot be satisfied when the subject is recalled to our attention and to the zeal of the faithful by the pope himself, who tells us of its recent developments and urges its needs. We cannot be satisfied when whole continents, until yesterday static tributaries of European civilizations, today move and call for an autonomy which the Catholic greets fearlessly as a prelude to closer brotherhood. We cannot be satisfied when modern life needs universal ideas to educate the new generations, and only the Gospel can produce ones that are genuine and beneficial. We must give a new impulse, new forms to our missionary co-operation. This should show not only our Catholic vitality but spur this vitality with the conviction that faith received must be faith passed on, and that the love in the Gospel enriches us insomuch as we can give Christ's love to others.

May Catholic thought and love, strong and universal, grow from our celebration of the Lord's Epiphany.

9

UNITY AND THE PAPACY IN THE CHURCH[1]

THERE ARE two differing, though complementary aspects of unity. First that of uniqueness or oneness. This is the aspect in our minds when, faced with the idea or claim that there can be a number of Churches, we affirm that there is only one, i.e. unique, Church.

This uniqueness is the outer aspect of the Church's unity. It concerns apologetics and basic theology. It involves comparing the position of the Catholic Church with that of the various bodies of separated Christians who use the name of Church; a name intransferable by its very nature, because the Church is one, unique.

The true Church can only be one. The Christian religion can admit no plurality of doctrine, of subjective interpretation. It cannot find expression in entities separate from each other, in differing structures and constitutions. It cannot concede that anyone may go to God, or more exactly, try to go to God, by his own formulae or his own means. The Church, and the Church alone, has the secret of man's true relationship with God as established by Jesus Christ. In fact, bearing Christ with her as she does, she is herself this relationship, the means, certain and exclusive, of achieving our salvation.

This aspect of unity characterizes the true Church. Christ did not found a number of churches, he founded one and this one he called his Church; it was that specific Church whose head was Peter.

If it is admitted that Peter had successors, and that they inherited the keys of the Kingdom of Heaven, that is, the same religious powers which Christ conferred on Peter, then the conclusion must be: in Peter's successors, that is in the Papacy, is realized that aspect of unity, of uniqueness, which distinguishes the true, living, perennial

[1] Lecture given to Christian Study Group, organized by 'Pro Civitate Christiana', Assisi, 29 August 1960.

Church of Christ. The unity, the uniqueness, of the authentic Church is established through the apostolic succession.

This doctrine, though accepted among ourselves, is of course constantly discussed, disputed, and contested in the world of Christian controversy. We may quote in its support just one among many: St Cyprian, Bishop in Africa, fourth century martyr, and great defender of the Church's unity. He was one of the first to argue that the apostolic succession proved the unity and authenticity of the true Church—the argument, we may remember, that led Newman to Catholicism. St Cyprian, writing to warn against the devil's insidious attacks went on, 'God is one and Christ is one, and the Church is one, and the Holy See is one, founded as it was by the Lord's words over Peter. No other altar can be set up, no new priesthood created beyond (that) one altar and one priesthood. Whoever gathers elsewhere, disperses.'[1] This is followed by strong words against those who attack this unity.

The basic idea of unity

But there is another aspect of the Church's unity to be considered, that of cohesion, of intrinsic unity. This is an inner quality rather than an outward one. It refers to the mystery of the Church's life, to a unity above all conceived by God, in his wisdom and goodness, for the destiny of mankind. This concept of unity, that of the cosmic Christ, was spoken of particularly by John the Evangelist and the apostle Paul, the latter in a synthesizing, vigorously phrased formula: '*Instaurare omnia in Christo*', 'to unite all things in Christ its head' (Eph. 1, 10). Christ is the world's focus, is at the centre of the human circle. Christ is at the centre of that human circle founded by him as a particular society of believers, illuminated by his doctrine and infused by his grace: it is the Church, a human society animated by Christ's spirit. We are expressly reminded of this in the encyclical on the Mystical Body:

'Our divine Saviour himself governs directly the society which he founded, for he reigns in the minds and hearts of men. . . . By this interior government he, the shepherd and bishop of our souls— (1 Pet. 11, 25)—not only cares for each individual but also watches over the whole Church.'[2]

Christ gives his Church unity of faith, of grace, of help. The

[1] *Ep.* 43, 5, 2.
[2] *Mystici Corporis Christi*, English translation, C.T.S., London, p. 24.

Church is one by reason of her single source, her head, her bride-groom. The union of the faithful with Christ bestows on the Church her real unity, both practical and spiritual. Listen again to St Paul's words to the Ephesians: 'I beg you to lead a life . . . eager to maintain the unity of the Spirit in the bond of peace. There is one body and one Spirit, just as you were called to the one hope that belongs to your call, one Lord, one faith, one baptism; one God and Father of us all, who is above all and through all and in all' (Eph. 4, 1, 3–6).

If we want to enter the orbit of Christianity we must be per-meated by this basic idea of unity. It holds the genius of Christianity, it holds within it the strength of its inner coherence, its indestructible capacity for diffusion. It reveals the mysterious depths of compassion and beauty in the divine plan for our salvation. Unity, one-ness, is a complement of being. So God, the Being of beings, the Being *per se*, infinite and transcendent, is the ultimate One. And all that lives and exists is one, is affirmed as one, and when it grows and lives it affirms a fuller unity. When it draws close to God it aspires to union, which is an intimation and approximation of unity. Unity is a need of philosophy, a metaphysical need without which all theories of reality and thought disappear. It is the need of the mystic, that is not only of those who try to understand life and the world by way of knowledge but of those who want to have, and do have, an incipient and transforming experience of its tremendous reality.

I insist on this final aspect of our theme because the concept of unity, which we must recognize in Christ's Church, leads to the doctrine of the Mystical Body. This is an affirmation of the Church's unity in a form that meets the spiritual needs of the modern soul; for on one side it refers back to sources in scripture, and on the other it applies to our daily lives.

Mystici Corporis, Pius XII's encyclical, which we have just quoted, begins:

'The doctrine of the Mystical Body of Christ, which is the Church, a doctrine originally received from the lips of the Redeemer himself, and making manifest the inestimable boon of our most intimate union with so august a head, has a surpassing splendour which commends it to the meditation of all who are moved by the divine Spirit, and with the light which it sheds

upon their mind is a powerful stimulus to the salutary conduct
which it enjoins'.[1]

Thus the concept of one Church should not be merely historical
and juridical, concerning only the human beings who are part of it,
the Church's visible, physical face. It should be understood also in
relation to Christ and God as a principle inherent in that reality
which makes the Church a mystery, a thought, a plan, a work of
God.

Before the Church was one in historical fact it was one in God's
plan. This plan was begun by Christ in the Gospel, develops
throughout time and is resolved in the mysterious kingdom of the
next world. The Church is one because she is his Church, because
she is the means of his redemptive mission whose purpose, according
to Christ's greatest prayer, is that all may be one: *ut omnes unum sint*
(John 17, 21). The Church is not only the means of our salvation.
Rather let us say she will be our salvation when, her sanctifying
mission completed, she will be shown as the formation of Christ's
Body (Eph. 4, 12–13). Now this profound unity, coming from the
divine idea, realized in Christ and tending to its final reality in a
future life, is expressed, must be expressed, in a unity of society, a
unity that is human, visible, indisputable, to which all men are
called and to which we have the good fortune and responsibility
already to belong.

That we do belong to it should be our joy, our pride, our
strength. We should feel passionately about the unity and uniqueness of God's Holy Church. From our sense of belonging to it we
should draw the riches of spirit which, according to the Old
Testament, were in the hearts and on the lips of the citizens of
Jerusalem; that city which was a symbol and pledge of the transcendental destinies of a people who throughout their tormented
history were always convinced of their vocation and sustained by
inextinguishable hope.

We are citizens of a spiritual Jerusalem, a homeland no less
human and historical, a Jerusalem descended from heaven to earth
in order to be peopled with human beings to be brought to heaven.
We should be enthusiasts for this religious homeland of ours, that is,
the Church, which anticipates in this mortal life our place in God's
eternal city, and introduces us into a network of relationships, first

[1] English translation, C.T.S., London, p. 6.

with Christ, then with God and with our brothers, which is a preparation and a prelude to final unity in Heaven.

The basic structure of the Church

The Church makes us part of a communion, a universal family. She is a society living in faith and by charity, a system of converging relationships which elevate human life and save it. The Church is one, but her unity is not uniform and passive, not only that of a band of brethren, but organic and active, that of a mother bearing children. In other words she is a composite unity with a structure most marvellously dovetailed.

Here we may recall some other words of St Paul on the composite unity of Christ's Mystical Body. 'Some should be apostles, some prophets, some evangelists, some pastors and teachers . . . for building up of the body of Christ' (Eph. 4, 11–12). Here we should consider the two basic components of the Church's living unity. One is the invisible element, the divine animator which we have said to be the mind of God, his grace, his help. The other is the visible element, the part of humanity which believes and is vivified by charity, the 'ecclesia sanctorum', the society of Christians. These two components we can call soul and body. These make the Church an entity simultaneously divine and human, invisible in the gifts which make her life, visible in the members which compose her; the continuation, that is, of the mystery of the Incarnation.

This second component we are talking about is the Church's living body, her organization, her hierarchy, which presents her under certain aspects as a community all equal among themselves, and under other aspects as a community of pastors and faithful, the first with specific faculties of sanctification, of magisterium and of government not held by the second. The Church is a mother. As St Bede put it, 'Ecclesie quotidie gignit Ecclesiam', 'every day the Church generates the Church'.[1] Before that St Ambrose affirmed 'Sola Ecclesiae gratia, qua redimimur'.[2] We are redeemed by the grace which only the Church gives.

How does it come about, that within and through the unity of the Church an active principle, a power emerges? How has a community of love become a community of authority? Is the governing organism born from within the community itself, as so many

[1] Explanatio Apocalypsis, i, 11.
[2] In Ps. 39, 11.

dissidents who are now forced to admit the need for a visible and operative authority in the ecclesiastical community try to maintain, or does the authority precede the community, convoke it, create, sanctify, and direct it?

To us the reply is obvious. We are surprised that it is not equally obvious to all who recognize the authority of the divine word in Sacred Scripture.

Recall only the famous passage of the Gospel of St John in which Christ, after the Resurrection, speaking to Peter of the love that linked Peter to him, says that the shepherd's motive force, the one with which he gathers and guides the Christian fold, is love. 'If you love me, because you love me,' our Lord seems to say, 'feed my sheep.' Our Lord, desiring to create a society of love, does not make the hierarchy which is to guide it come from that society itself, but confers the power directly on those who exercise it in his name.

Tommaso de Vio called Gaetano (1469-1534), famous during the Protestant reform and in scholastic theology, commented on this. He may help us evaluate a notable trend in modern Protestant theology which would make the community and not the apostles the heirs of the Christian message. Gaetano wrote:

'To understand the nature of her (that is, of the Church's) government we need only look at her beginnings. She did not begin through the work of any individual, nor through the work of any community. She was assembled around her head, Jesus Christ, and from him came her life and her power. It is not you, he said, who have chosen me; it is I who have chosen you. Right from the birth of the Church, her government was clearly apparent. Authority does not reside in the community; it is never seen to come, as in the civil order, from the community to one or several leaders. By the Church's nature, and from her earliest days, this authority resides in a single, recognizable head. As this head is the Lord Jesus, who lives and reigns yesterday and today and forever, it follows that it was his natural right, and not that of the ecclesiastical community, to choose a vicar at the moment of his Ascension, one whose office would not be to represent the ecclesiastical community, which is destined to obey, not to command, but to represent its Head who by his very nature is ruler of this community. That is what our Saviour deigned to do when . . . he chose . . . one apostle, Peter, as his vicar. And as the

Head of the Church does not derive his authority from the Church, nor does his vicar derive it from the Church but from him.'[1]

The history of the Church shows quite clearly that it is the hierarchy, the apostolate, the missionary who evangelizes humanity, fosters the faithful, forms them into a living Church, and not an amorphous, arbitrary community of faithful which draws from its midst the shepherd who will guide it.

This double duality (invisible animator and visible community, on the one side; teaching Church and preaching Church on the other), and this origin of the Church's functioning powers are essential to the genuine unity of Christ's Mystical Body.

Now, when we look for the highest and fullest expression of this ministry of grace, truth, and guidance, the ministry which, in dependence on and in virtue of Christ, mirrors and generates this mysterious unity in the history of time, we must come to the conclusion that its expression is a person, a human, living, and visible person, the successor of Peter: the pope. In him is centred the Church's unity.

The pope and the Church's unity

Let us remember this. The unity of the Church is not mere uniformity of doctrine. It is not, as Calvin's city was called, a 'bibliolatry'. It is not just disciplined homage to one hypothetical code of beliefs and morals; not membership of a community of faithful organized in one compact body which has attributed to itself the sacred name of Church; not the sum of different and divided bodies, joined by a vague ecumenical link. Neither is this unity merely the result of a religious society being governed by a college of bishops or a group of patriarchs, that is by a hierarchy without a head. It is the sum—the quality, the beauty, the life, the mystery—of persons[2] congregated in a visible religious society governed by bishops whose head is the bishop of Rome, the universal bishop, the pope.

This personification of the Church's unity implies much else that we must simplify here. But as one who has reached a mountain-top is impelled to gaze at the view before him, so we feel impelled

[1] Gaetano, *Apologia de comparata auctoritate papae et concilii*, c. I, n. 450–2.
[2] Cf. St. Ambrose, *In Lc*, 2, 86.

to point out the paths which have led us to this peak, to point out, that is, the connections between the Church's unity and the papacy.

The primary connection is one of derivation, from Christ to pope. Christ, sole and supreme Head of the Church, but now in heaven and invisible, makes Peter and each successive pope his vicar. As such the pope is the earthly, visible head of the Church, whose one Head, Christ, is always the same.[1] The word, the love, the authority of Christ were transferred to the first among the apostles, conferring on him a universal primacy which Catholic tradition celebrates with many names. The pope, as St Cyprian wrote to Pope Cornelius, alluding to the Church of Rome, is 'Ecclesiae catholicae matricem et radicem', 'the matrix and root of the Catholic Church'.[2] In another letter to the same pope, St Cyprian looked to the See of Peter and this matrix Church as the font of sacerdotal unity, 'Unde unitas sacerdotalis exorta est',[3] as did St Ambrose, 'Totius orbis Romani caput Romanam Ecclesiam'.[4]

Similar, or rather the same, is the pope's derivation from St Peter; a connection not recognized by Protestant theologians, who consider that Christ's investiture of Peter was a privilege personal to him (Cullman).

We may also refer to unshaken Catholic tradition, one of whose most incisive and authoritative spokesmen (among the many that could be quoted) St Leo the Great, defined the pope as: 'Princeps apostolici ordinis', Prince of the apostolic order.[5] Here we note another relationship, that of the pope with the bishops, which we might call of fraternity on the one side, and of pre-eminence, not only in honour but in authority, on the other. This pre-eminence is a well-known fact; as is that of the pope over all the faithful.

Pope John XXIII reminded us of this in the memorable words with which he announced his intention of calling an ecumenical council:

'Venerable brethren and beloved children' [exclaimed the Pope], 'a successor of St Peter, reflecting on the dual duties entrusted to him, at once realizes his double responsibility as Bishop of Rome and Shepherd of the universal Church. They are two parts of one supernatural investiture, two attributes which cannot be divided,

[1] Cf. Mystici Corporis Christi, A.A.S., 1943, 210–211. C.T.S., London, pp. 24–5.
[2] Ep. 48, 3.   [3] Ibid., 59, 14, 1.
[4] Ibid., 11, 4.   [5] Serm. 82, 3.

which must in fact dovetail with each other, for the encouragement and edification of clergy and of all the people.'[1]

This establishment of the pope not only in the centre, but at the very peak of the Church, is a fact which moves her greatly. She gives the pope the grandest, most solemn of names; Holiness, Supreme Pontiff, August, Sovereign Head of the Church, Vicar of Christ. He is the rock of faith, the representative of the whole Church (*Totius Ecclesiae figuram gerens*, says St Augustine),[2] not in the sense that the pope derives his functions from the Church, but that he sums up in himself the powers of the whole Church. At the same time the pope is given also the most human and familiar names, 'pope' means 'father'; he is the shepherd, the servant of the servants of God.

So high and so singular is the pope's position that we want to see it precisely defined. That is what the First Vatican Council did when it defined the pope's prerogatives in dogmatic terms, that is, terms that are certain and indisputable. These can be summed up as: primacy, infallibility, indefectibility.

It is worth mentioning these expressly and reading the opening part of the first dogmatic constitution (called the first because it was about the papacy, although in actual fact the second, which was to have concerned the episcopacy and the faithful, was not discussed by the First Vatican Council due to its interruption by the events of 25 September 1870). This constitution was promulgated by the Vatican Council in its fourth session, on 18 July 1870, under the title of the opening words '*Pastor eternus*'. It opens with this ample and lucid prologue:

'Jesus Christ "the eternal Shepherd and Guardian of our souls (1 Pet. 2, 25)" in order to prolong in time his work of salvation and redemption, established the Church which, as the home of the living God, was to contain all the faithful in links of faith and charity. Thus before he was glorified our Lord prayed to his Father not only for his apostles, but also for those who would believe in him through his apostles' words, "may they all be one: as thou, Father, art in me, and I in thee" (John 17, 21).

Just as he sent the apostles whom he had chosen into the world as he himself had been sent by the Father so he wanted

---

[1] *A.A.S.*, 1959, p. 66.   [2] *Ep.* 53, 1, 2.

pastors and teachers in his Church until the end of time. In order
that this Episcopate should be one and undivided, with all
believers kept in unity of faith and communion by a consistent
priesthood, he set Peter above the other apostles and made him
the visible beginning and foundation of both these unities. On
Peter's rock was to be built an eternal temple and a sublime
Church rising to the skies in firmness of faith.

But the flood-gates of hell open wider everywhere, in growing
hatred, to fling the Church down, if that were possible, from her
divine foundations. For the safe-keeping and increase of the
Catholic flock we consider it necessary to put before all the faithful, with the Sacred Council's approval, the doctrine of the institution, nature, and perpetuity of the apostolic primacy, on which is
based the strength and solidity of the Church, as a doctrine
believed and held according to the constant and ancient faith of
the Universal Church; and to prescribe and condemn errors so
harmful to the Lord's flock.[1]

Meanwhile we teach and declare, according to the testimony
of the Gospel, that the primacy of jurisdiction over the whole
Church of God was promised and conferred directly by Christ
our Lord on the blessed Peter.[2]

There follow canons declaring that Peter was the visible head of
the whole Church militant, with primacy of jurisdiction; that
Peter's perpetual successors are the Roman Pontiffs, also with
jurisdiction over the whole Church, and ordinary and immediate
powers both on all single Churches and on each single pastor and
layman; and finally that Christ gave Peter infallibility, which is
transmitted to his successors, when making a definition 'ex Cathedra', that is when, exercising with full authority the apostolic office
of pastors and teachers, the popes promulgate doctrines concerning
faith and morals.[3]

This definition convinces, and indeed comforts us Catholics, but
not those outside the bosom of the Catholic Church.

Unity has two implications which our dissident brethren, due to
their very separation, will not admit. One is exclusiveness, the other
obedience.

[1] Denz, 1821.
[2] Ibid., 1822.
[3] Ibid., 1823, 1825, 1831, 1840.

Unity cannot mean multiplicity. To say the word is to define it. Unity separates those who adhere to it from who do not. Thus Catholic unity appears as an exclusive concept, an exclusive programme, of religious life. This is why Christ said he came to bring not peace but the sword.

'The supposition that there could be several independent Christian societies within a "spiritual unity" is . . . contrary to the whole of the history of primitive Christianity,' wrote de Lubac.[1] Unity implies obedience; that is, it implies conforming to an order established by the competent authority. Unity and authority go hand in hand, just as do unity and obedience. These are harsh words for those who have not understood how the divine economy of the Church takes human weakness into account.

Some have argued that this is an impossible economy. The Chancellor of the University of Paris, later Cardinal Archbishop of Cambrai, Pierre d'Ailly, taking part in the Councils of Pisa and Constance, maintained that our Lord could not have founded the '*firmitas Ecclesiae in Petri infirmitate*', 'the firmness of the Church on the infirmity of Peter'. But Pierre d'Ailly overlooked the fact that Christ actually based the Church's stability on the rock-like firmness which he gave to the weak Simon-bar-Jonah.

Others have argued that excessive powers have been allowed the pope by the Catholic Church. To escape this power the first reformers affirmed, as liberal Protestants still do, that the Church is not a visible and hierarchic society but merely a spiritual and invisible one, without realizing that this would cause not only the Roman Catholic but the whole Church to melt away.

In a vigorous phrase of Father Louis Bouyer (the distinguished French theologian and writer, a convert from Protestantism), which echoes St Ignatius of Antioch, '"an invisible Church is the same thing as no Church at all"; without the hierarchy which is its point of crystallization, its organizer and its guide, "there can be no talk of the Church".'[2]

What people fear is a papacy that is despotic, imperialist, and political. To avoid homage to such a papacy they sacrifice the unity of the Church, of the one true Church. How do we answer this objection, which has been such a formidable obstacle on the road to unity? It is not one that can be removed merely by discussing apologetics.

[1] *The Splendour of the Church*, London, 1956, p. 57.   [2] *Ibid.*, p. 58.

We can only say that the fear of rendering obedience to an arbitrary and tyrannical power is quite groundless. Obedience certainly implies humility, loyalty, patience, and sacrifice. But it is not unreasonable if it is the will of Christ. It is not unlimited if confined to a definite jurisdiction. It is not harmful to the good of those who profess it; in fact it guarantees and defends their good. Nor is it isolated, motivated only by reasons that concern the soul of the individual faithful.

Here is what Monsignor Blancret, Rector of the Catholic Institute of Paris, has to say:

'When the pope exercises his doctrinal authority, it is not an external yoke which one man, in the name of his own will, imposes on a religious society, however talented he may be; it is the Church herself, whose faith he is defining. The Church is not subordinate to his consent, but he speaks in union with her. It is the truth by which she lives which he translates and renders precise. It is our own belief whose meaning he guarantees, whose content he analyses, whose misinterpretation he prevents, whose vigour he maintains.'

So we say to the Church what the apostle said to her Founder: 'Where else shall we turn, for you have the words of eternal life?' We say this not from weariness of spirit, not from wanting to leave the care of thinking and the fatigue of living to authority. It is, as Newman said, from a sense of reposing in the fullness of Catholicism.

In this connection we might also remember Newman's prayer: 'Let me never for an instant forget that thou hast established on earth a kingdom of thy own, that the Church is thy work, thy establishment, thy instrument; that we are under thy rule, thy laws and thy eye—that when the Church speaks thou dost speak.'[1]

We may quote too the testimony of another thinker, this time an oriental, Solovyev, who, on moving from Orthodoxy to Catholicism, confessed, 'the perfect circle of the universal Church needs a single centre, not in order to be perfect but in order to exist. The Church on earth is called to embrace all nations. It must, in order to remain a real society, have a definite and universal power to oppose all national divisions.'[2]

[1] From *Meditations and Devotions.*
[2] Solovyev, *Russia and the Universal Church.*

Let us call to mind our own experience of the papacy in recent years, since by the great blessing of providence the Vicar of Christ has no longer appeared in the trappings of a temporal sovereign— save of one tiny surviving state which is certainly no instrument of power but the smallest symbol of his liberty and independence. Now the papacy is totally absorbed in carrying out its evangelical mission; by teaching, by reawakening knowledge of divine principles, by diffusing light and faith, by indicating ways of social evolution, by warning governments and peoples about encroaching errors and pressing dangers, by classifying doctrines and events according to the scale of eternal values. For decades now the teaching office of the papacy has been exercised not only in the Church but before the world.

It also continues to guide Christ's fold, arousing within the Church energies that show her vitality in works whose resplendence does not come from the kingdom of this world but kindles in her children an ardour for good. It encourages every healthy advance and useful activity. It opens a new dialogue with art and culture, and with our modern civilization, so superabundant in means and so ignorant of ends. It continues to help sanctify this Church of God, quickening the flow of grace within her, re-arousing the appetite for prayer and charity, pointing out new roads of holiness.

In these past years we have seen how, amid the tumult of peoples at war, the pope remained alone, praying for peace. We have seen him bent over the wounds of humanity, making his evangelical message speak of the deepest motives of human life: goodness, justice and pity, liberty and dignity of the human person. Nearly always he was isolated and neglected; but his very position, remote from all earthly interests, extraneous to all human contests, often the target for fierce and inexplicable antagonisms, made him appear unique, solitary, as if he were humanity's point of convergence and comparison. There seemed a strange universal presentiment that around him should circulate the destinies of civilization, not because he disposed of riches, means, strength, or power, but because he sympathized with all human needs, loathed all human injustice, and had the principles, the humility, and dignity of a man of God.

The papacy rises over the world with the prophetic gift of one who preaches the Gospel and announces hopes which go beyond the confines of time.

Establishing unity

If the world paid more attention to the papacy how many 'useless massacres' it would avoid, how much dispersed effort it would direct to useful advance, how much unworthy behaviour it would change to its own honour and peace of mind!

If those who still look on Christ as the salvation of the world knew more about the doctrines which inspire the papacy, they would not be so scandalized by past events in which so many clerics gave such unfortunate proofs of human weakness; nor would they be so impressed by certain dubious and random aspects of Roman life, but see with joy and amazement how the mystery of Christ lives on in him who is called the Vicar of Christ. And if, instead of lingering over reiterated attempts at disassociating spiritual Christianity and corporeal Christianity (Luther), visible Church and invisible Church (Calvin), religion of authority and religion of Spirit (Sabatier), Church of right and Church of charity, the Church as institution and the Church as fact, hierarchic Church and charismatic Church, they took a dispassionate look at what the papacy really is and what its activities now are, they would realize how mistaken and unjust such abstract distinctions are today; they would realize that the Roman pontificate, supreme expression of the so-called juridical Church, is the most faithful custodian and generous diffuser of Christ's word, love, and grace throughout Christendom and the world.

And what about ourselves? We, too, are often intolerant critics of the papacy, imbued with the self-sufficient dogmatism of a liberal mentality, ready to judge its defects and discount its merits, prejudiced about presumed reactionary attitudes of the Roman Curia. Yet we bother little about supporting the pope's injunctions for the Christian regeneration of society.

If we paid more attention to that teaching, had a closer, holier sense of Christ and his Church, a more sincere, more burning wish for peace among men and unity among Christians, we would feel in our hearts, reborn and growing, a sense too often dim and vague in us, a 'Catholic' sense, an awareness, that is, of human universality achieved in the freedom of God's children. We would be aware of this unity, spiritual and mysteriously real, fixed in one centre to which Christ's plan is tending and established in one person, his Vicar the pope, and at the same time widening out in a vast extent which aims to encompass the whole world's dimensions, not from any yearning for grandeur or dominion but from an urge for communion and equality. This expansion is not a dream, but the aim and duty of apostolic love, anxious to call every man brother, to share with him the patrimony of truth and grace which we have not the merit but the good fortune and responsibility to possess. To build unity! To work at building Catholic unity! Why should that unity not come about when there is an urgent need everywhere for union and peace among men? When temporal civilization itself aspires to world unification and seems to open its ways to the Gospel? When the Church exhorts and urges all her children to be active missionaries and apostles within a society which is losing its Christian sense and morals? When a gentle and wise pope announces the convocation of that seat of unity, the Ecumenical Council, and calls on us all to prepare in spirit, by prayer and love, for its happy outcome? Why should not we all, with renewed Catholic consciences, help in some way to build this unity?

Then, with delight, we should see ourselves transformed into builders. We should see the marvellous plan of unity coming alive under our hands, and hear resounding in the ears of our souls the words of the divine architect: 'You are Peter, and on this rock I will build my Church' (Matt. 16, 18).

That is why there can be no true religious unity without the Church, and there can be no true Church without the papacy.

PART TWO

THE MODERN WORLD CONFRONTS THE CHURCH

I

MAN'S RELIGIOUS SENSE[1]

BEFORE US lies the whole vast spectacle of the modern world, pulsing with life, thought, activity, achievement. The earthly city is in a process of constant change; it is creating new forms of civilization on a vast scale. Man grows in numbers, in knowledge, in power. He is absorbed in research, in business, in new ventures and interests, in machines and money, travel and wealth, diversions and amusements, dreams, plans for the future, and his mind has become coldly calculating, wrapped up in his work, in his social consciousness, and in the pursuit of pleasure. The immediate reality enthralls him. Even his hopes have no inspiration beyond the present life. The earth is his kingdom.

And the kingdom of heaven? The future life? Man's supernatural destiny? The mystery of life and of the universe?

And God?

Modern man is in process of losing his religious sense.

The 'religious sense' as a concept

First I will try to show as simply as I can, as befits a pastoral letter, what exactly is meant by the expression 'religious sense'. It may seem vague and indefinite, but this is because it denotes certain activities of the soul which of their nature are difficult to define and which frequently receive very different explanations. On the latter I shall offer no comment, despite the fact that many of them have gained wide acceptance in modern culture, not only in the field of religion proper but also in the fields of philosophy, ethnology, and psychology.

I would here draw attention only to one of these explanations, that put forward by modernism which, starting from agnostic

[1] From *Man's Religious Sense*, Pastoral Letter to the Archdiocese of Milan, Lent, 1957 (English translation, Darton, Longman & Todd, London, 1961).

77

premises, has given an 'immanentist' explanation of the religious
sense as something welling up from the subconscious, a sort of need
for God that creates its own end and, becoming thus a conscious
thing and combining with certain historical and sensible facts,
finally emerges as religious faith. It will be remembered that this
false evaluation of the religious sense was explicitly—and deservedly
—condemned by His Holiness Pope Pius X in the well-known
encyclical, *Pascendi*, in 1907.

I say, on the other hand, that the religious sense is a natural human
aptitude to perceive that we have some relation to God. We call it
religious feeling when it becomes active and aware of its own
perceptions—though it is worth noting that today in ordinary
speech the two expressions 'religious sense' and 'religious feeling'
are frequently used interchangeably.

The first thing to notice about the religious sense is that it is not
equally active and developed in all human beings, whether in
respect of their natural endowment—there are people with a
naturally quick and sensitive religious perception like an ear for
music, others in whom it is slower and duller—or of their cultivation or neglect of this spiritual gift. Children, the pure in heart, the
spiritually alert, wise men and mystics, all in their own different
ways possess this wonderful aptitude in an exceptional degree.

It can be perfected by a supernatural factor, grace: we all know
how this divine gift can give strength and delicacy to man's natural
religious sense and accustom it to higher aspirations and insights.

When, for example, the Bible speaks of a spirit that gives life
(Isaiah 42, 1; Ps. 50 [51], 12; Zach. 12, 10; Ez. 36, 26; Acts 3, 17–18),
of 'newness of mind' (Rom. 12, 2; Phil. 1, 9; John 5, 20), or of 'the
mind of Christ' (1 Cor. 2, 16), these expressions may also, I believe,
be applied to the increased power and vitality of the natural religious
sense inspired by the presence of a supernatural gift.

The modern term used comprehensively to denote all these
rudimentary manifestations of the spiritual life is the word 'reli-
giosity', as meaning a general propensity towards the things of
religion. This refers to the subjective aspect of religion, the soul's
capacity for a rudimentary awareness of God, a capacity to seek
him out and commune with him, to believe in him, pray to him,
love him, to sense the sacred element in things and persons and to
view all human conduct in the light of a responsibility to something that transcends the human order. It gives in fact some indica-

tion of how far a particular human being, and not simply human nature in the abstract, is *capax Dei*, i.e. open to God.

For the sake of what follows, I must make some reference to the other terms that are commonly used, with varying degrees of accuracy and inaccuracy, to describe this human propensity for God. There is, for instance, what men of old, and good Christian people still today, call 'the fear of God', meaning not precisely the gift that presupposes faith[1] and grace,[2] nor precisely fear and perplexity, but rather a sense of some all-powerful, all-pervading divine being to whom, as soon as we become aware of him, we are drawn, and from whom we involuntarily shrink (Luke 5, 8).

We may, with St Thomas, describe this religious sense as one of man's natural appetitives—*vires appetitivae*—subject to the rule of reason but moving instinctively towards God as though led by some higher power.[3]

Some people call it 'piety', denoting thereby one of the most natural, elevated, and fruitful manifestations of the human spirit, to which human thought and love and art and life have given tributes of untold wealth and in which they have found an unfailing source of powerful inspiration. But piety in this sense is religion already perfected in act, and shows us man standing in the presence of God in loving worship.[4]

Finally, some people simply use the word 'religion' as a generalized term.

Here it will be sufficient to regard the religious sense as a state of being open to God:

man's natural movement towards his first beginning and final end;

a vague intuitive awareness that he is both responsible for his own destiny and at the same time dependent on another;

a natural, incohate utterance of the soul about its mysterious relationship with the supreme being;

a spontaneous gesture by human nature, in an attitude of adoration and supplication;

the soul's urgent longing for a personal infinite being, like the eye's longing for light or a flower's need of the sun.

---

[1] *S. T.*, II, IIae, 7, 1.   [2] *S. T.*, II, IIae, 19, 9.
[3] *S. T.*, I, IIae, 68, 4.   [4] Cf. De Luca, *Arch.*

It is important and comforting to note that this primordial human inclination derives from man's inner and essential nature. St Augustine's famous words come to mind, *'Fecisti nos ad te'*, 'Thou hast made us for thyself, O Lord.'[1]

Such, it seems to me, is the religious sense. It is not, obviously, a very precise term, but it has now passed into common usage as a description of all that is immediate and subjective in religion. In a sense it precedes human reasoning, but it derives its *raison d'être* from reality, being as Spiazzi has said, 'the religious movement of human nature, when not corrupted or even blinded by mental or moral evil'.

In more precise terms, it is 'pre-philosophical knowledge, potentially metaphysical in nature'.[2]

A close, impartial analysis of this direct kind of religious perception reveals it as an implicit train of thought of lightning-like rapidity, which I have not time to describe here; and that in turn takes us back to those 'ways' that lead to certainty about the existence of God and aim to discover something of his nature. Both show that this train of thought is substantially sound and moves in the right direction.

Recognized authorities classify the religious sense as part of mankind's 'common sense'. This, as they show, is a store of primordial fundamental certainties belonging to the natural untutored reason, takes existence as its formal object[3] and has an intuitive knowledge of first principles.

Others speak of 'religious experience' and yet others of the 'religious idea'.

But to bring this point to an end, we can include under the expression 'religious sense' all the manifold and complex manifestations—instinctive, conscious, rational, and moral, on both the natural and the supernatural levels—of mankind's general tendency towards God (Rom. 1, 19–20; 2, 15; 10, 17; 12, 1; 1 Thess. 2, 13, etc.).

First of all we must ask why our own day is less favourable to the religious sense than former ages. The fact is that the cultural, moral, and social atmosphere of the modern world does not provide

[1] *Confessions*, I, i.
[2] J. Maritain, *Approaches to God*, London, 1948.
[3] Cf. Garrigou-Lagrange, *Le Sens Commun*.

the best conditions for its defence and development, with the result that religious life easily decays.

This is plain for all to see. The general run of people today no longer have the religious sensibility of those of yesterday. Observance of religious duties is a harder task than it used to be. The people most closely involved in the characteristic activities of modern life—scientific research, factory work, mechanics, technology, bureaucracy, sport, economics, entertainment, and so on—are less inclined to practise religion than people who have not yet been caught up in the fever of this intense activity.

A great many young people are fascinated by the outward aspect of the world around them and soon get infected with a spirit of destructive criticism. If they achieve any sense of spiritual values, any feeling for religion, any sort of inner life, it is only after much patient endeavour and wise counsel and toil on the part of their educators. For the most part they are distracted from these things, more inclined to work for their own ends than for any heroic ideas, impatient of the interior life, and with little feeling for poetry or prayer. Religious vocations have to struggle to make themselves felt in this climate of external excitement which surrounds the formative years of such a great proportion of young people today.

Even woman who surpasses man in her instinctive concern with the essence of life, and hence with the religious sense, today responds less than formerly to her natural impulse towards piety and goodness.

Even among Christian believers the active life and external activity are more highly regarded than prayer and the inner life, and sometimes human means seem to predominate over supernatural ones. The contemplative life has almost been abandoned; modern society lacks men of silence, solitaries, men rich in inner life, as it lacks spiritual powerhouses and choirs of contemplatives to guide and accompany it on its precarious human way towards its final destiny.

Worldly activity prevails, even among Christians, and not only as a duty imposed by present necessity but as being to most people's minds the only practical thing, the only really effective thing to do.

Why all this should be so, is a difficult question; it involves a study of all the vast and highly complex movements of the modern mind. Fortunately, this has already been undertaken by experts in the field; and so I can simply indicate, among all the many causes, some very general ones that summarize the explanation we seek.

The first is 'secular humanism', that is to say the attempt to make man the end of all things. Man takes the place of God. This has a long history behind it, as we all know. Man, drunk with his own knowledge and power, his discoveries and inventions, increasingly asserts his independence, his supremacy, his self-sufficiency. From studying being he passes on to the study of consciousness, and comes to regard himself as the master of his own mind. How he can do this in the light of reason and his own practical experience is difficult to see; indeed, sooner or later it becomes a manifest absurdity; but given such premises, the conclusion is logical; the worship of man is taking the place of the worship of God.

This obsessive exaltation of man lies behind a number of philosophical attitudes that have diverted the human mind from God, thereby extinguishing the religious sense and having innumerable pernicious consequences quite beyond the wit of man to describe. I will mention just a few of the better known and more baneful by name—rationalism, illuminism, naturalism, agnosticism, idealism, existentialism, and today, in a more immediately practical sense, secularism and atheism.

And it must be remembered that though a humanism of this type, utterly committed to the exaltation of man and the neglect or denial of God, imagines that it is enhancing human dignity and delivering man from a tedious and unnecessary state of subjection, it is in fact forfeiting man's real title to greatness and dignity, which resides in his relationship with God and Jesus Christ. 'Man', as we are reminded by the noble and forthright words of Pope Pius XII, 'is made in the likeness of God, One and Three, and hence he too is a person, brother to Jesus Christ who is both God and man, and with him and through him heir to eternal life. In this is man's true dignity.'[1]

The second point is the tendency to manhandle the moral order. This, too, is very widespread, very many-sided, and is characterized by the strangest and most ingenious theories. For the moral order, like everything else, has its source in God and in God its object. All human activity is subject to an influence drawing it beyond human limitations, which if followed can lead it up to the threshold of God: 'So he that doeth truth, cometh to the light' (John, 3, 21).

[1] *A.A.S.*, 1949, p. 265.

But what is most characteristic of today as regards human activity is the attempt to free it from anything that lies beyond a human law bereft of any natural and absolute foundation, or beyond a human consciousness reduced to the narcissistic level of psychological analysis. Liberty is no longer regarded as freedom to do what is right but as license to do as you please, and has become its own end.

The study of moral obligation, deprived of divine laws and sanctions, finally loses all urgency and meaning. Sin no longer exists. And to uphold this terrible principle which cannot but be the source of moral anarchy, all genuine remorse, all repentance which might lead back to the Father's 'house' is suffocated at birth. Man's moral and religious senses stand or fall together, and a moral crisis becomes in the end a crisis of faith.

The third and perhaps the most widespread of these causes would not in itself be an evil if it did not in practice hinder man's normal spiritual development. I mean his conquest of the world of nature. The world of nature, as such, is exactly matched to man's intellectual capacity and so is of immense interest to him, but today a vast number of minds are absorbed in it almost to the exclusion of all other things. With the conquest of the world of nature in our own time, man has become so engrossed in the properties of matter that he no longer has eyes for anything else. Matter has shown itself to be riddled with secrets and rich in energy. From the passionately intense study of these, science has been born, and the kind of certainty science has achieved has banished every other kind of certainty from men's minds as being either without foundation or a form of superstition. Science has enlisted the industrious energy of man and man's industry in turn has tamed nature and turned it to his own uses. The distraction of utility has been added to that of certainty. Technology has turned all things into instruments for man's own ends.

Thus the art of producing *things* has triumphed: industry and commerce have surrounded modern man with such an abundance of sophisticated material riches that he is constantly tempted to give way to the intoxicating illusion that he is happy, and to believe that the whole circle of objective reality—his world, and of subjective satisfaction—his spirit, can be summed up in this wonderful, heady, temporal experience. And so man has barred his own way out of his vast materialistic cage. He has forgotten and denied his God.

So it has come about that the religious sense of the people has grown weak. Is this to the good? In order to quench in man the desire for God, it has been necessary to blindfold him, that is, to deprive him of the power of seeking what lies outside himself and the world of sense, without minding that through this fatal blindness people and things lose first their true significance and then their value. Religious sensibility and, following that, religion itself have been discredited by some as rudimentary phases of human progress which has now reached the scientific phase. Others have regarded these things as primitive manifestations of the human spirit, which have now been dissipated within a fully self-conscious mental activity that is no longer preoccupied with the idea of a First Being. Many more have dismissed them as useless things, in order to direct human activity towards the concrete realities of the everyday life of society. And in our own day they have been stifled by insidious oppression or brutal persecution.

Modern man has neglected the study of 'being' in itself and of the human soul; he has confined himself to external phenomena and psychological experiences. He no longer concerns himself with his angelic but innate capacity to reach out to something beyond the realm of natural experience, with his unquenchable urge to pass beyond the frontiers of the finite world, with the elementary necessity that constrains him to derive his logical processes, even those governing the positive sciences, from an Absolute, a Necessity. And this is what lies behind all the tragedies—spiritual, cultural, social, political—of the world today as it spins on its giddy course devoid of the central axis of security, order, and peace.

2

THE MORAL SENSE[1]

ANY ADEQUATE discussion of the moral sense[2] involves clarifying a number of terms; in particular, that by *moral* we mean human.

Today there is general suspicion of anyone who mentions morality, as though it were boring pedantry, an antiquated and artificial way of considering human activity. People nowadays prefer to study human activity from other viewpoints—psychological, economic, political, scientific, artistic, etc.—rather than from the strictly moral angle.

[1] From *On the Moral Sense*, Pastoral Letter to the Archdiocese of Milan, Lent, 1961.

[2] To avoid possible confusion of terms, we should define what we mean by 'moral sense.'

The term 'natural law' means the moral obligations of the human state, which reason may discover, almost intuitively, through its 'moral sense', or through rational enquiry, and which precedes the formulation of juridical norms by the legislature. It is the sense of equity inherent in the human condition, which claims effective application first, before a formal legal system gives it expression in positive law (cf. *Ad. Rom.*, 2, 14; *S.T.*, I, IIae, 94).

And what is 'conscience'? This is the knowledge one has of oneself, i.e. the reflective act by which we bring reason to bear on our actions, and by means of which we seek to know ourselves at the tribunal of our inner awareness and action. This may be psychological knowledge, which merely takes note of how an act begins and develops; or it may be moral knowledge, when reflection judges how our actions are brought to completion, and are fulfilled in terms of the norms which should guide them, in terms of what is good, in terms of their morality. The moral conscience is consequently a mental act by which an action is judged good or bad, and hence it constitutes the immediate yardstick, from instance to instance, of what we do. Hence it has a resemblance to the moral sense, which includes conscience but has a wider field of reference, embracing not only the inner view of the action but also that external moral canvas which spreads out before human activity.

Can we then make the moral sense and prudence synonymous? Prudence is a perfect virtue of the reason, i.e. of our mode of evaluating, in terms of the good of our actions. Prudence teaches the conscience and the moral sense to judge aright, governs the application of our judgment so that it may function well, gives integrity to our thinking, particularly with regard to how we act; it introduces moral considerations to the practice of reason (cf. *S.T.*, II, IIae, 47). Prudence is a useful rational act, whereas the moral sense has a less specific meaning.

85

These people do not realize that to consider the moral aspect of
an action is to emphasize its specifically human element, which lies
in the use of freedom; this in its turn involves reason and the will,
the higher faculties of the spirit. '*Idem sunt*' affirms St Thomas
'*actus morales et actus humani*',[1] 'moral actions and human actions are
the same thing'.

An action is truly human if it proceeds from a voluntary and
personal choice. 'We call human those actions of which man is
master. And man is master of his actions through reason and will;
from which it follows that liberty is the said human faculty, both
rational and voluntary.'[2]

Thus the moral consideration in human action should be neither
omitted nor discredited; it is the highest and most noble consideration in human action, the most personal and indispensable.

St Ambrose confirms us in this conviction: '*mores proprie dicuntur
humani*'[3], morality is proper to man.

Such an explanation of morality should convince at least those
who have a spiritual and not merely an animal concept of man.

What is more difficult to state precisely is how the concept of
morality includes that of finality, that is, the concept of the end,
the aim to which human action is directed, which is the good.

A human action intentionally performed for a good end is a true
moral action. If the good befits our nature, the moral action is good;
if it is not fitting, the moral action is bad.

Thus the important thing is to establish this suitability to our
nature which is determined by the law and the conscience.

The conscience is the subjective and the immediate guide of
morality. But is its subjective judgment always certain and does it
always correspond objectively to what is good? The objective

Then may the moral sense be the expression of 'synteresis' (the sting of conscience),
i.e. the possession of the first moral principles (I must do good, I must avoid evil)?
Yes, the moral sense is, like the synteresis of the philosophers, the innate disposition to
perceive the fundamental principles of moral action (cf. *S.T.*, I, 79, 13; II, IIae, 47, 6,
ad. 1 and 3); but, when we study it, we find in it a greater inherent meaning, and a
broader one. We may say that it is a habitual orientation towards the good, an alert
and spontaneous awareness of the responsibility of our acts, a summary but deliberate placement of human action on a scale of values higher than life, an appreciation of what we are and of what we do in terms of the requirements of our religious
obligations.

[1] *S.T.*, I, IIae, 1, 3.
[2] *S.T.*, I, IIae, 1, 1.
[3] *In Lc.*, praef. 7, prope. finem.

judgment comes from another guide, the law, which should direct our actions towards what is truly good, and lay down before us an ordered system which we must put into practice.

What subtle and difficult ideas! Human action, liberty, end, good, conscience, law, order. And there are more to come.

Two others should be remembered: the final end, which in its turn leads to the concept of perfection and beatitude; and moral obligation, or duty, to carry out given actions towards the fulfilment of an aim, a good, which appears to be necessary.

All this indicates not only how vast and complicated is the field of morality, but also how important and interesting it is.

We will leave the analysis of these concepts to students and scholars, and content ourselves now with noting that they are implicitly recognized and operate explicitly in that general estimate of human actions which we call the moral sense.

The moral sense is man's natural orientation towards honest good, that is, towards a good which is rightly desired for itself. This honest good can also be useful or pleasant, in so far as it is co-ordinated with the good as such, which in the end is the supreme good, God himself. The moral sense is the realization of order, the intuition of true morality. It is the awareness of good through natural inclination.[1]

We must now consider the moral sense as a habit of mind which puts integrity in human action above all else.

The moral sense, we can say, is the search for the good in our actions. We may not always agree as to what the concepts 'integrity' and 'goodness' mean, because we term an action integral and good according to different criteria; whether, for example, it complies with the dictates of the conscience, or with the wisely interpreted needs of human nature, or with certain laws.

Integrity and goodness can therefore have different meanings. But in general we may say that an action has integrity and goodness when the duty or motive guiding it directs it towards the semblance of good as such, that is to say, when it 'informs' the reason's choice of good because it is good. Such a choice refers, whether we realize it or not, to the absolute Good, the supreme Good which we know to be God, in whom this reason for Good finds its essential and complete realization.

The moral sense therefore eventually becomes one with the

[1] Cf. *S. T.*, I, IIae, 94, 2.

religious sense. It confers on those who possess it a degree of dignity, nobility, and grandeur which man by himself cannot attain. We recognize such people as men of integrity, the heroes and the saints.

An aura of holiness surrounds a person who is truly good because of this relationship between a good action and the good itself, the transcendent aim of human life.

We should remember that the moral sense, the disposition to consider our own actions and those of others in the light of integrity, is not only the best ornament for each individual, but is also a nation's most precious and civilizing heritage.

Today we are witnessing a very important and momentous phenomenon; the moral sense of our people, and indeed of the whole contemporary world, is in a state of crisis.

It is changing and is neither as watchful and regular, nor as active as it was in the past.

To say this is not to adopt the mental attitude which sees the past as good and the present as bad, as with the famous *'laudator temporis acti'* but rather to observe a general fact that is characteristic of our time: a change of custom.

Custom, a people's way of life, is made up of the regular and long-established modes of behaviour of most of the individuals in a community; it is their normal and traditional behaviour. 'Custom is what has always been done, what continues to be done and what . . . should still be done.'[1]

This regularity and persistence are related to moral principles.

It is important to be aware of this relationship. Custom presumably derives from moral principles and so serves to recall and impose them. Thus a change of custom raises the question of whether the moral observance and the expression of the moral sense has changed.

We will not stop to describe practical changes in ways of life today because these are obvious.

But let us observe first how *action* has today acquired an esteem, an importance, an intensity, a scope it never had before. Nowadays action is setting the whole field of modern life into motion, throwing it into agitation, transforming it.

He who acts, lives. Action is the great criterion of modern life.

[1] Cf. M. Gentile, 'I grandi moralisti', p. 6, *R.A.I.*, 1955.

At one time life was dominated by such static ideals as wisdom, order, law; now it is the dynamic ideals that move and excite, such as progress, renewal, revolution, evolution, etc. Today speed is sovereign. Energy, movement, productivity, transformation, discovery, give the continual excitement of novelty. In these terms life is presented as becoming rather than as being, a becoming that goes ever faster and deeper, makes more and more impression on what was once considered motionless and stable.

Work itself, a primary factor of human life around which gravitate ideologies, sociologies, and economies, is only an expression of human activity directed towards its true end. As St Ambrose taught, 'Work is the law of life'.[1]

It is plain that the world is in a state of flux. Also plain are some of the consequences and special aspects, negative and positive, of this febrile agitation of modern man. Let us glance at some of the distortions of the moral sense deriving from the instability of modern life.

First, doubt: instability has even invaded the command post of human activity, thought. This has certainly resulted in an increase of intellectual ardour—*studium*, the ancients called it—but it is an ardour directed towards shaking foundations and principles.

We need only point out now that while doubt is increasingly thrown on the validity of speculative thought, scientific exploration grows ever stronger. The intellect doubts itself, and conquers the universe.

For while vast new fields of the external world are conquered by science, the human mind is inwardly insecure and tries to prove vain the intrinsic consequence of its own logic. Since thought lacks absolute values, it cannot impose them on action. So action remains blind.

The attempt to discover an absolute imperative in moral obligation while denying the mind any objective certainty may be noble, but it is weak and does not work in practice, which is left to the mercy of transient relativism.

Such is the primary and basic negative result of modern activism.

Human activity has grown enormously today. But it seems to have lost a sense of awe, a sense, that is, of supreme ends, for which it has substituted immediate means. It has weakened moral obligations and made precarious the respect for the laws that

[1] *In Lc.*, praef. 6.

guide it outwardly and justify it inwardly, that determine and en-
noble it.

Hence modern disquiet, the cult of action for its own sake, the
urge for revolution, the prevalence of might over right.

But order must be found somewhere.

And here we come to an important aspect of the flux of contemporary life. All this anxious activity needs must tend towards
some co-ordinating factor, some form of perfection, and it finds
this in the powers and resources which man's scientific experience
has enabled him to dominate.

Man may no longer be master of himself, but he has become,
to a much greater extent than before, master of the things surrounding him. He has learnt to know and harness energy for his
own profit and enjoyment. Around him everything must be
practical, comfortable, functional. Nowadays he seeks perfection in
objects for his own use.

This perfection in objects to be used is called technology.

Technology has become the great law, the great yardstick. It
rules this life of modern man, because by it he rules the field of
his immediate experience. Science itself plays a great part in this
utilitarianism, with all its marvellous machinery and superb
organization.

The human spirit is more alive, more glowing here than ever
before. The results of this projection of the spirit on to nature's
hidden resources are vast and impressive. They form our modern
civilization of science and technology, this industrial civilization of
ours which puts such means at man's disposal and demands such
discipline in return that it has radically changed traditional ways of
living.[1]

As a result, modern society and its habits are different. So is the
normal rhythm of life. And the tastes, the interests, the forms of
human activity have also changed, outwardly, almost completely,
and inwardly, not a little. Today man studies, thinks, works, plays,
as he never did in the past.

This increased capacity for action and for progress also makes
him wonder whether the canons of morality till now inviolable are
still valid.

If customs change, why not morality too?

[1] Pius XII, Radio message for Christmas 1953; *A.A.S.*, 1954, pp. 6 ff.

Things modern and novel exercise a great fascination on mankind, and particularly on young people: they induce a sense of dizzy elation, of uncertainty and daring. From these changes of custom come dangers of an intellectual order—changes in those ideas which should be firmly anchored to immutable realities and truths.

Such changes in ideas can give rise to grave deviations in the moral order. The basic error is to consider that the moral law, stemming as it does from the essentials of human nature, can ever change, cease to be absolute and universal and become relative to man's judgment and particular circumstances. This is in fact said of the moral law, whose fundamental precepts, constituent elements, and eternal sanctions have been taught us by Christian revelation.

Such moral relativism has a great attraction nowadays, particularly because it exalts human liberty, divorcing it from principles that are both objective and necessary, and giving it complete autonomy.

The exaltation of liberty threatens to encourage licence of every kind, almost to become a principle of anarchy. Liberty, without subjective obligations, objective rules, and transcendental aims, becomes utterly vague, open to any capricious and illogical impulse. With such liberty man can wander in any direction whatsoever, like a blind man in a desert.

Liberty is indeed a supreme prerogative of the human personality, a sign of man's likeness to the divine, a source of his greatness and dignity, of the inviolable dominion of his conscience, the stupendous faculty which makes man generator of his own actions. But it is a relative, not an absolute, faculty; relative to the good, towards which the human will is directed by reason. That is to say it is not an end in itself but an instrument by which the good is chosen.

This good is not something irrational. It is not even man in himself. It is man in the complex of the particular connections and surroundings in which he spends his life. These connections and surroundings postulate an objective order, a rule to be followed, a purpose which is outside man himself and with which he must integrate.

Man is made up of autonomy and heteronomy. Liberty as an end in itself means a liberty that is irrational and uncontrollable. This is why supporters of this absolute liberty eventually find life an agony and the world absurd. It also explains why absolute expressions of liberty correspond with absolute expressions of despotic, totalitarian authority.

Another very important and serious moral consequence can and does derive from the inevitable—and in itself good—evolution in habits. This is a matter not so much of specific doctrine as of mental attitude, of a mistaken conception of life. It is the idea that temporal goods can answer all man's needs and satisfy his deepest aspirations.

The great effort made by modern man to know and conquer the world of nature, the hard work he has put into transforming this world and making it useful to him, have brought him vast riches and a concentration on economic and material good. It has also followed that the benefits to his physical health, to his culture and pleasure, have produced in modern man the facile illusion that he has achieved, or at least is able to achieve, happiness by this means, and so he is convinced that he must seek it by this means.

The whole of life has thus come to be considered in terms of economic good upon which all man's personal and social efficacy depends. This is the materialist conception of life with its vast moral repercussions.

The main if not the only motive force of human activity becomes self-interest. Individually this frees a man from moral obligation and fear of God; socially it leads men to struggle for the possession and enjoyment of economic goods, source of every other good.

Men who concentrate on material goods are filled with an extraordinary zest and energy to produce, administer, own, and keep possession of them. To such people every manifestation of life seems to derive from the economic structure of society.

This is historical materialism, with all its simplifications. It cannot understand the complex reality of the universe, but it can torment man by stimulating his appetite and by making him hope in a justice whose only scale of values is economic and temporal. Historical materialism, with its spiritual blindness, cannot grasp religious values. And it ends by denying God.

The idea that happiness is or can be reached through the possession and enjoyment of temporal goods is very prevalent in our era. It even has a hold over those who do not accept the theories and principles of materialism. Its fatal consequence on moral life is hedonism, the search for pleasure as a result of riches gained or as reward for riches not yet achieved.

Modern hedonism as we all know has had expressions every whit as extreme as the most refined and corrupt paganism of the past. It has its own treacherous literature, its own vast and varied press, its own formidable organization. It has invaded the theatre and the cinema. It is particularly evident in some of the habits of our upper-middle class and aristocracy.

For it is becoming a habit, a bad habit. Sexual immorality is characteristic of this false view of life, sharing both its attractions and its consequences. It has a strong attraction, makes a deep impression, and is easy to indulge in repeatedly; and it leads to mental and moral distress, obsessive passion, scandal, and social disintegration. But its main consequence is loss of that inner beauty which is innocence and grace, without which it is easy to lose faith in God and even hope in life.

The atmosphere of our age has been impregnated with the attitude of mind which allows such latitude and priority to the flesh, to sensuality, pleasure and vice. It is aggravated by the morbidities of psychoanalysis, the flaunting of luxury, by art which is careless of its influence on the soul. And now there are also the far-reaching effects of some of our films and television programmes.

All this is assuming such proportions that it needs careful watching by those who care about the highest and most delicate human values. The moral sense really is changing, and as far as we can see today this change is not in the direction of raising and strengthening the moral sense, developing a strong and healthy humanism, the worthy and sacred use of life or any virile and Christian virtues. Usually the changes seem to distract and confuse, weaken and disorientate the moral sense.

These few remarks about moral change resulting from changes in habits could lengthen into long, dreary lists supported with weighty evidence.

These erroneous moral tendencies are summed up in the Gospel in one word: the 'world'.

This word, used by Christ and in the first Epistle of St John the Evangelist, does not mean the complex of created things that we call the universe, nor the sum of human beings in this world nor any particular field of human action. It means the state of mind and the habits of those who do not follow Christ. The world is life lived outside his light. It is the result of all the vague theories and expedient opinions that have not passed through the needle's eye of truth. It is the effect of habits unjustly established by passion and self-interest, not by duty. It is the outer, pharisaical, form of virtue. The morality of the world is the so-called easy-going morality, freed from rules that are too demanding and too severe.

The world today exercises a great fascination and imposes its own seductive conventions on people who think themselves free. A glimpse of it should be enough to make us feel the call of the moral sense and to understand more of the world's admitted opposites, true honesty and true sanctity.

Signs of today's moral crisis are a refusal to accept suggestions by authority; an antipathy against paternalism, obedience, heteronomy, law; an inclination to accept whatever is imposed by authority, leading to a sympathy for state-control and totalitarianism; a rejection of custom or tradition and a consequent reaction against all conformity, regulation, or stability. On the other hand there is insistent pressure to follow current fashions, manners, and styles, to do what others do or what they will be doing, and to do what is expedient.

Another sign is the rejection of what is easy, of solutions already reached, of the providential, the balanced, the comforting, and a preference for what is difficult or problematical, for the anguished, the tormented, the rebel, the absurd, etc. There is scepticism of virtue, chastity, religion, goodness, sacrifice, and resignation to our own weakness, a lack of will to carry out promises or intentions, to be coherent or happy. Truth, understood as the relationship between thought and reality, or as between what is and what should be, is replaced by 'sincerity' or 'authenticity' (Nietzsche), understood as psychological and amoral awareness of one's own state of mind, of one's own movements of spirit. Hence the tendency to think oneself honest and wise when exploring and expressing this 'awareness', which does not tell us our duties but describes them, thus escaping both moral obligation and responsibility to others. Hence the tendency to lay oneself completely open to hedonistic spontaneity, to intensity of pleasure of whatever kind, even if selfish, animal, corrupt, and corrupting, even if designed to destroy all scruples and remorse.

The result is 'amorality', the gratuitous concurrence in or refusal of an action according to one's own arbitrary convenience. Finally comes immorality, the rejection of all life that is not spontaneous and freed of what is considered artificial.

This is pure egotism, which thinks itself free but is actually in a state of servile receptivity, making an aesthetic and despairing precept of evasion.

At the root of every mistaken concept about human action lies a mistaken concept about our relationship with God.

The basis of the integrated human system regulating our actions is religion. Why? Because God is the first cause of being, the guiding light of thought, the basic law of human action. This triple synthesis is from St Augustine.[1] When our reason respects the laws of its own working and the exigencies of reality it must necessarily adhere to it. The normal human being has an intuition of this order and so is naturally led towards that religious sense which we call 'fear of God' and which is the beginning of wisdom (Prov. 1, 7; 9, 10; Eccl. 1, 9 ff; 1, 18).

When God is intentionally denied, the whole moral system is compromised. Morality loses its reference to an absolute principle, to a transcendent aim, to a necessary obligation. The concept of good becomes relative and so insufficient to satisfy human aspirations. If it were sufficient it would become only a relative and limited good; first illusion, then disillusion, would dominate the human spirit (cf. Eccl. 1 ff).

Liberty can become licence—no longer a rational faculty for choosing good but a vague and floundering activity, mere blind spontaneity lacking the dignity and joy of willing and loving.

Moral obligation is particularly sensitive to the conscious denial of God, which deprives duty of its grandeur and strength.

Of course, when action conforms to healthy reason, a moral system can develop and function without explicit avowal of God; it implicitly refers to principles which in their turn refer back to God.

This is the morality of many who are honest but not religious and also of many who are religious but untrained in speculative thought. This morality persists in a society whose principles derive from Christianity.

But this morality eventually finds support in other principles

---

[1] *Contra Faustum Manichaeum*, XX, 42, (*Deus*) *nobis est initium existendi, ratio cogitandi, lex amandi.*

which seem simpler and more convenient but which in the end
reveal their own weakness. Moral scepticism lies at the base of
morality without God. At first it is sustained by habit, then its ethic
is supplied by exterior legality. Moral laxity and practical indifference follow, together with inability to see any true distinction
between good and evil; the final result is amorality, which calls
what succeeds good and what fails, bad. Our era has had tragic
experience of this in the ideologies that have generated totalitarian
absolutism and revolutionary anarchies.

If we may briefly sum up the moral crisis we are passing through
we might say that:

(a) If, by morality, we mean the faculty to act, freedom, the
will to work, activism, intensity—i.e. the capacity and will for
action—then our era shows definite progress.

(b) Likewise, if by morality we mean knowledge of human
action, we may note a great revival of interest which, in the field
of Catholic culture, is developing rapidly. Likewise, the theory
and practice of various education and teaching methods are today
making great steps forward and are held in high esteem.

(c) If, by morality, we mean duty, the observance of the law,
the search for moral standards, the principle of authority, religion,
whether we think this is the basis or the result of ethics (Kant),
then there is a definite decline.

(d) Finally, if by morality we mean that which is human, then
it is difficult to define the position. For from one point of view
man has become the centre of everything. All the new movements, whether spiritual, cultural, social, or political are guided
by an aspiration to create a new humanism. But who is man?
What should his ideal be? On this central point of human
morality there are deep cleavages in the modern world, and these
cause the most varied and strident contrasts.

Even so we would like to think that modern man's absorbing
interest in these matters is a good omen. For it shows modern
thought moving from matter to life, from the external world to
humanity, from aims that are purely economic and political to aims
that concern the individual and his spirit, from purely scientific
knowledge to a sense of man's mystery.

And behind this mystery, now and again, can be glimpsed the
ever-present Christ.

Let us try in all honesty to look for the good in moral action today. For good there must always be, even if partial and deformed; even if, lacking co-ordination with life's final purpose and with the authentic plan for human perfection, what is good in itself must be udged bad in relation to man's true good.

Let us remember that we are always directed towards the good, even when we go astray. Man lives to act, and the object of action is always a good. Basically we are directed towards the good.

We should be as punctilious in looking for the good in every manifestation of life as we are in searching out defects and deviations. This does not mean glossing things over and making ourselves and others believe that for a human phenomenon to possess one good feature is enough to qualify it as good. We want to encourage that partial good, make it an aspiration towards a genuine and complete good.

We must do this because there is a great deal of good in humanity's general progress towards the ideals that guide it to ever increasing perfection. Otherwise we can neither understand our era nor benefit it, nor will we be faithful to the redemptive message of the Word whose disciples and teachers we want to be.

Yes, there is much that is good in our era; even though there are deformations and contradictions in certain aspects of human behaviour which nevertheless are definitely good.

Firstly, there are ideals which merit our praise and trust. These ideals, if examined carefully, turn out to be as Christian as they are humane. We may even say that they derive, in their absolute and binding formulation, from Christianity. We might call them the guiding beacons, the motive forces of the modern world.

Briefly these are: the respect for the *human person* as the pivot of civil rights; the cult of *liberty* as the source and explanation of every honest human activity and as the irreplaceable criterion of all true and responsible morality; the duty to promote a constant improvement, a continual *progress* in the conditions and forms of human life; the ideal of social and international *peace* which, if justly understood and loyally applied, can change many of the false concepts of sociology and politics that many men still profess in open contradiction to their often hypocritical and rhetorical exaltation of the sacred Christian word 'peace'; finally, the *unity* of the world in a harmony that respects each component part; this ideal no longer

seems utopian and oppressive but ecumenical, having as its goal
and guarantee that Catholic unity begun in history by Christ and
promoted doggedly and fearlessly by the Church.

To these great and wonderful ideals could be added others
characteristic of our time; they all generate changes which are
reasonable in so far as they spring from natural, moral, and Christian
principles which are still insufficiently expressed in positive equity
and actual conditions.

First among these ideals is that of justice. We will not discuss now
which type of justice the modern world seems to want, or the
oppressive and unjust forms it sometimes takes. We will only say
that this concept, which is an irrefutable argument for the existence
of a natural right, preceding and promoting positive right, arouses
powerful energies in our society; it urges on the continual process of
law which works to adapt to social realities those needs which the
'moral sense' tells us are both legitimate and imperative.[1]

The need for truth is less general but its principles are no less
noble; sometimes, however, in its concrete forms of expression it is
as little deserving of praise.

Young people in particular are conscious of this need. In them it
is a need not so much for speculative truth as for truth lived. The
ancients called it 'veritas vitae' and distinguished it from 'veritas
doctrinae'.[2] It is a truth stripped of rhetoric, cliché, conventional
enthusiasm, pretentious ambition; an attitude of the spirit rather
than a logical system, it springs from disillusion due to the ghastly
wars inflicted on the generations of this century. The young reject
the wisdom of the past with intolerance, even with contempt.
There is a danger here of scepticism and cynicism, even of disintegration, as certain books and paintings reveal. But the young
and generous also feel a need to recover basic certainties of thought
and to accept the obligation to bring their conduct into line with
these certainties.

These attitudes are not rife where the Christian religion is an
inner ferment of sincerity and truth, rather than mere outward
show. In this connection we recall Pope John XXIII's words to the
world in his Christian radio message on the duty of thinking,
honouring, and speaking the truth and acting truly.

These words can be the foundation of a moral life.

[1] Cf. Pius XI, *Divini Redemptoris*, pp. 24 ff., C.T.S., London.
[2] *S.T.*, II, IIae, 109, III, ad. 3.

Another positive and very fruitful aspect of the moral sense in our time is the tendency to make a duty of giving spontaneous help to those in need.

The concept of human solidarity has made a great deal of progress. Vast developments in charitable organizations and health and education services, the science and practice of social assistance and social security, the emphasis on the duty of rich nations to help backward countries, are great and growing realities in contemporary life.

They bear witness to the approach of a humanism that is Christian in origin and impulse. We are, we must be, pleased by this moral and social evolution and see it as an encouraging expression of the moral sense, by the generation of a genuinely humane civilization.

We must also mention another factor of great importance today which is bringing about a dynamic reform of our way of life: democracy.

Democracy has been discussed and elaborated as a system which recognizes the people as the primary source of sovereignty. It fits into the Christian concept of authority as coming from God: 'there is no power but from God' affirms St Paul (Rom. 13, 1). We may observe that the people possess this authority by the natural law, of which God is the author, when they form a society and entrust its material and moral functions to chosen representatives (*potestas a Deo per populum*).

Today, though, democracy is considered more as a system of organized social life founded on the primary concept of the dignity of each human individual; from this develops the gradual process of man's emancipation from a state of having no basic civil rights to responsible participation in promoting the public good.

In a democracy, therefore, man figures as an individual free and equal to others and subject to the law and to duty in their most complete expression.

Thus democracy is also a factor of first importance in man's life, capable of producing a 'moral sense' of great value to a people's education and spirit. So Pius XII said, just before the war ended, in his Christmas radio message in 1944.[1]

Let us hope that this is so. For democracy must be sustained by a vigorous and austere moral sense. This should be a rule which is lived rather than imposed: a result of the collective conscience

[1] *A.A.S.*, 1945, pp. 12 ff.

on the respect which every citizen owes to himself and others and on every man's collaboration and solidarity for the common good.

This high, inner concept of right and duty holds together really well—we would like to say *only* holds together—if society's conscience is pervaded by religion. That is why we consider that religion, when properly understood and practised, has a new and indeed indispensable role to play in our democratic era.

Let us hope this may be so, and that the word 'democracy' will no longer engender and conceal abusive forms that are a disintegrating force within the social order. For this word can be interpreted in a sense which is opposed to its true meaning: exclusiveness, collective egotism and privilege, and therefore social struggle and class war. It can also mean giving free-play to irresponsible and indiscriminate activities harmful to the public peace and public good. Again, it can mean the excessive influence of political parties which, while pretending to help citizens exercise their civic rights, substitute their own interests and manoeuvre the electorate towards aims which are not their own.

Thus the ideal of popular sovereignty which is proper to democracy can, when it has no higher ethical or juridical principles, become arbitrary and violent in the apparent service of freedom; or turn into class or state despotism.

If, on the other hand, democracy is permeated by the moral conscience it can help bring about, in justice and love, the brotherhood which is humanity's highest good and which for us Christians has its fruitful and incorruptible source in the fatherhood of God brought to us by Christ.

3

THE SENSE OF SIN IN THE MODERN WORLD[1]

THE NEED for redemption begins with awareness of sin. Let us explore for a moment what this awareness means in the world around us.

We absorb the mental climate, the currents of thought and public opinion which surround us. What place has awareness of sin in all this?

I would like to make these few observations. The first is that where God, or liberty—'moral liberty'—or responsibility, is denied, there is no longer any concept of sin. We find that these constituents of moral responsibility, which combine to form the true moral sense, are denied in the world we live in—sometimes widely and resolutely denied.

The atheism which surrounds us denies God and thereby denies that any relationship with him can exist; if there is no relationship with him then there cannot be that violation of this relationship, which is sin. Thus mankind, by abolishing God, becomes completely innocent and completely irresponsible.

It is this lack of any fear of God, this ignorance that we are responsible to him for our actions, which produces so much confusion in the world and alters so deeply its ways of living, judging, and acting. The Babel we can see around us is due mainly to these basic denials.

What happens then? The awareness of sin and evil is not destroyed but altered. We often hear about self-accusal in certain trials: 'I am at fault, I have done unworthy things and am a wretched creature; I stand here to be condemned!' When awareness of sin breaks out in such tragic and ridiculous ways it shows that even under atheist regimes where every effort is made to blot out any idea of God and so of moral responsibility this responsibility survives and is somehow

[1] From Sermon given on Monday of Holy Week, 1956.

reborn. It is deformed of course, but it is reborn in the heart of man and expresses itself in ways that are so unnatural that we ask ourselves whether the world has not gone mad. A sense of evil, of sin, persists even while it is denied.

Another denial of sin is contained in the word 'freedom', used as a sophistry by the youth of today. Young people feel that rules limit their field of action, that God's commandments are all prefaced with the unattractive word 'not'. 'Thou shalt not kill, thou shalt not lie, thou shalt not commit adultery, thou shalt not steal.' Always not, not, not. The young, full of exuberant life, their instincts anticipating their intellect, feel the moral law to be a strait jacket. Then they say, 'Suppose I try to break this "not", this negative rule? Suppose I ignore it?' So they try; and have an immediate sense of freedom, freedom from scruples, freedom from fear, from the awe of God. At last, they think, they can do as they like.

This form of liberation from the sense of sin cuts people off from the logical and spiritual order, the order of the will and the intellect, and leaves them at the mercy of instinct and impulse.

According to certain writers today, in this way man becomes sincere with himself; as if it were sincere for man to let his lower, his animal side prevail over his spiritual side.

What happens next? A general darkening. Then come crises of faith, followed by all kinds of accommodating philosophies and justifications that put thought after action. Action should be regulated by thought. Instead of which, now, action creates a justifying philosophy. This leads to action that is arbitrary, to an easy and open corruption of manners. It means the self-ruin of youth, dissipating its own vitality, wasting the physical and emotional, moral, and spiritual energy which it could have. Then comes satiation; a hint of sadness and bitterness is to be found in many young people today who are experienced in this false form of liberation.

There is a third way of shaking off our sense of sin; by sophistry—what we might call the sophistry of adults—the separation, that is, of one order of actions from the general complex of human life. People say every action has its own technique: I act according to this technique without caring whether my particular segment of life or action is in harmony with all the rest or not. If an instrument in an orchestra said: I am playing my own music and do not care about the other instruments, and the other instruments did the same, then there would be confusion and disharmony. This disharmony is produced by the person who separates a part of his activity from the equilibrium of the total order to which life should submit; and so his justification for sin is a false one. This happens all the time, and it is one of the factors that most influences social life today. How often people say, 'business is business'; and then do their business according to their own law, which is the law of their own advantage. It does not matter to them if gaining this advantage means violating justice, law, conscience . . . 'Business is business'.

A subtler formula of the same kind is, 'The economy is autonomous and sovereign; it cannot be subject to moral scruples; we must make a free economy.' By 'free' they mean an economy determined solely by the intrinsic laws of self-advantage and the play of the market. These people do not consider that the economy is also a human factor and should obey human laws. Above the economy is man, and the economy must be subordinate to man's advantage, an advantage understood not only subjectively, in an egotistical way, but as the advantage of the whole social fabric. The goods of this earth should in fact serve mankind as a whole. If not, by separating economic life from the ordered complex of human action, we deny the sense of sin. Politics tend to do this.

Politics which leave the moral order out of account have no laws but their own. They become the art of succeeding, the science of means, of immediate ends.

With such reasoning it is easy to be precipitated into disorder, into war. This very isolation of politics from the general considerations which should govern the balance and unit of life led to the last world war.

Art is a splendid thing in itself, people say; it has its own laws and needs, even, one often hears, its own inner purity. But if it causes harm to life, to moral life, to childhood, youth, then art is no longer a splendid thing. Art too must bow to what is more important, to the hierarchy of the whole human order. It is not right that art should be a kind of forbidden fruit for the younger generations or for those who could be harmed by some of its products. Art too must be part of the superior harmony which respects man's supreme ends.

To isolate one field of our actions, to follow prevalent custom without bothering about the harmony of the whole causes the loss of a sense of sin; and not only its loss, but denial that there is such a thing as sin.

How often do we hear, 'One can't avoid doing wrong, some
rules just can't be observed whatever the priests tell us. They just
can't.' In other words, good is impossible, so is moral law, honesty,
or innocence. I have heard a mother justify her son, who had
fathered a child and refused to recognize it, with the words: 'What
can one expect? He's young . . . He's got to live.' Ah, how ingenuous! He's got to live has he? To dishonour his own home and
others? Are these the rights of youth? Sad to say, the young often
find indulgent mothers, fathers, and judges who tell them: 'Try
everything once.' How often in young minds the temptation arises,
'Let's give it a try; if I don't I won't know life.' Evil has its own
dynamic, its own experience, its own power. Its kingdom must be
entered, even though it makes us dizzy. There is a moment of
excitement, of apparent grandeur. . . . All illusion, my children! To
prove this just look around and read modern books for yourselves;
you will see that when they stem from this principle and try to describe this way of acting—sin as justified, sin as strength, sin as
power—these books always end with a bleak sense of souls lost in
despair and absurdity.

4

MODERN UNBELIEF[1]

NOWADAYS THE sin of unbelief, as you know better than I do, rises like a tide. The world around us calls itself Christian because it is heir to a Catholic past which in two thousand years has covered our land with sacred buildings, including the one we are in now. It has given our society rites, customs, noble traditions both human and civil, and it has created organizations which continue today to perform innumerable good works. It has given us knowledge, scholarship, and culture.

Yet the characteristic sin of our time is incredulity, apostasy, the forsaking of faith, the crisis of conscience and thought. The abandonment of our holy religious tradition, of our venerated spiritual patrimony, is nowadays almost usual. This is a very serious sin and one which weighs heavily on our society.

What will our Lord say to us who have received so much from him, yet who are so careless about gathering, nourishing, and revivifying these traditions? If St Charles Borromeo were with us now what would he say of us disciples so feeble and so faithless to his teachings on the very matter he cared most about, fidelity to Christian doctrine? Many are no longer taught Christian doctrine at all. Religious instruction survives only because there is legal backing to support it. But where, my people, is your spontaneous eagerness for instruction? Where is your care and responsibility towards the Word of God who came down from heaven to teach and save us? Where is your urge to know God's truth, to let our Lord guide you, to be pupils of our divine master?

We have come so far and yet now we go out in search of human teachers. We have burnt all that incense to freedom, created a free citizenship, given a free circulation to every theory, and now allow renegades to teach us and to print and give the widest possible

[1] From Sermon given on Maundy Thursday, 1959.

distribution to depraved books. Our very press gives daily proof of the absence of religion in our lives. This tenacious, polemical, ferocious attack on Christ's truth is an inherent sin of our time.

All around us we find varied proof of the wish to suffocate the faith. Why is this? One could give innumerable answers to that question; the reasons are many and lead to lengthy diagnoses. Try to make these diagnoses yourselves, but let us discuss them together elsewhere, for to do so here would take too long.

Yes, we are tempted with the sin of apostasy. Our society is becoming irreligious and atheistic. Atheism, which was once exceptional and ineffective, has now become a disease deliberately spread by its own printers, its own books and propagandists, and by its own political parties. Sometimes we allow ourselves to be fascinated by the thought; may they not be right? Deep down we begin to make excuses for their unbelief. Our idea of God, of religion and the faith in our souls is so vague that our minds are inert, we give way to intellectual laziness, play with impractical ideas, even try at times to cut a figure with some phrase of doubt or criticism.

Utopianism and sophism have become fashionable. If you want in a few words the main reasons for the modern crisis of thought, by which I mean the modern crisis of faith, they can, it seems to me, be reduced to two, both taken from the Gospels.

First: prejudice. Why did the Jews not believe? Because they had already defined their own truth among themselves and did not want to submit to a new teacher announcing a new truth, even though this truth seemed more persuasive, had better intrinsic reasons, and was outwardly supported by astounding miracles. The Jews were too prejudiced.

How many of our brethren and fellow-citizens are prejudiced too! How many of them judge religion before they know it! Rooted in their own mental systems, they will no longer even discuss it. In much of the activity we think of as intellectual there is an implicit dishonesty of thought.

The second reason for incredulity is self-interest; that is, avoiding the encumbrance of a message which would change our lives. We are afraid of God's word, and try to avoid hearing it so that it cannot come and disturb us. We try to silence it because its acceptance could become binding for us and we do not want to be bound. We have our business affairs, our careers, our pleasures to think of. Do not come and tell us things which would give us other worries. We are hard workers, people who consider ourselves well set-up in this world.

And so, as St Augustine says in his comment on the Gospel for this morning, by our ignorance we are losing both this world and our other heritage, heaven. The earth will swallow us up and be our tomb. That was the first sin, the first dramatic sin to enter the gospel scene.

The second sin which our Lord found on his path, and against which he was very severe, was pharisaism.

What is pharisaism? Why did our Lord launch out so against the representatives of official virtue? The Pharisees were observers of the law; they tried to be just and they practised their religion scrupulously. Why, then, did our Lord not esteem them, these saints of his time, nor praise their organized and official virtue?

To analyse this would introduce us into another world of morality very close to our own. Our Lord saw in the Pharisees a virtue which was apparent but not real. He called them 'whitened sepulchres'. Jesus, who is truth, has what I might call an irrepressible repugnance for a living lie, for hypocrisy, for imposture. Because he is the radiant truth he reacts against a mask of virtue, against the legal virtue practised by the Pharisees, the virtue which is all surface, and follows the letter of the law. Such virtue is isolated; under its formal label is hidden all the inner rottenness of bad thoughts, bad actions, bad habits. This was what most angered our Lord, and his anger was expressed not only in blistering words, but in famous parables such as that of the Pharisee and the publican in the temple.

Exterior virtue is ostentatious, and Jesus could never tolerate it. He called it hypocrisy, imposture, pretence. He reacted vigorously to overthrow it. He preferred the publicans and sinners, who denounced their sins in a spirit of truth and humility, to those who walked erect and made it quite plain that they were fasting, giving alms, following the Mosaic law.

Is there hypocrisy, pharisaic virtue among us, too? If we look around at our society we have to admit that we are not immune from this terrible vice. Sometimes people are heard saying: we venerate and respect the judiciary and want it to be great, free, and wise. But are not many of us content merely with the legal justice of the written code? How many of us fail to move on from this to its application in real life, in human reality, in morals?

Think of the crimes that go uncondemned because there is no

formal accusation. With our legalistic outlook we are content with
this. And how much more could be said of the emphasis on outer
show in modern life! Fashion, art, luxury, with their outward semblance of perfection, of beauty, of an advanced form of life—what
do they hide? The film-star system, so wide-spread and so highly
publicized, does it not hide ignoble, cruel, pointless, selfish lives?
Film-stars are the heroes and heroines of newspapers and magazines,
and the delight of many, far too many, readers. Hypocrisy, false
morality, is the façade that hides reality.

Nor are these the only evils that our Lord finds in us.

Just now I mentioned the violent outbursts of Christ's eloquence
against evil which is hidden and camouflaged.

Another evil which made Christ angry was scandal. What is scandal? It is the propagation, the contagion of evil. Notice that our
Lord adopts an unexpected attitude towards it, one which is not
always realized. He did not want evil to be repressed by force or
external means. He hoped that what is today called self-criticism,
that is moral force, would impose itself on its own, and he said,
'*Oportet ut veniant scandala*'. It is inevitable that human weakness
must produce evil, a succession of evil acts like a contagion or an
epidemic. That is humanity's sad fate.

In the parable of the cockle our Lord told of servants who, impatient to put a field into order, wanted to tear the cockle up. No,
he said, do not touch it, leave it to ripen. Our Lord does not want
violent physical repression. He puts the modern problem of tolerance in terms that are incredibly liberal and generous; but he
launches out fiercely against scandal. His words were metaphoric,
I know, but he could have chosen metaphors less crude. Instead, he
said:

> 'If your hand causes you to sin, cut it off; it is better for you
> to enter life maimed than with two hands to go to hell, to the
> unquenchable fire. And if your foot causes you to sin, cut it off;
> it is better for you to enter life lame than with two feet to be
> thrown into hell. And if your eye causes you to sin, pluck it out;
> it is better for you to enter the kingdom of God with one eye
> than with two eyes to be thrown into hell' (Mark 9, 43–7).

See how severe our Lord is, how he challenges on the inner, not
the outer, plane. On this inner plane he also challenges what others
consider proper to oneself, one's natural powers, the eye, hand, and

foot. Jesus wants us to mortify ourselves. If this mortification is necessary to fight the evil within us, better be mortified than sinning. No, we do not expect such severity in the gentle face of Christ, who strokes children and says: 'To such belongs the kingdom of God', and then goes on to those tremendous words: 'Whoever causes one of these little ones who believe in me to sin'—and Christ's imagination creates a torture that is metaphysical and apocalyptic—'it would be better for him to have a great millstone fastened round his neck and to be drowned in the depth of the sea'. To such a point does the responsibility of scandal weigh on the conscience. My children, the world which we live in is all scandal; '*totus in maligno positus est*' says St John. We, too, say so; our whole world is full of evil and scandal. Evil has a liberty, a diffusion, an organization, a power which seems irresponsible but is in fact responsible.

Here I want to say: woe to those who write certain things, woe to those who use the theatre to scandalize the innocence of our youth; woe to those who organize certain television programmes and so often project worldly values into our homes and present debased forms of amusement; woe to those who write novels that corrupt life at its source, at its roots, in its highest and worthiest manifestations: innocence, love, life, hope. Woe to them, for above them is a hand that will not forgive and will ask them to account for every soul they have scandalized.

Let us tremble, brethren, if we too are accomplices. Let us tremble because the just God who announced our salvation also announced so energetically the ruin of those who want evil and spread it.

I feel that perhaps I am becoming too serious but I do not want to end without mentioning other evils which our Lord fought openly: avarice, for instance, the search for earthly goods and the forgetting of eternal good, the preference for exterior rather than interior good.

Avarice ossifies the soul and prevents the heart feeling for others. It destroys the possibility of opening our lips in prayer. Woe to you, oh rich! Blessed are you, oh poor. These phrases in the Gospel have a fundamental significance. How Jesus denounces the life of the rich man who spends his riches only on himself and for his own enjoyment! We see this especially in the parable of the rich man and Lazarus.

You may be wanting to ask what our Lord said concerning yet another epidemic in our society, sensuality, the sin against life, the sin against the flesh. We are surprised at not finding a categorical denunciation, as though this suggests that Christ, knowing how delicate this subject is, never dealt with it directly. But he did, and very firmly too. When the crowd was pressing around the woman who had been taken in adultery and was about to be condemned and stoned, Jesus was bending down and seemed to be distractedly writing in the dust with his finger. When the crowd asked, 'What do you say about her?' Jesus got up, looked around, reading the souls of those people as his eye passed over them, then pronounced the words which show how well he understood our miseries: 'Let him who is without sin among you be the first to throw a stone at her'—you are all hypocrites, all marked with the same sin. And one by one the questioners moved away.

No, we find in the Gospel that our Lord has not forgotten sensuality, humanity's running sore. We find that he treated it with great human delicacy, that he tried to present the problem as a positive rather than a negative one. To convince us that we can recover from it, Jesus made Mary Magdalene a privileged person, the first to hear the news of the resurrection, his vision, his message. Take the case of the Samaritan woman: Jesus made revelations to this lost soul whose sins of the flesh he denounced bluntly yet discreetly. Our Lord knows that we too must be most careful and severe in our examination of conscience about this sin, but he wants us to be sincere about it. Jesus is discreet about this sin for he knows that it is not the most serious one. The most serious sin is one of thought, the sin of pride. But he also knows that the sin of the flesh is the most contagious, the easiest to fall victim to. He seems, one might almost say, to be wanting to limit the chances of contagion by speaking of it with the utmost delicacy, summing up his teaching in the lovely words: 'Blessed are the pure of heart for they shall see God.'

You see, brethren, where the Gospel has led us? It has brought us into the hospital of sick humanity. For we live in the midst of a world infected by many sins. Should we just curse it? No, of course not. How are we to behave then? All I ask for as the result of this evening's meditation is sincerity. Let us call things by their names, 'est est, non non'. Behind this sincerity, believe me, there is only God's judgment, his law, his requirements, and also his sanctions.

Let us prepare for Easter by making a humble and sincere examination of conscience before God.

5

THE FAMILY IN THE MODERN WORLD[1]

OUR FIRST observation is that people today are far more conscious than they were in the past of problems connected with family life. The word 'family' is on everyone's lips. There are studies of the history of the family. Even a philosophy about the family has grown up. The family is analysed demographically. Theories are launched about its nature, its fecundity. Its juridical aspects are discussed. New laws concerning it are promulgated. A vast literature has grown up around it, and new institutions are founded for it.

In the religious field, too, there are notable signs of interest in the family. Charitable and social organizations are beginning to occupy themselves with the family as a unit, and not only with its individual members. The sacrament of matrimony is studied today as never before. Special pastoral care for the family is developing. The spiritual life of the family now has its own theologians and experts.

This increased awareness is due to the fact that family patterns are in a state of transition. This is obvious to everyone. We need only mention the lessening of paternal authority which was the cornerstone of the old pattern of family life; the growing importance of the wife; the change in the distribution of money and so of the family's economic function; the growing number of jobs which take members away from the family group; the increasing role of society in education, welfare, travel, amusement; the changes in the design of houses; the calculated drop in the birthrate; the different internal relationships between members of the family. All this makes us realize how the family nucleus has gone, and is still going, through deep and inevitable changes.

Because of this we now have to face the delicate task of distinguishing between the essentials of family life, which should be

[1] From *For the Christian Family*, Pastoral Letter to the Archdiocese of Milan, Holy Week, 1960.

defended and encouraged, and features which may be no more than optional or transitory and so may be altered.

We can see at once that some aspects of this transformation are positive and others negative.

The vast majority of marriages today are freely entered into. That is, the wishes of one's parents or of other people's considerations of inheritance, dynastic obligations and class pressures are not determining factors nowadays in the formation of a family. Today the protagonists of a marriage are the bride and bridegroom themselves. The crystal clear definition of matrimony by Ulpian (expressing that wisdom of Roman thought which the Church has always defended for Christian civilization), *consensus facit nuptias*, is now being realized. It is consent, free spontaneous consent by the contracting parties, which gives cause and consistency to the pact of matrimony.

This is an advance, for freedom of consent has not always been so full and so autonomous as it is today. It can lead to dangers and disturbances which should not be forgotten; but in itself it is good.

If the family today is freely entered into, this shows that spiritual and emotional factors, with love first and sometimes exclusive, are at the origin of the modern family. This too, if well understood and practised, may be considered an advance.

Love comes first; that is right for an association that should be founded on love. Love precedes marriage and does not only follow it; this also is good, if preparation for a family is to guarantee happiness, honesty, and stability later.

In the modern family children hold a far higher place than they did, both in terms of affection and of education. In the past a child was apt to be considered merely as a consequence of marriage. Births were of course more numerous (an element which is good, and of the highest importance, which should be properly appreciated). But children then received less attention than they do now. Often mothers handed over their children to be cared for by others, and people were resigned to a high rate of infant mortality.

Today the child is considered a major purpose of marriage; *the* major purpose, so the Church teaches. And children are far better looked after, more protected, helped, trained, educated, and loved than they were at one time. Modern education has even begun to condition the lives of parents in relation to their children, and indeed to make the child in a way the educator of its parents.[1] This too, if

[1] Cf. Montessori, *The Secret of Childhood.*

understood and encouraged, is an advantage. It is due not so much to natural reason (which, sad to say, often alternates the idolizing of children with birth-control and abortion) as to a phrase in the Gospels which has gradually made us see children as the most authentic citizens of the heavenly kingdom (Matt. 18, 3).

As children receive greater consideration, so too do their mothers. This again is something about which we should be very pleased, for thus human life is honoured in its loving and mysterious dawn.

Tenderness, compassion, love, sacrifice make motherhood something sacred and sublime. Because of its utter weakness, the new life of which a mother is the source demands the shield of a habitual and unalterable protection. When this new life flowers in a good honest family the mother gains resplendent dignity. It puts her by the side of our blessed Lady, Mother of Christ in the flesh and of ourselves in the spirit.

Thus new, wider family rights are growing up, and these should be recognized as one of the best signs of modern progress. Every man's right to form his own family is now defended and help for the family in hygiene, health, education, has developed. There are praiseworthy efforts to give every family a healthy and adequate home. The principle of family allowances is spreading; large families get favourable treatment; systems of small-holdings, insurance, and pensions develop. There are attempts to promote the well-being not only of each member of a family, but of the family as a whole. And it is to be hoped that the recognition of certain public rights should help consolidate the family as a social nucleus, to give it back some more responsible function, and confer on it more civil dignity as a fundamental unit of society.

With these positive aspects we are bound to mention other, negative, considerations.

The most salient of these are: first, an apparent lessening of family solidarity by comparison with the past. Many extrinsic causes combine to produce this. The economic evolution of society has brought about the organization of labour in industry; this has made the family unit cease to be a means of production and has created the proletarian family. It has encouraged various kinds of emigration and caused some members of a family to tend to move away to more distant places of work. It has also opened up for women occupations outside the home, and so on.

There are many intrinsic reasons, too, for the weakening of the family. Family rules are less strict than before; the patriarchal family has vanished and the power of the father has diminished; each member of the family seeks his own advancement outside the home. What is more, the strong influence of various modern doctrines has corroded the very concept of the family on a fundamental point: its permanence.

Divorce, which denies the indissolubility of marriage on which the permanence of the family is based, has become part of many countries' legislation, and even finds supporters in Italy. These, starting from incomplete or mistaken philosophies of life, now threaten to change the basic concept of the family and do it incalculable harm.

Ignorance of the nature of humanity and denial of the Christian mystery of man are combining to spread a purely naturalistic concept of marriage. This brings with it, as the blind positivist logic of naturalism often does, a degraded, materialistic concept of marriage as something dependent on the whims and passions of the contracting parties. From this follows the specious argument that as marriage is made by the free consent of these contracting parties so it can be dissolved whenever these parties want. This means an appalling collapse of the home, an appalling injustice to innocent children, an appalling desecration of love and of the sanctuary of the family.

The concept of the sacred permanence of the family is still strong and healthy among our people. But unfortunately it is less sustained today by a due sense of responsibility. People are often resigned and indifferent to the break-up of a family and are apt to explain, often to justify it. They feel less like sacrificing one good for another, higher good, and this induces an apathetic indulgence, maybe even a sympathy for those who break up a family. The declining sense of a morality based on transcendental and immutable principles influences many people to accept things which would formerly have been considered scandalous and disastrous.

Another negative fact may be noted: the falling birthrate in the modern family.

This too has varied reasons, not all of them immoral. A high birthrate requires a healthy, strong, united, well-protected family. Families today are often not in that ideal situation.

But there is no doubt that one important reason for a falling birthrate is that widespread and dangerous doctrines have been made available to all. Although these are nearly always inaccurately expressed, they are wrapped up to look scientific. We are alluding to two in particular: neo-Malthusianism and birth control. But we will come back to these later.

Two serious mortal sins result from these mistaken principles: the vicious practice of avoiding conception unlawfully and the criminal suppression of new life germinating in the mother; that is, onanism and abortion. There is a great deal of casuistry about both these, as we all know. Here we need only observe that the range of these sins is difficult to calculate; but those who study the matter have alarming figures to show. We are facing moral deviations, crimes which are an offence to God's plan for the transmission of life and they throw a shadow of infamy over our civilization. These are personal sins which extend into social sins. The devastating epidemics of ancient and medieval times were not perhaps as disastrous as this systematic corrosion of our people's vitality. Perhaps even wars cost fewer human lives than this cold suppression of human beings called to life and death by their own parents.

When selfishness rules the kingdom of human love, the family, it embitters, saddens, and disintegrates it. The art of loving is not as easy as is usually thought. Instinct is not enough to teach it, still less passion or pleasure.

The two opposite poles of love are selfishness and sacrifice. The tendency of the first is to extinguish life; of the second to give it. Christ said: 'For whoever would save his life will lose it, and whoever loses his life for my sake (*propter me*, that is, according to the law of Christ), will find it' (Matt. 16, 25). The marriage union has its basic paradigm in the love of Christ, who sacrificed himself for humanity, redeemed it, and made his Church for this supreme purpose (cf. Eph. 5, 25). When love leaves this supernatural path it deviates towards a sterile and cruel fear of new life.

Then true, pure, transfiguring love is replaced by eroticism. That is what happens to human love when it is deprived of its sacred character, its mysterious spiritual light, its sublime aim, its moral law.

Sexual energy stands as its own arbiter. Man feels that he has discovered the most positive reality in his nature, that he is drawing on the secret sources of his mind. He feels he is deriving from this sexual energy the sincerest and fullest emotion, an experience of the life force. Man opened the way to the depths of his heart, which was empty now of all higher spiritual happiness. He even handed over the region of thought, allowing only an animal definition of his nature. And he found this intoxicating.

Then he began to describe himself and so came the books and songs and films which have such a prominent place in modern life. All this he called sincerity, normal experience, genuine expressions of human nature, freedom at last from all scruples, all hindrances, all moral supports. In so doing man, having broken away from the old Christian rules, is following a course that always seems new but is fundamentally monotonous. Its curve is bound to be a downward one towards domination by instinct. This eventually always means defeat to the free man who is enslaved by a fate stronger than himself. And all he can do then is bewail his lost strength and rail against the evil and absurdity of life. If not he may pretend to resign himself in the supreme hypocrisy of false peace, the spiritual man definitively imprisoned by the animal man.

These dreams are normal today. They are given wide publicity to tickle the public imagination and so permeate and influence the younger generation. This is very dangerous.

Parents, teachers, artists, priests, doctors, magistrates must defend society from this immorality which is flaunted so proudly and cynically. And young people in particular should know how to defend themselves against the eroticism offered them in false exchange for true love; or they may make a bad bargain between a true, everlasting happiness and one that is soulless and ephemeral.

One could, sad to say, point out other negative sides of family life today. But what we have said should be enough to make us more aware of the necessity of preserving and indeed increasing the dignity and function of the family.

We would like now to point out the extent to which the basic cause of weakness and decadence in modern family life stems from a lack of spiritual preparation. Instinct is usually considered to provide the preparation for founding a family, but instinct can fail in its function if not itself instructed, disciplined, and enlightened.

For us Christians, who know that matrimony is raised to the dignity of a sacrament, adequate preparation is indispensable; the more so as home education, once the school of life, virtue, and good habits, no longer has the authority or capacity to prepare sons and daughters for the great act which will determine their state and their future, the act of matrimony. A modern, specific preparation for marriage must be thought out, one in which couples to be married are reminded of its nature and duties, its moral and religious values, so that they can found their new family with an informed conscience and in a whole-hearted way. The engagement period thus acquires great importance as time of education. Everything important, fine, and delicate requires suitable preparation. The great and, in a sense, supreme thing which is matrimony requires a high degree of preparation within the family and on the social and pastoral levels. Here is a new field for the zeal of our teachers and pastors.

6

MATERIAL PROGRESS[1]

Is THE material well-being and economic progress of the modern world genuine? Competent people say that it is and we are all aware of it to some extent. It is not yet general, nor sufficient, nor assured, but the impression is that we are moving towards the increased satisfaction of our economic needs.

We do not want to linger over the many consequences of this modern phenomenon, important though they are in themselves. Hunger, poverty, unemployment, insecurity should vanish. The great social problems that have rent the world since the last century should vanish or at least be attenuated. Social classes should grow closer to each other and the standard of living become more homogeneous. There should be an end to the difficulties of earning a livelihood, a diminution of avarice, of the defence and accumulation of property. The dependence of one man on another, because the economy is such that he cannot earn the means to live, should be lessened.

Tremendous results, these, that change the face of the world and the course of history, as they are beginning to change individual lives, family relationships, popular culture, population stability, etc. Let us take a careful look at this transformation of the world scene.

As we do so, two feelings are uppermost. First, admiration for those who are producing this well-being, for all the scientists, technicians, organizers on one side, and for the workers on the other. We feel admiration for all the brain-power and labour and, let us add, for all the capital instrumental in generating and directing the economic transformation of our society; and admiration for all the work of organizing and putting into practice, for all the sweat and toil which has made such a transformation possible.

[1] From *The Christian and Temporal Goods*, Pastoral Letter to the Archdiocese of Milan, Holy Week, 1963.

118

With admiration goes hope; a tacit hope, reviving once more, of improved relations between management and labour, those two coefficients of modern civilization. One asks oneself whether one should go on regarding them as forces locked in perpetual disastrous opposition simply because they are bound to meet. One asks oneself whether they should not eventually be seen as complementary elements of a productive and social organism—capital and labour, financial means and human labour, those who organize and those who carry decisions out in practice—with mutual interests that seem to come from the very nature of the dual organism, destined to co-ordinate and not to set in opposition the two terms that compose it, and to establish links not of contrast or mere respect but of collaboration and solidarity.

We would like to examine more closely the relationship between these remarkable phenomena and our moral and religious life. First let us look at the negative side.

In an age of material well-being emphasis is laid on the achievement of this well-being. There would be nothing wrong in this, indeed in itself it would be good, so long as this emphasis did not hold up the expansion of the human spirit.

That work should become the rule for all; that it should dignify men and nations and be the main source of a common well-being; that it should grow and render ever-increasing results, using constantly improving techniques to increase production and diminish human effort: all this is excellent.

But can work be an end in itself? Can man's need for activity be satisfied by exercising it on work alone? Can work so satiate human aspirations that it prevents the search for and enjoyment of moral and spiritual good? Can man's religion be a purely secular one?

Is it enough for man to solve the problem of *how* he should act and neglect the *why*? Is the science of means enough for a civilization, without the science of ends? Are economics to guide life and hold first place in it? Should what serves man as a condition of life become his aim in life?

Material well-being, we observe, brings with it the danger of practical materialism. This is favoured by present historical circumstances. The danger is not remedied by the hedonistic satisfactions which material well-being brings with it, such as amusements, luxury, pleasure. We know all too well how when these are considered to be the highest level to which life can aspire they quickly and tragically degenerate into idleness, pride, vice, and boredom. Often, too, they lead to radical pessimism about life and an incapacity to seek and appreciate the moral and spiritual values in which life abounds.[1]

When Christians become watchful and, using their capacity for higher vision, take up an attitude of reserve, criticism, or cautious conditional approval towards the world around them, particularly, as in this case, towards the well-to-do, then a wide sector of public opinion becomes openly hostile to them. That branch of public opinion is aware that the Christian does not entirely conform to the concept of life based on prosperity. It treats him as an outsider, one who does not understand that temporal well-being deserves full support because of its abundance, vitality, and usefulness. Thus the Christian tends to be excluded from the decisive moments of economic activity, the moments when it is given sanction and direction. His moralizing, people say, spoils their fun, robs them of carefree enjoyment, spreads gloom and scruples everywhere.

This is one of the reasons for contemporary secularism. The Christian seems to represent a concept that opposes the temporal expansion to which our era owes its power and splendour. The Christian, in face of economic well-being, is on the side of renunciation, poverty, flight from the world; he is a bearer of the cross; how can he be a citizen of modern civilization?

We Christians should think over this objection, for it generates around us an attitude of distrust, alienation, even hostility. It is an objection prevalent in circles where trust is put in the primary role of the economic factor, that is, among capitalists and Marxists. It also has a hold over the young, who lack any exact concept of life. We see it around us every day. And we have come to think that one of the most serious and urgent problems of today is to find a proper relationship between Christian life—by which we mean loyalty to the pledge of the Gospel—and modern life—the pervading search for and achievement of temporal well-being. In other words the problem is to examine the significance which the Christian should attach to the temporal sphere.

[1] Gen. 1, verses 4, 10, 12, 18, 21, 25, 31; Lessius, *Opuscula*; Bouyer, *Humain ou chrétien*, English translation, *Christian Humanism*, London, 1958, pp. 30 f.

7

WORK TODAY[1]

RELIGION AND work; these two expressions of human life are not only distinct but actually separate from each other. Sometimes they ignore, sometimes suspect, sometimes oppose each other. Often they exist side by side without helping each other, without forming a spiritual link, without finding mutual balance or harmony. When urged to lessen the distance between them, they are suspicious of each other. If forced together the first hinders the second, the second profanes the first.

Some might say that the two are not made to understand each other. Some might say that the opposition to religion in the worker's mind is now too deep to be overcome, that it has about it an air of vindication, liberation, progress. Some might say that this is a characteristic of labour today, as compared with the past. Modern work is insensitive, and, in fact, opposed to religion. It wants to be secular, it wants to be atheist.

Why does this opposition exist? It was different in the past, as we can see from a few historical examples.

Take, for instance, the foundation and development of rural parishes which in Italy lasted until our own day. These were small ethnic groups in which economic effort, of which they were the main source before the shift of labour to industry, was permeated with the religious spirit. The calendar, time-table, liturgy, art, and poetry were based on religion, giving rural labour a popular and sublime spirituality which seemed to make for an intimate and indissoluble alliance between labour and religion.

A modern historian, Daniel-Rops, member of the French Academy, wrote about the Dark Ages:

[1] From *Religion and Work*, address given at Turin, 27 March 1960, to industrial workers.

'Those who see (our) village communities as represented first
and foremost by the belfry and the churchyard, which tell of
man's fidelity to the earth and his aspirations to heaven, must
pause a long time before this fact. What would our villages be if
they were not parishes too into the bargain?—remote places,
miserable slums, lost in the midst of the countryside, bodies without souls. For the folk who lived on the land the foundation of
the rural parishes was an event as important as the emancipation
of the communes was for the folk in the towns.'[1]

Then there were those singular medieval institutions, the monasteries, with the character, as Luzzatto wrote, 'of a small community
of equals working and producing for the good of all, renouncing all
profit from their own work and sharing its products.'[2] Another contemporary economist comments:

'The faith and culture diffused by the Benedictine Order was
equalled by its influence on the formation of agrarian institutions.
This revolution was all the more marvellous as it did not come
about by planning or by imposing programmes, but by the
spiritual and juridical wisdom of the Benedictine *Rule*. This, in the
many monasteries of the Order scattered throughout Europe, was
able to realize the social ideal of the Gospel, founded on the dignity of manual and agricultural labour, in a love which united all
men of whatsoever condition in the name of Christ.'[3]

Such is the historical picture of a community, the monastery, in
which the two aspects, religious and economic, of a house of prayer
and agricultural enterprise were so fused that they presented a single
whole. No one could deny that the monasteries functioned with
high dignity as centres of humanity and civilization.

Similar observations can be made about the relations between
religion and labour in medieval organizations of technical and artisan
production, the trade guilds, forerunners of the trade-union organizations in modern industry. These bodies were wholly social and
economic, in which religion, though not a qualifying element as it
was with rural monastic labour, was yet always present as a complementary factor. Religion was very much part of this collective
labour, giving it integrity and dignity. It also gave champions and

[1] Daniel-Rops, *The Church in the Dark Ages*, London, 1959, p. 262.
[2] Luzzatto, *Storia Economica d'Italia*, Rome, 1949.
[3] Barbieri, *Fonti per la storia della Dottrine economiche*, Milan, 1958, p. 263.

protectors in the patron saints; these heavenly prototypes represented this body of labour, ennobling it, pointing its moral, and associating it with the great heritage of faith and hope.

'As is well known,' writes Monsignor Civardi, 'in those days every economic guild had its own confraternity. . . . It is no exaggeration to say that the Christian religion was the soul of the medieval trade guilds. It permeated their admirable programme of liberty, justice, charity, and fraternal solidarity.'[1]

Something still survives here of this inherent sympathy between labour and religion. It shows in the spontaneous requests by the most varied categories of labour for the assignment by the Church authorities of a patron saint. And even today it is easier to bring some workers close to religion by referring to the particular characteristics of their jobs than to aspects of their personal lives.

But the fact remains that generally today there is a deep division between religion and labour. To analyse this split we would have to go back to the origins of the crises of the modern mind; for example, its protracted efforts to intensify the rational and exclude recourse to transcendental principles; its attempts to break free from any consideration of God and a binding relationship with him; its falling back on itself until it is terrifyingly alone, incapable of absolute judgment, resigned to systematic doubt, to scepticism, and to the nihilism of that very reason which was trying to be self-sufficient, to be its own light and guide. The modern mind made a double attempt to evade its own inner emptiness, the first by making human thought the source of all being and reality, in the philosophy called idealism, the metaphysic of the gratuitous; the second by issuing from the labyrinth of subjectivism and solipsism, and making contact again with exterior reality by way of the senses and the logical and scientific processes deriving directly from them. This *positivism* seems the right philosophy for those who content themselves with experimental observation or utilitarian exploitation of what they have observed.

This is the vast and prolific field where the mind of labour stops to draw its nourishment, unwilling to venture further, as if beyond lay myth and fantasy and to proceed were useless.

Another cause of the break-up of the unitarian conception of life lies in the political and social history of the modern world since the French revolution.

[1] Civardi, *Cio che il lavoratore deve a Cristi*, Pescara, 1959, pp. 71-2.

This political and social rupture has detached first the cultivated and well-to-do, and then the working classes, from the Church and the profession of religious faith.

At the roots of the conflict between religion and labour lies a great deal of political and social resentment. These have produced a stubborn anti-clericalism that has now become almost traditional, a matter of prestige, an insoluble misunderstanding, which in some areas and sectors makes resistance to priests and to religion almost obligatory.

Now, after a period when such anachronistic attitudes seemed about to change, they have been reinforced by atheism imported from abroad. And now these prejudices are no longer individual but collective, no longer interior but openly professed and organized, no longer limited to certain moments and forms of life but raised to an absolute system, almost to a religion, in their own right, a religion determined to mould despotically and on unproven assumptions the whole of human life.

But here we must limit our brief review to the relationships between religion and work which today are either uneasy or intermittent. We must look at the mind of the worker when confronted by religion, leaving aside references to any specific or even local conditions. A few general points are enough.

The mind of the worker—be he the executive or the workman—is strongly influenced by the field of observation immediately before him. It is external to him: that in itself makes him suffer from a lack of interior life. What he can actually see can be tested, it is tangible and definable; the worker has difficulty in conceiving of the invisible, in admitting any reality which does not enter into the ordinary life he sees every day. The experiences this life offers him are measurable, subject to calculation, linked continually to the material by quantity. The worker finds it hard to set his mind on things that have no comparison with quantitative measurement and bodily consistency. His field of observation lies in the present, in this part of time he actually experiences. The worker feels no links with the past and lacks an historical sense, or if he has one it is often scrappy with regard to the past while the future is regarded as almost mythical.

His surroundings can in fact be dominated, and this is perhaps the most attractive and impressive part for the worker; he feels that between himself and the particular fields of observation in which he is involved there exists a kind of struggle or duel.

What is work if not man's activity in mastering the things around him and transforming them from what is extraneous, inert, and useless into things that belong to him, that move, that are useful and pleasant? The final purpose of work is the victory of human action over objects, their conquest by man and their integration into his life. Hence work is wealth, completion, happiness. The cycle of human activity is fulfilled and completed by the purpose of work—by its economic results. Work is the tangible framework of life, the proof of human capacity, of man's powers.

Today this conquest, guided by brilliant scientific research, sustained by prodigious and progressing techniques has spread vastly and is still increasing. To it the world of work looks with all its attention, trust, and pride. It is difficult nowadays to get the working world away from this circle of impressions, thoughts, and hopes. It trusts itself and its own methods so much that it cannot imagine that there are any gaps and will not admit that any reasons, principles, and superior ends could surpass, condition, and explain those methods.

Work is only the exercise of human causality; that is, it depends on man's strength and will, on his efficiency and organizing capacity. So the worker feels himself to be powerful and free, lord of nature, riding the crest of the future. Though his work wears him out, as well as imposing a severe discipline, he is intoxicated by his own creative capacity. All this is his own doing, he thinks; he is superior to natural causes, though in fact his only superiority is in his capacity to use them. He puts himself as beginning and end of all things, though in fact he is the beginning and end only of that world of techniques and economics to which he has restricted his vision. He can conceive of no other cause superior to himself, and if called upon to recognize one that transcends him he is suspicious and rebellious, then puts it out of mind and denies it. Order begins and ends with himself.

This is why the worker is so seldom religious. He thinks he is self-sufficient. And he is satisfied with himself. This is the point, I think, from which Marxist atheism starts. Marx wrote: '. . . from the fact of man's substantiality, from the fact of man becoming felt and seen in nature . . . it is practically impossible to ask if an extraneous being can exist, a being placed above man and nature'.[1]

We must also, to be objective, mention other factors due to the

[1] *Das Kapital.*

workers' circumstances which exacerbate his spirit and make access to the religious world difficult for him, particularly in its concrete expression, the Church.

Here we must distinguish between the two main categories in which we usually classify labour (though today they are assuming different aspects both in concept and practice). These are the categories of those who own capital and those who work for a wage; in other words, owners and workers. Each of these categories has its own specific objections to religion and the Church—familiar, well-worn objections which should nonetheless be patiently considered and unravelled by anyone who wants to re-establish a regular and helpful relationship between labour and religion.

The first category is that of management, whose contribution to labour is thought, study, science, technical application, and organizing ability in both the economic and structural fields. This category is still easily paralysed by the rationalist objection, by the illuminist claim to know more by its own scientific and practical means than do all the prophets of religion. To this kind of mind religion does not appear to stand up to confrontation with modern rationalism, which goes beyond religion, explains it, and makes it superfluous. Only science is valid. Religion, for those who are still imbued with this way of thinking, is a substitute for thought and valid only for the primitive and uncultivated. It can be useful as making for order and morality; it can be picturesque, a religion of the people. 'People' in this connection is a synonym for the ingenuous and sentimental, the non-rational, the non-scientific; religion is good enough for those others but not for the intelligent and advanced.

Not even the abstruse speculations of theologians can, according to this school of thought, resist the inevitable victory of scientific certainty.

On the other side, we have the workers' objection to religion. It is a practical and formidable one and is deeply rooted in their minds. They hold, clearly and tenaciously, that religion distracts them from what should be their most important preoccupation, their economic and social interests.

According to them religion deceives and placates the worker, fixing him in a social and juridical system where others live in plenty, security, pleasure, and privilege while he, the worker, lives in need and subjection. He considers religion an accomplice of this strident social inequality, ally of a conservatism which sacrifices the working classes to the profit of the capitalists.

Let us examine how this false opinion grew up in the workers' minds during the last century and has been inherited by many in our own.

In the era preceding our own we do indeed find people who believed that the conservation of the established order—if it can be defined as such—was a supreme good. We do find people who tried to use religion to defend their own prosperity, without considering first of all how this prosperity should have been used for the common good, as a social and economic organization to bring bread to all. We find people who even tried to turn charity into a means for the rich to keep the poor at a distance.

Necker, in 1788, just before the French Revolution broke out, praised charity as: 'a most estimable virtue' in the service of the 'imperious laws of property'. We find men of the Church, not of the Catholic but the schismatic church (so Solovyev, a Russian philosopher, tells us) who forgot the social function of the Christian religion, and allowed the opinion to spread in the mind of the people that religion was party to the authoritarian imposition of wretched social conditions.

But no honest observer of history can really maintain, as people still try to do for purposes of anti-clerical propaganda, that religion is a means of exploiting the masses and enslaving the workers.

There are some practical objections of a general character against religion which seem common to all kinds of workers, and not just those two, capital and labour, to which old socialist theories have accustomed us.

These are: first, a sense of detachment. What has religion to do with work? Distinctions between various activities and qualifications are becoming more and more marked in the modern world. Specialization increases. Now the two forms of thinking and acting, religion and work, have become detached and distant from each other. Why confuse the sacred with the profane? Why link the seeking of the kingdom of heaven with the seeking of the kingdom of earth? Are the two aims not quite different? Had they not better ignore each other?

The secularist conception of modern society seeps everywhere, and gradually suppresses the religious concept of the world. One can live without religion, people say.

This leads to the second objection. What use is religion anyway? It must seem useless to people whose lives do not see beyond the temporal sphere. This sphere is occupied by work and its criterion is usefulness—what is economically useful, what is useful to the senses. Religion transcends this sphere: so what is the point of it? Is it not evasion of concrete experience, a waste of time?

We might add here a third objection to religion; it is incomprehensible. Its doctrine, its rites, and its economic organization are full of stumbling blocks. This is particularly true of the Catholic religion, which is not content with vague ideas but has precise dogmas; is not satisfied with sentimental effusions but requires firm clear acts of mind and will; is not limited to amiable exhortation, but demands a continual observance of definite precepts.

How can religion, when presented in terms so complicated and demanding, be any comfort to a man tired out after his work? A day-dream in a cinema, a football match, a country outing is a better restorative for a man who has spent his week amid the movement and monotony of machines or stuck to a paper-laden desk, than the arcane atmosphere of a church.

PART THREE

THE CHURCH CONFRONTS THE MODERN WORLD

I

THE DISCOVERY OF THE HUMAN PRESENCE OF CHRIST IN THE WORLD[1]

THE BIRTH of Christ, as we all know, took place in the greatest humility; only a few Jewish shepherds were told of it. Shortly afterwards the great event was discovered by some Wise Men, who lived far away and were Gentiles. These mysterious personages have been seen by the Church as representative of peoples outside the Jewish tradition, also called to know the Incarnate God.

The Incarnation of the Word of God may be considered from the aspect of the relationship which has been created between Christ and man, a first relationship, effected by his coming into the world, and the consequent discovery by the world of this new and totally unique presence. But we should always remember that God, by his nature, by his infinite transcendence, is inaccessible, incomprehensible, ineffable. Our search for him ends in mystery, a mystery that is not without certainty and joy. It stimulates, but is infinitely superior to thought. There is always a dramatic tension about man's relationship with God. Man is God's creature; he needs him, longs to reach him; and he can never come sufficiently near to him. As God shows himself in some degree knowable, man becomes more aware of his own blindness, realizes that he is more capable of loving him than of knowing him.

For God is at one and the same time knowable and ineffable, mystery and light. This explains, if it does not justify, why most men are inert and almost bemused before the problem of God, and do not know how to set about searching for him, praying to him, turning their lives to his light. Often indeed, weary of the arduous climb towards that transcendent summit, they stop along the way to make idols for themselves, or to bask in the momentary illusion of being able to do without God, or to drug them-

[1] From Sermon on the Feast of the Epiphany, 1956.

selves with self-contemplation, mistaking his reflection, sublime and humble, in the human spirit, with the great sun which only he is.

Humanity was in a haze about religion. Its sky was darkened by a pall of cloud, its directions vague, its movements stumbling. The night of incredulity had fallen over human history, leaving men to disperse in every sort of deviation.

Then what happened in the world at a certain moment?

What happened was that God, in order to lead man out of his bewilderment, revealed himself.

God appeared!

How did God come into the world? We might have expected him to come, in a manner more appropriate for this marvellous encounter, as the crowning point of human thought, as the terminal point of philosophic speculation, as quintessence of wisdom. Pascal, who was overwhelmed by the discovery of God, tells us why he did not: 'God of Abraham, God of Isaac, God of Jacob; not God of philosophers and scholars.'

We might have expected him to come in the marvel of his majesty and power. But the divine revelation did not respond to this appointment made by messianic imaginings and superstition either. St Paul described this dual disappointment in memorable words, personifying one expectation in the Jews, the other in the Greeks: the Jews expected prodigies, the Greeks wisdom. Neither of them were to be satisfied.

So how *did* God appear in the world? There are two aspects of his appearance that we might dwell on now. First, he appeared in history, that is at a given moment and a given place, in a given form. He entered the web of human life and so marked the meeting point between religious and philosophical thought on one side, and history on the other, between the idea of religion and religious fact. Second, he appeared humbly, '*humilis Deus*', as St Augustine says, that is without violence or upheaval, without exterior domination of that world and that history in which he became a presence. This means that man's search for him, sure now of reaching its goal, must continue not along paths of miracle and speculation but by following a human figure, unique and worthy of infinite contemplation. At the end of man's natural search, God's name was a mystery. At the beginning of evangelical history, his name is Jesus.

God appeared in the world humbly, silently, quietly, and became

And what does this enquiry involve, if not the beginning of a spiritual movement to raise, stimulate, and urge all men towards a search for truth? Christ's coming should provoke a mental and practical dynamism that will shake the inertia in those near to us and those afar. Apathy is no longer justifiable.

But what is in fact the state of affairs? Religious sloth is the dominant note of our era. Each day the world seems to grow less sensible of the riches of religion. Modern progress induces a need for truth; and one can understand that religions which are inadequate or inconsistent should lose their appeal, that the superstitions of the pagan world should be seen as vain or the doctrines of schismatic and heretical sects as weak. But that people today should be unresponsive to the call of a religion willed and initiated by God himself, based both on historical fact and on logical reasoning, and answering man's deepest and most legitimate needs, is a very serious and very sad thing.

It is particularly sad to see that just where the announcement of Christ is most clear the resistance to it is deafest and most sophistical. That happened, too, at the time of the three Wise Men. Those close at hand were indifferent and disregarding, but some of those afar were serious and responsive.

Here we are led on to examine the motives for this resistance to our Christian vocation, and to distinguish various categories among those who hang back from it; there are some who think they have already answered the call, and do not realize that it requires a more logical, more binding response; some who try to elude Christ's invitation; some who smother it with secularist claims and pretensions; some who oppose it with arguments, materialist or atheist, that flatly contradict it. To examine these would take us a long way. Today let us remember particularly that there is no one who is not summoned by Christ's light if he but open his eyes, but move a step or two in his direction. Those who want, will have. Those who think, will understand. Those who pray, will rejoice.

The barriers raised between us by social and other conditions can be overcome by the star of the Epiphany. Those far from us may be the chosen ones.

How many there are who live outside the sphere of religion, and think themselves free of it, or excluded from it, or incapable of crossing its threshold! Philosophers, for instance, who build for themselves ideological systems which they presume impervious to the rays of Christ; or practical men, strangers to spiritual values, who think they can contain reality within the limits of economics; politicians, who think that people should be defended from the sovereignty of religion, or that history and the social order can be interpreted by dogmatic and quite inconclusive principles. Do these seekers after certainty not realize that certainty is just what they lack, and that the very absence of Christ in their systems is a call to him? Do they think he is far away, when he may be near at hand?

So let us pray that this revelation be given to the souls of those who are indifferent or hostile, that they too should have the courage to get to their feet and walk. '*Surgam et ibo*', 'I will arise and go to my father' (Luke 15, 18).

We too feel the same duty in another form. The duty to go towards Christ also presses on us who call ourselves Christians, who call ourselves faithful. No one is ever close enough to God. Those closest to him burn most with the desire to come still closer. As St Augustine exhorts: '*Sic ergo quaeremus, tamquam inventuri; et sic inveniamus, tamquam quaesituri*', 'We must search as one who expects to find; and so find as one who would search further'.[1]

1 *De Trin.*, IX, 1.

2

THE DIVINE INITIATIVE AND HUMAN LIBERTY IN THE SEARCH FOR TRUTH[1]

THE EPIPHANY poses questions that are many and far-reaching, about the way in which Christ, and through him God, revealed himself; about the signs which made him recognizable and his revelation credible. It makes us think of the suitability, the manner and scope of an apologetics which should lead men to knowledge of and faith in revelation; and of how men have behaved and should behave towards the manifestation of Christ, and hence of all the problems connected with our own acceptance of Christ. Looking further afield, it brings us to the problem of religion in general, the greatest problem of thought and action, the problem of truth in life, seen under the initial and basic aspect of man's meeting with God, of the acquisition of truth. And then we think of how the Christian revelation, destined for all mankind and all nations, is restricted in its diffusion by practical conditions and exterior difficulties, the complexities and contradictions of man's acceptance and often of his resistance to the Christian message.

The canvas is vast and of the greatest interest. It mirrors the spiritual history of the world in terms that are clear and full of meaning. Take the story of the three Wise Men. They expect, seek, and find the mysterious star, set off on their journey, ask the authorities for news, and act on it, while others either ignore the news or attempt astute betrayal. So the Wise Men set off joyfully on the last lap of their journey, and eventually find Christ as a humble baby. Then, instead of being affronted, they fall in humble adoration, offer symbolic gifts, and eventually set off home by other routes. This story of the three Wise Men, which we know so well and recall on this day, recounts a chapter in man's adventurous journey towards the Epiphany of God.

[1] Sermon on the Feast of the Epiphany, 1957.

137

Let us pause for a short meditation on the search for Christ, for God, for truth. The three Wise Men are the exemplary seekers, the brave and lucky explorers of the great problem of religion. They are seeking for a solution to bring their thought into line with the historical fact of the Messiah's birth. They sought long, studying the skies; and so the study of nature and science led them to the sign. They sacrificed time and peace of mind in search of human proof of the divine voice, persevered between heavenly light and human teaching, unashamed of the purpose of their journey and unmoved by having no precursors or followers more fully informed. They seek and find in joy and humility, adore, make their offerings in joy, and then disappear.

That mysterious trio teach us some of the basic laws of our relationship with God. Firstly that God must be sought. Ignorance, indifference, agnosticism, systematic doubt, boredom, a vague religion contented with inner experience, the reduction of knowledge to mere tangible data and rational evidence, those and other expressions of modern anti-religious feeling, the three Wise Men teach us, are abdications of human thought before its ultimate aim, the first duty in life: to know God.

To know him we must do something about him; think, study, and learn about him, pray to him. Another law, still more necessary and even more profound, is that we need help, an initiative, from God himself, not only in order to find him but in order to seek him. This is true in the natural order, due to the fact that human nature is orientated towards God and is the work of his hands; 'Fecisti nos ad te,' says St Augustine, 'Thou hast made us for thee.'[1] It is all the more true in the supernatural order, to which we should never have aspired and reached had God himself not come to meet us, not arranged a whole mysterious and loving economy to reach him.

There is a third rule too. That God, even when he reveals himself, remains mysterious; mysterious in his infinite transcendence and the veiled manner of his appearance. 'This is why I speak to them in parables,' he warned his disciples about those on the lakeside, 'because seeing they do not see, and hearing they do not hear, nor do they understand' (Matt. 13, 13).

This means that the good fortune of accepting the revelation, of believing and entering the blessed circle of communication with

[1] Conf., I, I.

God's very life is a free and total gift of his on one side, and requires on the other the co-operation not only of our eyes and minds, of our imagination and reason, but of our hearts and wills, our honesty, our thought and our life, our worship and our love.

This duty to seek, though, is exercised differently by those who already have the faith and by those who do not. A man who walks in the light walks differently from one who walks in the dark. This difference leads us to a specious and dangerous objection, dear to many modern intellectuals; that to seek truth is worth more than to find truth, because the latter stops the movement of the spirit while the former stimulates it. This is a false assertion; it is also unjust when applied to believers as opposed to non-believers, or to Catholics as opposed to Protestants, as if the former were at a dead end in their own certainty and dogmatism and had no further incentive to intellectual and spiritual activity, while the latter were urged by their very uncertainty and consequent freedom to fertility of thought and inner experience.

The assertion is a false one, for truth does not hinder but rather provokes a conquering process of the spirit. The truth is fertile, not sterile. Thought proceeds from one certainty reached to another certainty as yet unreached. Logic is founded on this principle. From it science draws its own tradition and its own progress. And from it religion draws its sustenance. A first conquest of divine truth makes it possible to achieve a second, a third truth; to derive prayer, moral law and, even more, a new desire, new thirst, more love.

Remember Pascal, 'You would not seek me if you had not already found me.' Remember Salmo, '*In lumine tuum videbimus lumen*', 'by thy light we shall find the light'. Remember St Augustine, '*Sic ergo quaeramus, tamquam inventuri, et sic inveniamus tamquam quaesituri*', 'we must search as one who expects to find, and so find as one who would search further'!

To have formulated a religious truth in terms that are exact and for us intangible, that is, to have acquired a dogma of our faith, does not stultify our thinking about that truth, nor suffocate our prayer. St Leo the Great, in one of his sermons on the birth of Christ, taught: 'No one draws so near to truth as he who understands that in divine things, even if he has been able to progress much, there are always things still to seek. Thus whoever presumes he has reached what he seeks, will not reach it, but will fail in his search.'[1]

[1] *Serm.*, IX.

People who speak, as someone did recently here in Milan, of 'open religion', claiming to direct religious search and intending to loose religion from any duty towards truth and God's will, should say, rather, that they want to demolish religion, not to renew it.

If there is one recommendation we can take to heart on the Feast of the Epiphany it is this: do not let our having the benefit of the faith and the Church's teaching prevent our trying to progress in the knowledge and understanding of God. The act of faith does not dispense us from the study of religious truths, on which we should meditate; from the love of religious truth, for which we should pray; from acting in accordance with religious truth, by which we should lead a life of Christian virtue.

So may Epiphany be a call for us to the great principle quoted by St Paul, 'my righteous one shall live by faith' (Heb. 10, 38). To apply to our lives the light of faith already seen means to make ourselves capable of seeing a yet more splendid light. This progressive process is possible for the believer also because in this ascent towards supreme truth he is using not only his brain but also his will and his heart. *'Caritas abundet in scientia'* (Phil. 1, 9), 'Charity merges into capacity to know'. Again it is St Paul speaking; and he is echoed by St Augustine in this superb plan of spiritual progress; God 'is called by love, sought by love, implored by love, revealed by love; finally it is by love one keeps what he has revealed'.[1]

What shall we say of those others who are far from the Church, who *'in umbra mortis sedent'* (Luke 1, 70) are in the darkness of death, do not have, that is, the light of faith?

First of all we can say that this is their particular feast. The Epiphany is the calling of those who are distant. It is their great occasion to overtake those nearer the goal. It reveals a Providence so all-loving that it seems almost over-adventurous. It shows what surprises, visions, experiences, torments, and mysterious influences can encompass those who are far off. It tells of the divine compassion for the circumstances they are in. It shows the divine initiative which pursues them, surprises and blesses them. A world of spiritual marvels is unveiled at Epiphany; of journeys in the spirit, of unexpected vocations and conversions, of early experiences leading to late returns. Mary, our mother, and with her the saints, the angels, and

---

[1] *De Mor. eccl.*, I, XVII, 31.

men of prayer are working to draw from the darkness of materialism, paganism, and sin those destined to become children of light. Today is the feast of the prodigal sons; it is the feast of the missions, the feast of the universality of Christianity, of the vocation of peoples, of a general invitation to all. This should be a true feast for the whole world.

So let us greet now as possible brothers those, wherever they may be, who are far away. Let us call to them as to virtual children of God's Kingdom: Come too! We are awaiting you, we want you, love you! Do not leave empty the place reserved for you. The way is shorter than you think. The goal is lovelier than we ourselves can describe. The light, the faith, the certainty of Christ! Come!

Look out into the night of modern agnosticism. Does no star appear, calling you to move a few steps closer to Christ, the Light of the World? Does no experience, maybe some spark from this week's fires, startle you, awaken you, make you fear and make you hope? Yes in Hungary, which at this historic moment has become a theatre of supernatural conflict, a pressing, an overpowering need for truth has led to spiritual revolt. Disgusted by the false, materialist 'humanisms' of the regime, some writers and artists made what the papers call 'a pact of truth'; and that began the revolt for freedom. Truth frees.

We would like to ask our own writers and artists who still use the weight and considered judgment of their culture to support inhuman communist slavery, if they can still calmly affirm—I quote— that 'dialectical materialism frees the development of the human conscience . . .' and if 'one thing seems historically certain; that Marxism represents and defines the humanism of the contemporary era'? We would ask them not to commit other mortal sins of dishonest thinking; we would implore them to let facts speak for themselves, to stop questioning the truth as it has been learnt by the appalling experience of whole peoples who have been victims of that barbarous form of humanism.

Because here there is a definite responsibility for those away from the Church, the intelligentsia in particular. A duty, too, for those without the light of religion. Even those in darkness have a duty to search. This duty is one merely of natural honesty, a duty of man towards himself, to use thought honestly. Thought is by its nature orientated towards truth, even if it can easily lose the way. Those who overcome weaknesses, deviations, utopian fantasies, hypocrisies, utilitarian calculations, interior lies, and search for the truth are likely to find it. Those who respect their own thoughts are already on the road. 'He who does what is true comes to the light, that it may be clearly seen that his deeds have been wrought in God' (John 3, 21).

3

THE RESTORATION OF THE RELIGIOUS SENSE[1]

VENERABLE BRETHREN and beloved children, our mission must be to restore the religious sense to men's minds.

This vocation is imposed on us both by the mere fact that we live in such an age as this and by our responsibility as Christians.

It is demanded of us by the religious decadence of our time and by the yearning of spirit and long-suffering expectation evident both in the world of thought and letters and in everyday life.

It is demanded of us by the critical condition of modern society always in turmoil yet always hoping for something better.

The signs which proclaim this demand need to be given careful attention, explanation, and thought. They have been set down and discussed by many scholars and other experts, and you can without difficulty find out all you need to know about them.

Here my aim is a simple and practical one, and I shall therefore try to sum up in a few paragraphs our chief duties, if we are to see the religious sense lively and flourishing once again.

First of all, the religious sense needs to be rehabilitated at the rational level. We need to realize that it is not only a natural and spontaneous element in human psychology but a perfectly legitimate one, and not only a legitimate one but a necessary and excellent one as well. It has been equated far too often with the human spirit's lower manifestations of an imperfect, infantile, simple-minded, or superstitious kind, and it needs to be accorded its proper place and function.

We must be convinced that it is absolutely necessary to give religion its rightful position of primacy and its specific field of action.

We must be prepared to defend this necessity at the bar of

[1] From *Man's Religious Sense*, Pastoral Letter to the Archdiocese of Milan, Lent 1957 (English translation, Darton, Longman & Todd, London, 1961).

contemporary world opinion and hence to foster the religious sense with all the respect and care it merits.

People who are insensitive to religion are not creatures who have been liberated from some ancient inferiority complex; they are themselves diminished, atrophied beings.

The greater freedom they seem to enjoy is the freedom of the ignorant man who does not know the rules of the game yet thinks himself an expert.

This is primarily the responsibility of thinkers and of those whose task it is to argue in defence of Christianity, and it is my hope that the soil of Catholic culture, in Italy as well as elsewhere, will go on producing an ever-increasing number of new, penetrating, original, and convincing voices to proclaim the truth.

This is not the place to say how—and no less because they are Catholics—they should constantly keep their knowledge up to date and should draw upon a more immediate and accurate knowledge of modern science and the modern mind in venturing to give original and ever deeper expression to orthodox beliefs; it is sufficient here to applaud all who are working to this end, and to encourage them in their efforts to achieve new and striking success.

The battle for Catholic culture must continue with more vigour than ever.

For any defence of the religious sense a thorough familiarity with the two main modes of attack upon it is needed. One is secularism, found chiefly in the middle class sections of society, the other atheism, which makes itself felt more in revolutionary and marxist circles; both spring from negative tendencies in the spiritual aspect of life in our day, especially in the field of public life. Both are vast subjects, and I have no intention of going into them in detail here.

I cannot, however, fail to remind you that, in Italy at least, the first is simply a survival from bygone days, even though it tries to present itself as the culmination of a historical, cultural, and political movement of emancipation of the State from the Church, and hence from religion—and is seemingly justified in this by the fact that a sovereignty in temporal matters is rightly conceded to the State by the Church no less than by non-believers, while on the other hand, the State has no authority in religious matters.

According to this secularist attitude, public life should be kept free from any moral and religious influences deriving from Catholicism —hence the anti-Church and anti-religious zeal of so many public figures in whom liberal principles have been transformed into an attitude of suspicion, dogmatism, and intolerance.

They are driven by fear of 'clericalism', as they call it (another word which it would take a long time to examine thoroughly), fear of the undue domination of religious influences and the organized Church in the very wide field of the State's authority and secular life in general.

They do not realize that fear, if it becomes a decisive factor, is—like all emotional reflexes—a baneful source of unpleasant political manifestations out of which secularism would make an evil amalgam tending not to unite the vital forces working for the common good, but to detach them from their spiritual context and to re-open ancient divisions. Nor does this fear of theirs seem to be in any way justified, considering the steadfast care with which the Church limits her own sphere of action, and considering the standards of civil liberty that prevail in public life in Italy today.

How can they fail to see that modern secularism disavows the spiritual—and religious—history of civil life in Italy and ignores fundamental elements of the utmost value in the soul of the Italian people, besides offending, at least in intention, against precise requirements of the civil law which protects religion, like all other free manifestations of the human spirit, by special legal enactments?

I should like to remind the advocates of political secularism through which in the end the religious sense would wither, how much this sense has contributed over the ages to the great affirmations of Italian political life. Let one example stand for all; in the words of Dante: '*Romanum imperium de fonte nascitur pietatis.*'[1]

Atheism, the second mode of attack, is the result of an extreme form of materialism. This first takes the form of a thorough-going 'scientism', dumb as regards all the great problems of being and life, and insensitive to every form of thought except a narrow preconceived positivism.

Subsequently it appears, especially in anti-social mass-movements, as a form of spiritual revulsion when people are so exasperated by a sense of the injustices they have to endure, or by unsatisfied longings, that they will turn any doctrine—today it is dialectical materialism—into a fanatical messianic creed. From this they draw the energy for stubborn, violent, and sometimes impressive action, which is equalled only by the strength of the inevitable reaction—on

[1] *De Mon.*, II, V, 5.

both the theoretical and practical planes—against the principle which (blindly or deliberately) they have taken as their starting point; witness the recent Hungarian tragedy.

And so God who can bring light to human minds and happiness to human living, but is no longer sought for, no longer accepted as man's ultimate aim and object, reappears in both tendencies as a source of fear and deadly anguish.

Our main problem today is, therefore, to re-educate the modern mind to think in terms of God.

Not long ago in one of the main streets in a certain city a banner appeared bearing the words, 'Remember God'.

First of all, in the hope that any unbiased mind will face the position frankly and patiently, I want to state once again the simple fundamental fact that the religious sense is not a perverted manifestation of the human spirit but one that is natural, worthy of respect, legitimate, dignified, and indispensable. Let me explain.

Considered as instinctive, the religious sense is, to begin with, quite a primitive thing; it must be integrated with the development of the higher faculties of the intelligence and will, and, for the purpose of action, it needs to be directed by the mind.

Spontaneous expression is not enough; left to itself and its own impulses it can lead to many aberrations, to whims and superstitions, to a lamentable and dangerous pietism.

Moreover, it is not confined by the measured logical tread of the critical intelligence; it soars up into the world of poetry and prayer and attempts to reach an object above anything that can be clearly and immediately apprehended. To this end it needs guidance.

Being, as it were, a line cast upon the wind, what message of ours can it truly carry to the kingdom of heaven or what message bring back that will not be uncertain or even deceiving, unless there is some heavenly hand to draw it upward and bring it into contact with the reality of the divine mystery?

The whole history of religion is proof of the human soul's endless aspiration, humble but sublime or bizarre and ignominious, towards God; but it would have been perpetually fruitless had not God in his infinite wisdom and goodness taken the initiative and revealed himself, thereby instituting the one true religion.

Indeed, a true religion is needed to defend the religious sense from the danger of disintegration that is only too real.

Spiritual or religious manifestations which have not the truth as their guide offer no guarantee of salvation and are the source of much error, illusion, and disaster.

Today for example spiritualism, which is a capricious and superstitious form of curiosity, has in some countries become a plague to society. There is also 'indifferentism', the idea that one religion is as good as another; this tends to create a false peace in men's minds that turns whatever remains of their religious feelings, manifested now in the most diverse creeds, into a source of spiritual and social confusion and prepares the way for scepticism and religious indifference, while at the same time being quite unable to draw the proper saving energy from religious values thus emptied of significance.[1]

Shrewd people—and most positively-minded people are so today —are not prepared to swallow mystifications such as this, and so they grow suspicious of the trustworthiness of the religious sense as a guide, they grow impatient with its unpredictable demands and obvious extravagances, reject it, and stamp it out completely. That is the explanation for a good deal of the irreligion of our day. But there is no need to act in this way—after the fashion of Pilate's, 'Let us make an end of these fanatical and useless disputes'.

The right way is to realize that man's natural religious sense is not a criterion of truth, it is a need for truth; to stifle this need is to thwart human nature and violate the work and the design of God. There is a solution to this problem and it is my duty to show you what it is.

As I have already said, a consequence of modern life is that men's minds have become engrossed in the conquest of the world around them. The result is that modern man is interested in phenomena rather than in substance, in appearance rather than reality, in the visible rather than the invisible, matter rather than spirit, secondary causes rather than fundamental ones, himself rather than his neighbour, the present rather than the past or future, earth rather than heaven, the useful rather than the good, pleasure rather than duty, this world rather than the world to come, man rather than God.

Modern man's main activity is work; he takes a proper pride in it and finds due satisfaction in it, but it has also made him feel that here alone lies power, and this has limited his field of vision. Thus is born a state of mind that easily grows indifferent to religion and with a little encouragement becomes frankly hostile to it. But this is not wholeness of mind; it is a one-sided, atrophied state of mind. The

[1] I John 4, 1.

human mind can attain wholeness if, keeping its curiosity about, and knowledge of, the scientific laws that are so useful to man's work, it studies them more closely and discovers that they postulate a transcendent Mind, creating and ordering all things.

And so it is, also, with science which today is supreme in the sphere of man's work, which seems to satisfy the mind's desire for knowledge and does indeed satisfy it, but focuses the mind on the *how* to the exclusion of the deeper and more essential *why* of the marvellous universe which it surveys and explores. If science remains sole mistress of the human mind, it will even hamper and stultify the mind, denying it that further development which comes through philosophy and religion and is the mind's final goal.

Modern man therefore must not allow the material things which so absorb him to blind him to what lies beyond them. A more intelligent impulse must be awakened in him, he must re-discover a metaphysical curiosity, a determination to go back to the *raison d'être* of all that lies before his eyes.

This speculative movement which is the crowning glory of the human mind, arises naturally from observation of what God has created.[1]

Could it not arise today from the contemplation of what man has, so to speak, 'created'—the products of his ingenuity, his industry, his tools, his machines.

Modern man sees in these things the reflection of himself and is proud and satisfied to contemplate these tokens of his own intelligence and industry.

And yet is it not possible with a further leap in human understanding to see in them a revelation of the mind and work of God?

This is the leap man must make today to fulfil his powers of understanding and to revive his sense of religion.

As always in the field of religion, this will call for an act of humility which means simply honesty and truth. The technician standing beside his apparatus may well say with satisfaction, 'This is new, this is mine', but he should add, thoughtfully and with even more satisfaction, 'It is rather my discovery than my invention. I have discovered laws and properties which existed before I thought of them. I have only applied them. I have moved one step nearer to the natural unfolding of a Wisdom which I did not know or dream of. Without expecting to, I have stumbled upon God.'

[1] Rom. 1: 20.

If, in the past, nature was the intermediary between God and the human mind, why may not the works of technology and art be this today?

This, in my opinion, is one of the keys to the problem of bringing back the lost religious sense into the realm of industry and technology, science, and art. This is the way to restore a spiritual significance to man's work. This is how in the factories, loaded as they are with material wealth, the flowers of prayer and joy shall flourish.

And perhaps the dawn of this new movement of the spirit is not far off.

The intense research into the newly revealed properties of matter, the urge to produce not only utilitarian abundance but also works perfect of their kind, and machines and products that excite admiration, the parallel endeavour to give to factories, to the tools of work, and to the finished article a beauty of line, the desire to exalt devotion to work as an ideal—all these are signs of a spiritually imbued humanism that is about to arise out of the materialism of our age.

The portent is stupendous, for in this way the material world, far from being repudiated, is ennobled; human work is not degraded, it is redeemed; the development of civilization is not arrested, it is baptized and made more truly human.

Is it perhaps possible that the intellectuals have not perceived this? If they have, why do so many of them still persist in burning a servile incense to a dense and outmoded materialism?

Is it possible that 'fellow-travelling' politicians should fail to realize that a window is about to open on the world of labour that will show how poverty-stricken and out of date is their philosophical thinking and hence how devoid of any real authority to guide the onward march of working people? And that when it opens it will give to these people a new breath of hope and a new vision in their labours?

So far as our own field of action is concerned, I should like to see the workers given every assistance, social, professional, and religious. I should like them to realize not only the wrong done to them by forcing on them a materialistic view of life, but that our own spiritual view of life has far more respect for them as persons and, while allowing for their attainment of every legitimate temporal good, also recognizes in them the boundless treasure of a soul that thinks and prays and believes. I should like to see technical schools helping them to realize that there can be a vocation, a redemptive value, a

religious dignity in human work. I should like their days of rest to
be sacred and inviolable. I should like their public holidays to be
marked with flowers and song and thought and prayer and to become truly occasions for recreation of the spirit. I should like to see
prayer once again linked with work, sustaining it, ennobling it,
sanctifying it. The working people are on their way towards such a
spiritual outlook and the Church of Christ looks forward to the
attainment of it.

Such is also our wish for the world of modern industry, that world
whose good fortune in the possession and production of wealth can
prove a serious obstacle to progress beyond the pursuit of economic
aims to those of religion. How difficult this task is is clear from the
Gospels, so stern and menacing in their warnings to the rich.

Fortunately in these days wisdom is gaining ground also among
those who possess and exercise control of material wealth. The
social or, in other words, no longer self-centred function of such
people is today unreservedly insisted on in theory, while in practice
those reservations that still exist are gradually yielding to the influence of a collective or, to use a current term, democratic wisdom.
The subordination of economic interest to moral law goes steadily
forward, with manifest benefit to both. The concern to promote
fruitful and peaceful human relationships is spreading to such an extent that it bids fair to change the terms of the social dialectic from
'class war' to 'co-operation'. Such is the road ahead: it is a good
road, a road which leads upwards.

When it is at last realized that the possession of material wealth is
not a privilege but an opportunity of service, to be made use of in
accordance with the mysterious designs of Providence and with the
brotherly love that knows it is better to give than to receive,[1] then
the triumph of the religious sense will bring tears of relief to the dry
eyes of those who still imagine that they can satisfy the soul's secret
hunger with the stale bread of materialism.

At this point I need to say a word about the religious sense in
children.

It is mainly addressed to their Catholic parents and devoted
teachers.

They need to have the clearest possible conception of their duty
towards their young charges in respect of the religious sense no less

[1] Acts 20, 35.

than of anything else. In this field too the characteristic principle of modern education applies: try to draw the child out, not to force things on him. The religious sense is a natural endowment of the child, just as much as the other gifts he possesses.

It may be potential only, it may be unformed, but in the unspoiled soul of a child it is there.

A baptized child has a higher potentiality still, for to his endowment of natural piety has been added a supernatural gift. His real condition has been raised from son of man to adopted son of God. God is near him, watching over him, loving him as a Father.

When one remembers this, one cannot but have an immense reverence for children.

This is due to them in any case, as tender creatures newly come into the world—you will remember the pagan saying, 'Great respect is due to the child'. Remember, even more, our Lord's momentous words about these same creatures, regenerated by his grace and ministered to silently and mysteriously by the angels: 'Woe to that man by whom the scandal cometh' (Matt. 18, 7).

In this respect our present world is guilty of flagrantly contradicting its own principles and all its sage concern for children and adolescents. For while it never ceases to surround the modern child with all the latest developments in teaching and physical hygiene, it then allows him easy access to books and magazines, films and theatre shows, games and amusements, that set up harmful disturbances in his mind, and may prove fatal to his moral and psychological balance.

It grows beautiful flowers, then treads them underfoot—grows them with jealous care, then tramples on them with culpable indifference.

The child's craving to get to the root of things can be satisfied perfectly and comparatively easily by any wise teacher who talks to it about God and thus shortens the young mind's journey to the mysterious Fountain of all wisdom—a journey that the grown man turns into a long, complicated, roundabout route until he is thoroughly exhausted and bewildered, only to arrive in the end, a weary victor, at the same conclusion, to hear our Lord's blessed words, 'Unless you become as little children, you shall not enter into the kingdom of heaven' (Matt. 18, 3). Children find it easier than adults to approach God, and in this a child becomes the teacher of the teacher who has known how to develop its Christian religious sense.

At the same time the teacher must make it clear that he takes the child seriously, and above all set it a good example. And at the times when they are worshipping together both must be united in thought, word, and deed.

To pray together in a spirit of piety—or, as Grandmaison has said, with that 'family and above all filial spirit which unites the faithful to God'—is an experience that should come early in any Catholic upbringing. The first religious lesson we give our children is to transfer the dearest and most natural of human affections from the domestic hearth to God the Father of the universe, so that it reaches out towards the infinite without any dilution and even with a welcome access of fresh vigour. If this lesson is well given, if it is really alive, it can implant in their hearts for life a clear understanding of the wonderful bonds of love that bind man to God and incline God towards man.

We need to teach children not only to say their prayers but to put their heart and soul into them, not only to learn their catechism but to learn that in it is summarized their own and their neighbours' destiny, not only to go to church but to look upon their church as a holy temple of the laws of life. In this way they will become aware that they live always in the presence of God, they will develop an inclination towards goodness and truth, a disinterested love of duty, and confidence amid all the uncertainties of life.

It follows that regular use of the sacraments is, as we well know, of the utmost importance to children: confession, the searching but kindly training in good and evil; communion, the anxious awaiting of and the joyful encounter with the Friend of Friends, and confirmation—which needs special emphasis and a special kind of instruction in a child's religious upbringing—as the dawn of a real sense of personal responsibility in the heart of the adolescent.

And what am I to say about our young people in adolescence?

This is a subject which deserves a discourse all to itself, and I am deeply moved when I turn my thoughts to it. Adolescence is the age of crisis, of decision, and it is youth that is most open to the irreligious and anti-religious influences of the day.

Yet adolescence is also the time of strenuous intellectual searching, the time when love bursts forth, the period when people are most able to perceive religious values in life and to give to their inherited religion a deep and personal significance. When this happens, it may find expression in a dramatic moral decision or in the form of some absolute and self-sacrificing loyalty full of passionate though un-stable enthusiasm, a splendid burst of generosity, a wonderful surge of aspiration soaring upwards to the heights of heroism and poetry. All I shall say here is that the religious sense needs to be helped and tended at this time of life more than at any other and that spiritual direction thus becomes a providential matter, of great importance for the future, requiring great insight.

It is also the age when 'some are called'.

This is one of the most interesting and most mysterious pheno-mena of human psychology—the time of 'vocation', the moment of spiritual fulfilment. For some it has merely a moral sense but for others it involves religion as well.

This comes about when the religious sense manifests itself so com-pellingly—whether as a spiritual torment or as some kind of attrac-tion or as a sense of joy is not important—that it gives rise to an exalted inward contest between the person's freedom and his sense of duty, a contest which is morally crucial for the rest of his life.

It is at this time, usually, that the 'inner voice' sheds the appearance of belonging to the person himself and reveals itself as the echo of another voice that is far off yet close at hand, clear but indescribable —the voice of God.

At moments such as these the religious sense finds one of its highest and most decisive forms of expression.[1]

Not only when we are young, but at every period of our lives the religious sense should be encouraged by a competent teaching and ministry.

The Church, as teacher of the truths of God and the minister of our relationships with him, does this. It is the Church's great mis-sion, all the more providential and necessary today at a time when modern man is so little concerned to preserve, to nourish, and to follow aright his natural tendency towards God. He is spellbound by the fascination of his own achievements which create in him the illusion that they can satisfy his longing for the Infinite.

The voice of the Prophet might well ring out again for our own day: 'My people have done two evils. They have forsaken me, the fountain of living waters, and hewed out cisterns for themselves, broken cisterns, that can hold no water' (Jer. 2, 13).

Led astray and deluded, modern man suffers torment and exas-peration, and abandons himself to the most capricious and perverse

[1] Heb. 5, 4; John 15, 16; 1 Kings 3, 4 ff.

instincts condemned long ago in like circumstances by St Paul,[1] and
documented again in all their shameful misery in so much modern
literature.

The desperate thrust of the human spirit towards some unattain-
able perfection testifies yet again that we are called to some unknown but specific destiny which Christ our Lord—and he alone—
has prepared for us.

Our Lord comes to us. First he attracts us to him and stirs our
feelings, then he teaches us and converts us, yes, converts us, by
means of that great and fearful lesson of the cross. After that he
opens to us his own ineffable presence, the presence of the true living
God, in the glorious mystery of the unity of one nature in three
distinct persons: Father, Son, and Holy Ghost.

Truth, beauty, goodness, peace, happiness, and life are his to give,
and we have already received a foretaste and a promise of them.

He comes to those who learn at a humble school—the school of
the Gospels, to which we must return as children if we would renew
the strength and vitality of our religious sense and fill it once again
with *spirit and truth*.[2]

He has made known to us the supernatural meaning of life. He
has taught us to see a sacred element in all things, and especially in
the face of humanity.

Our relationship to God appears in all we do, and at every moment of our lives; our dependence on his creative action and his
loving Providence is so vividly apparent in the Gospels that from
this point of view there is nothing that is not sacred, because nothing
exists of itself and for itself. Let us think, if only for a moment, of
the way our Lord regarded the circumstances of his human life: just
as we see the light of the sun reflected in the shapes and colours before our eyes, so he saw, and enables us to see, in all things God's
fatherly and all-embracing presence. In his eyes the things of nature
are the reflections of a loving Providence[3] and mirror the wisdom
and beauty of God.[4]

For him everything is a symbol, everything speaks of God. Think
of the mysterious religious artistry of his stories and parables: in his
hands, an ordinary familiar object or a simple everyday happening
becomes, as it were, a kind of chrysalis from which emerge vast
principles governing the relations between man and God.

[1] Rom. 1, 22 ff.   [2] John 4, 23.
[3] Matt. 6, 26; 10, 29.   [4] Matt. 6, 28, 29.

Our Lord has shown us the true and profound religious sense in his teaching about man (Matt. 18, 2; 18, 14; 21, 34), about human conduct (Matt. 11, 16, 17), about sorrow (John 16, 22), joy (John 19, 20), sin (Matt. 12, 36), authority (Luke 23, 27), death (Matt. 18, 8; Luke 15, 7), about anything that happens (Luke 16, 19 ff; John 11, 25). I cite these at random to show that his teaching introduces us to mysteries without provoking idle speculation, transforms the anguished—but, for those still far from him, most fruitful—restlessness of humanity in a luminous and heartening synthesis of justice and love, and gives to those who accept him an unassailable peace of mind (John 14, 27; 15, 11).

It is sublime yet simple teaching, from which we can draw two practical lessons for our present purpose. The first is that love of the Bible and careful study of it, especially saying the Psalms and meditation in detail on the Gospels, are indispensable and inexhaustible sources from which to sustain within ourselves a deep and true religious sense. And secondly, we must learn to project the religious sense itself into our daily lives, as Christian practice teaches us to do—in each day, hence our daily prayers, and in whatever comes into our lives, hence all the Church's simple blessings of our food and our home, of joy and sorrow, of our toil and recreation, our working tools and our flag, of health and sickness, school and office, of cradle and grave.

The giving of blessings has become a frequent and widespread religious custom. They are often asked by people far from the Church and for things remote from what is strictly speaking sacred.

But if the wish is sincere and the thing itself good, if the action is pious and worthy, then all is well. The Church has a very large store of ritual, precisely because she is remarkably broadminded in her interpretation of the sacred *understanding* spoken of in St Paul's Epistle to the Philippians (1, 9). With this in view, a small book entitled *Family Ritual* has been distributed to homes in our own city, to help in developing the confident practice of family prayers.

But, as we know, Jesus Christ specifically instituted certain sacred 'signs'—the sacraments—and created a special order of people—the priesthood—to dispense them. He taught a particular doctrine and entrusted the apostles with the task of keeping it intact and spreading it far and wide.

Thus was born the official hierarchical form of the religion he had established—the teaching, sanctifying Church.

Two things are involved—preaching and the liturgy.

Certain persons, places, temples, books, objects, gestures, rites, have become sacred. Art in particular has become a sacred thing when it has been willing to follow the path of contemplation and worship and when, through a sincere experience of the gifts of the Holy Spirit, it has sought to capture in sensible form the intimations of the divine mystery and the beauty of its unseen depths.

Preaching and the liturgy—these are the two great fountain-heads of the religious spirit. I will say no more about them here.

I would only remind you that the treasures I have mentioned are bound up with the observance of the Church's chief precept—assistance at Holy Mass.

This is the practical basis of the spiritual life, the indispensable nourishment of the religious sense and of all Christian living. We must do all we can to uphold this wisest of all observances, to prevent manual or professional work from becoming so exhausting as to hinder people from going regularly to Mass, and also to prevent leisure activities from making the practice seem inconvenient, tedious, or unnecessary.

We must do all we possibly can, and I say this to both clergy and faithful, to all in authority, and all orthodox believers. And let this be the fatherly exhortation, the loving watchword with which, while giving you all my blessing, I close this Pastoral Letter.

I cannot finish, however, without imploring God, who has implanted the religious sense in man, to give us the gift of piety.

Venerable brethren and beloved children, may the inner impulse of the Holy Spirit, through the intercession of Mary most holy, Mary most loving, help us to direct towards God in the highest, the God of all perfection,

—our living souls, that his presence may enlighten the thought of our minds;
—our questing souls, that they may open to the revelation of his mysterious wisdom;
—our weary souls, that they may be sustained by trust in his providence;
—our darkened souls, that they may be awakened to the brightness of his beauty;
—our restless souls, that they may find rest in the harmony of his peace;

—our sorrowing souls, that they may rise upward through self-offering to his goodness;

—our guilty souls, that they may be cleansed by the tears that his justice has declared blessed;

—our unfathomable souls, that they may be overcome with joy at his infinite love.

4

BASIC CHARACTERISTICS OF THE CHRISTIAN MORAL SENSE[1]

WE WOULD like to say something about the Christian moral sense, with a view to helping to renew it in our faithful.

Can a Christian lack a moral sense? No, he certainly cannot. Obviously the very word Christian has implications in the moral field.

The Christian is by definition a man for whom the moral valuation of life has supreme and decisive importance. An action for a Christian has value if it is moral, if it is good. For him all things are subject to moral judgment; all things come into the supreme classifications of good and evil.

This moral sensibility does not paralyse the Christian, but guides, fortifies, and urges him to action. For moral action is the search for good, and the good provokes love, and love provokes life and movement.[2]

Here we might bring up a well-worn question; that of the relationship between Christian morality and natural ethics, which was summed up in eternally valid expression by the moral law of the Old Testament.

We know that Christian morality absorbs within itself both the natural and the Old Law. From the Old Law it has dropped the purely legalistic and ritualistic sanctions, while it has confirmed and perfected the natural law.

In the Sermon on the Mount, Christ clearly announced his programme of reform: 'Think not that I have come to abolish the Law and the prophets; I have come not to abolish them but to fulfill them' (Matt. 5, 17).

---

[1] From *On the Moral Sense*, Pastoral Letter to Archdiocese of Milan, 11 February 1961.

[2] Cf. particularly St Ambrose, *De officiis*, and Manzoni, *Osservazioni sulla morale Cattolica*.

The Ten Commandments were a compendium of the natural law expressed in the positive law of the Old Testament. They remain the intangible principles of the evangelic message and of Christian life too.

Christ has always been recognized as the custodian of all the moral values that humanity is capable of desiring or expressing. At the same time he has always been recognized as the wisest and boldest reformer of moral deficiencies which humanity was unable to resolve by its own efforts.

This vigorous and incomparable position which Christ has assumed at the heart of human action has made him accepted, even by those unable or unwilling to recognize his divinity, as a man of supreme goodness and a teacher of the highest quality, in purely human terms. How much more we would like to tell these people about him! And how greatly, too, we would like to see those who still call themselves Christians meditating more deeply on the teachings which he brought into our lives! He not only reveals God, he reveals man to himself.

That eternal question of ancient philosophy 'Man, know yourself' can only be answered by the divine master himself.

We will not dwell long on this vast subject. But I do want to put forward a few ideas concerning the Christian moral sense, and indicate some points about it which seem basic to Christ's teaching.

He gave a new, deep, inward meaning to moral action. He aroused the conscience and made it into a source of morality, a tribunal. He told us that outer semblance is not enough, legality is not enough; semblance of good, expediency, respect for forms, material observance, praise from others, is not enough. It is the heart, the conscience, the free and rational exercise of the will, that counts.

From this inner pivot he traced the way to the transcendent pivot —God.

All life takes place before God; his presence exposes every detail, endows every action with responsibility. But the relationship of man to God is no longer uncertain, no longer timid. It is that of love, the supreme precept, the supreme source of energy. This relationship between man and God leads, as we know, to a relationship between man and man. Love for our neighbour follows on and mirrors our love of God.

That is why the Christian's moral life must be incomparably the most human and the most fruitful of true social harmony. Man's moral life thus becomes a dialogue in which God has the initiative. God creates, loves, and calls. Man responds by loving, by imitating Christ in practice.

This dialogue, man's response to God's law as taught by Christ and as he helps us to practise it, assumes the highest importance because our future life depends on it. Yes, this future life, which we forget, which we no longer know how to co-ordinate with our present life as we should, Christ has proclaimed imminent, certain, for ever defined in one tremendous alternative: heaven or hell.

Their foreknowledge of this final choice, their eschatological vision of human destiny, has made Christ's disciples ready to do their utmost, eager to live this earthly vigil as well as possible. It has been one of the first and strongest arguments for a Christian asceticism, a striving towards perfection.

Our Lord not only taught that we must observe his precepts, but that those among us called to a more generous loyalty to him would do well to follow his particular advice. The future life has always been a strong motive for conversion and for vigilance in moral discipline; and the terrible threat of eternal punishment has always impressed on the conscience of believers the absolute character of divine law and the huge responsibility we bear for our actions.

For there is a dark side to Christ's wonderful picture of moral life. This dark side is man's sin.

It is very important for us moderns to be aware of both the idea and the reality of sin. This is something that the contemporary world has lost. One of Pius XII's most significant remarks was that 'perhaps the greatest sin in the world today is that men have begun to lose the sense of sin.'[1]

For by losing the sense of God, of our relationship with him, we lose the true concept of sin, which is an offence against God. This definition, short as it is, embraces the vastest concepts; in the first place, that of detachment from God, who is life.

Sin is a form of death (cf. Rom. 5, 12). We must remember the real, if mysterious, transcendental relationship which each free action of ours has with God himself. We are responsible before God. Our life takes place in his presence. Each of our actions is registered by his

[1] Pius XII, Radio Message to National Congress of Catechists, Boston, 26 October 1946. *Discorsi e Radiomessagi*, vol. VIII, p. 288.

gaze. So each of our actions must have a rightness in view of its supreme end. If this rightness is lacking, then this is a fault, a sin.

This indicates that a law to be followed is constantly put before us. And the voice that declares this law to us is conscience. Whoever does not follow it, sins. And as the conscience is a voice within ourselves, whoever does not follow it violates himself above all else.

Evil is born in us; it is a discordance between the reason and the will.[1] The reason judges good a thing which the will refuses to desire or to do.[2] Sin is an offence done to man which reverberates in God because man must respect within himself the work, the law, and the image of God.

And as the whole of life is linked with the external order, with our neighbour and the rules of living together, the violation of conscience and of God's law usually also means a violation of our solidarity with other human beings and with the order which we should respect for society.

Sin therefore does a threefold harm: subjective, spiritual, and social. But the most serious is spiritual harm, which of its nature is measureless and irreparable because it refers to God.

The Gospel, which draws human life close into God's presence and into familiarity with him, emphasizes again and again the possibility and the gravity of our sinning. Unless he is aware of this a Christian cannot call himself a Christian.

This 'sense of sin' generates thoughts, feelings, and intentions of great importance in the Christian moral system. And it is from this awareness of sin that the need for liberation and salvation comes.

The message of salvation would be vain had man no need to be saved from this radical and in itself irremediable disaster which is sin, the loss of God's friendship and of the life, the true life, which comes to us from him.

That is why repentance, penance, and conversion stand on the threshold of Christian life.[3] With these things, the moral life of Christians begins its concrete expression.

It begins, that is, from the desperate condition of human life. Man is a fallen being; man is a sinner; man has broken the vital relationship which should unite him to God; man is incapable of saving himself.

[1] Cf. Rom. 7, 18; St Augustine, *Contra Faustam*, 22, 27.
[2] *S.T.*, I, IIae, 3.
[3] Matt. 3, 2; 4, 17.

Do not say that this is simply supposition, as naturalism affirms.[1] That is an optimistic lie. The spirit of our generation, with its anguish, bitterness and despair, alarmingly and openly proves the contrary.[2]

How then can man raise himself? How gather within himself again faith, confidence in the world, hope in life, relation with God?

We must realize, with joy, that God himself has come to our aid, and has set in being a new economy, the great economy of mercy.[3]

How does one enter into this economy, into this plan of salvation? By faith. Faith is the starting point of our justification (Eph. 1). Faith therefore has a moral aspect and function of the first importance. 'Without faith it is impossible to please God.'[4]

But faith is only a beginning, a condition; a positive intervention by God is needed, which we call grace. Grace is conferred first by Holy Baptism.

Baptism is a capital event in man's life. We know the effects it produces, how it raises us to a state of life which is above our nature, because it makes us in a sense participants of the divine nature and adopted children of God (Heb. 11, 6). Baptism is an inestimable good, an ineffable destiny.

But what we want to emphasize here is that baptism brings a form of new life. It is a solemn pledge; it makes an inescapable demand; it is the beginning of a wholly new way of living.

We do not give enough thought to this stupendous newness that baptism should introduce into our way of looking at life, our manner of spending and directing our life.

From baptism come those customs and habits which can be called Christian. From it the conscience should draw sustenance. And from it should come the way of evaluating human actions which we have called 'the Christian moral sense'. This has its roots in the memory and character of baptism, and finds expression in a manner of looking at everything, judging everything, regulating everything according to the spontaneous, almost innate inspiration of the 'new man', born again at baptism.

It is very necessary that this basic conception of life should take on fresh light and vigour in the modern Christian. It is a mystery and

---

[1] Cf. Maritain, *Three Reformers*.
[2] Cf. 'Le rire contemporain' in *Études*, February 1961; Pascal, *Pensées*, 526, 527.
[3] Eph. I, whole chapter.
[4] Council of Trent, Session VI, 8 Denz. 801. Cf. Heb. 10, 38.

a pledge often forgotten, together with the sacred and noble duties which derive from it. This forgetfulness leads to a progressive conformity with the profane, corrupt 'world', to a facile and disastrous lapse from belief and then to a habit of not living in God's grace. Thus the image of the modern Christian is too often a deformed and degenerate one.

We must restore our awareness of baptism in order to restore in ourselves the likeness of Christ.

The Christian, who longs to restore and keep the sovereign beauty of baptism, is not alone in his efforts.

There is the divine action of grace, the only truly operative force in our salvation. And help is to hand: the Gospels; participation in the sacraments; the Church's teaching; the example and company of the saints.

Each of these could be commented on at length. But anyone who understands the value of these aids, which act together in making man a good, strong Christian, and in particular anyone who has experienced them, is well aware how the 'Christian moral sense' is fed at these sources.

The Christian moral sense can be trained. This axiom should always be borne in mind by those Christians who are worried by the disturbing influences and changing customs of modern life. The moral decadence so obvious around us causes distress to those who are good and those who really love life. We must not lose heart and think that we should surrender to indifference or moral compromise in order to be modern. Exterior conditions of life change, habits change, but the principles which make our existence Christian do not change.

If man in his progress through life does not remain a good—that is a true—man, and if his moral sense does not develop either, it cannot be said that he has done himself any good in the end.

Hence the importance of morality.

On the other hand, morality cannot and should not be thought of as an obstacle to the development of modern civilization from which come these changes in general habits and in positive law. Morality should be a guide and mentor in these developments, in fact it should be their stimulus and purpose.

We must see the moral law not in life's contingent and changeable expressions, such as popular traditions or habits, not in specific rules that are arbitrary or transitory, but at the roots of life, in what is essential and lasting, in its immutable demands and intangible laws, both natural and Christian. So we must strengthen our capacity to find and act on the truly moral and Christian aspect of every step we take. We must, in a word, revive in ourselves a really active moral sense.

Obviously the best way to acquire a stronger, deeper moral sense is to train our personal consciences.

This does not involve moral science or psychological research, though both can contribute to give the moral conscience greater clarity and certainty. It means we must activate the 'heart', that is the intimate judgment of the soul about the goodness or badness of our own actions.

We must remember that at the roots of our moral crisis today lies the obscuring of the concepts of right and wrong. What should and should not be done today are no longer determined by an inner law, but by a positive, external law, and even that is accepted less and less and called more and more into question. Right and wrong are being identified with useful or harmful, often in terms merely of personal pleasure, convention, good manners, or hygiene. We, on the other hand, must train a good conscience if we want to realize our responsibilities to God. Christ strongly called us to do so in special and repeated recommendations to be *vigilant*.

His religion is not one which muffles the conscience or makes it sleep. His is a religion which awakes the spirit and makes it tensely aware of what is happening inside and outside ourselves, 'Watch, therefore'.[1]

We repeat it ourselves in his name, 'Watch, therefore', in those circumstances which call for prompt and sharp moral perception.

Each one of us today should be aware of the dangers and evils surrounding him. Each one of us should know how to defend himself from them. We need a critical sense of good and evil, personally choosing the first and frankly rejecting the second, and a firm self-control. And these should go with an affirmation of our moral personality, with a new bearing, easy but firm, worthy of the name of Christian.

Inner vigilance is trained by the *examination of conscience*. Yes, this age-old and humble Christian habit is as useful and up-to-date as ever.

[1] Matt. 24, 42; 25, 13; 26, 38 and 41; Luke 12, 37; 21, 36, etc. Cf. Apoc., 3, 2.

The wisdom of the ancients held it in honour,[1] and that of Christians has made it a daily rule for those who want to walk the way of Christ.[2]

That famous phrase 'Know thyself' finds fruit in the examination of conscience. When this self-exploration is made in the mirror of Christ's light, then self-analysis is no longer a morbid and vain narcissism but a discovery of the self in sincere yearning for perfection.

This brings us to *spiritual direction*.

This, as we know, is the help, advice, and exhortation offered by a priest to a member of the faithful, that the latter may know himself and his particular duty better, and so progress in forming his spiritual personality in God's order.

It is not the passive subordination of a soul to a so-called superior whose authority creates a definite duty of obedience.[3] But it is authoritative and private help by an expert and friendly guide in developing the moral conscience and the personal energies of one who chooses that help freely.

Spiritual direction has a very fine function. It could be called indispensable for the moral and spiritual education of young people who want to interpret and follow with absolute loyalty whatever the vocation of their particular lives may be. It can be helpful and important at every age of life, when pious and prudent advice can help us realize we are on the right path and reassure us that we are doing our particular duty.

It is a teaching method of great delicacy, but also of great value, a psychological art of grave responsibility for the director, a spiritual exercise of humility and trust for the recipient.

We think it deserves the attention and respect of all those who have at heart the formation of a firm and vigilant moral sense.

Now we must mention that incomparable school of the moral sense, the *sacrament of confession*.

---

[1] E.g., Seneca: '*Quotidie apud me causam dico totum diem mecum scrutor, facta et dicta remetior. Nihil mihi abscondo; nihil transea*' (cf. *Ep.* 83, 2; *De Ira* 3, 36, 1). Cf. Lebret and Suavet, 'Rajeunir l'examen de conscience' in *Economie et Humanisme*, Paris, 1952.
[2] Cf. Can. 125; St Ignatius, *Spiritual Exercises*, 1.
[3] G. Leclercq, *La conscience du chrétien*, Aubier, Paris, 1946, pp. 247 ff.

Manzoni says:

'An institution which obliges man to form a severe judgment about himself, to measure his actions and dispositions by the rule of perfection, which gives him the strongest motives to exclude all hypocrisy from this judgment, teaching what will be reviewed by God, is a supremely moral institution.'[1]

In the practice of sacramental confession Catholic training has an instrument of the greatest efficacy for the formation of souls.

It only remains to us to recommend that this ministry be carried out not only assiduously, patiently, and zealously, but also with great care and tact.

Catholics have their own original and providential contribution to make in the modern teaching aimed to form the ideal man for contemporary life: autonomy of the personality, sense of responsibility, self-control, capacity for choice, coherence in action, awareness of duties to society and disinterestedness in carrying them out, initiative for good, constancy in action, endurance, generosity in sacrifice; all these qualities we usually indicate by one word: *character*. The ancients called it *virtus*. It was and is the expression of the true, the complete man. It makes one think of champions, of heroes. And it makes one think of saints.

The moral sense would have its part in the ideal man.

We want in conclusion to call the attention of our clergy and faithful to some of the temptations which require a particularly lively moral sense today. These are, moreover, the classic temptations which lie always in ambush on the path of virtue.

Today temporal goods and riches are a particular temptation. Their conquest is now almost the height of temporal ambition. It is certainly so among those with a materialist concept of life, both proletarian and capitalist.

Christian hope has been supplanted by economic and social hope. This is undermining the concept of honesty—in the payment of taxes, the play of the Stock Exchange, speculations by monopolists, commercial swindles, bribery. Any dubious transaction that does not actually conflict with the penal code is justified by self-interest.

Then there is the enjoyment of these riches. Luxury, vanity, pleasure, amusement, worldliness have become idols to which

[1] *Osservazioni sulla morale cattolica*, VIII, 3rd edition, S.E.I., Turin, 1934, p. 241.

modern man must sacrifice: the fascination of the 'world' has become collective, the fever of the senses endemic, the life of self-indulgence an ideal.

The moral sense must be strong and vigilant to maintain 'the primacy of the spiritual', honesty and justice in business, sobriety in enjoying the goods of this world without being degraded by them.

Then there is the great temptation of the flesh. Perhaps this is the most dangerous today, because it is the most visible, the most available, the most tolerated.

St Paul's 'animal man' seems to have first place in modern writing, plays, films, press, and habits. It is a vast and depressing subject. These characteristic manifestations of our time are surrounded with such overwhelming publicity that it is difficult to avoid them. Criticism itself, though it may react to technical and aesthetic judgments, is apt to tolerate and sometimes encourage the immorality of certain manifestations which it considers to be cultural and artistic.

The good must be watchful, must take action.

The moral sense must not weaken before the spread of evil and the forms that lead towards it. Authorities, parents, teachers, honest citizens, have all the more obligation today to show moral sensibility, because the law, leaving objective criteria vague, has now become almost the only criterion of right and wrong.

The defence of the younger generation, the need to keep the family strong and integrated, the honour of our people, the dignity of our artistic expression, the healthy manifestations of life, and the sacred character of the human personality and of the baptized in particular, and above all the loving and tremendous command of God's law must all infuse new strength into our moral sense.

Rather than be scandalized and alarmed, we should be restoring integrity to modesty and love.

Finally, the third temptation, that of pride, the temptation so difficult to define because it creeps in everywhere.

We can find it in our contemporary world, wherever man thinks that he is an end in himself, that he is self-sufficient, that he should be concerned with nothing but himself. Then man becomes an idol to himself and denies, by word and deed, that preamble of God's law from which the rest of his commandments takes force, 'I am the Lord thy God. First, thou shalt have no other gods but me.'

Atheists deny this. Secularists exclude it. The indifferent do not bother with it. Those who concentrate exclusively on things of this world forget it. The hedonist substitutes ephemeral pleasures for it. These, among many others, are all forms of the eternal temptation which shatters the moral axis between God and man, and shatters it at the human level, as if this were the supreme level and enough for a 'good life'.

This modern illusion has insinuated itself into every social class, into those of all ages, into everyone who breathes the heady atmosphere of our world's power.

The Christian moral sense gives another, truer, more vital breath to life. It brings it a vision and aspiration of the infinite reality and gives a guarantee of being able to achieve it.

This does not mean that we oppose or invariably criticize the world around us, in which Providence has called us to live. Indeed we want to say that we feel friendship and admiration for it, even if we look at the world as followers of the cross.

The world around us, as we have said, is in a ferment of activity, progress, and transformation; science, technology, industry, culture are changing things all around us.

We greet this fast and dazzling evolution with pleasure. But let it not make us dizzy, not make us lose the true sense of life, which is the moral sense. On the contrary, this should be more alert and active than ever. It should keep man on his true point of balance which is indispensable not only if he is to achieve his supernatural aim but to avoid falling victim to his own conquests.

We want modern man to join the conquest of inner perfection to that of the exterior world. Man must remain man. But he must progress morally, lest in progressing only materially all the splendid work he has done should turn to his own harm. So he must remain a Christian and come to understand better and live better his vocation of salvation.

In the turmoil of this critical juncture of his history, let him remember the words of Christ: 'Watch and pray, that you may not enter into temptation' (Mark 14, 38).

5

THE REMEDIES FOR MODERN SOULS[1]

How ARE we Christians to deal with moral evil? Are we powerless before it or have we remedies? Shall we try to battle against it or elude it by verbal palliatives?

Here, too, Christianity has a remedy. And this remedy can be studied in the very person who brought it into the world, our Lord Jesus Christ, who defined himself and his mission as: 'the Son of Man came to seek and to save the lost' (Luke 19, 10); the purpose of Christ's coming into the world was to restore man. He made this bold challenge to evil, 'I will come and save the world. I will come and put myself in contact with humanity, and I will redeem it and regenerate it.'

To conceive such a great plan, even if it were a failure—which it is not—shows a heart so vast and potent that it deserves all our admiration.

What other great man has ever dared say: 'I will save the world'? Great men, remarks a contemporary writer, may at one moment during their climb to power claim they are saving the world; but they do so in their own way; and sometimes this way of theirs is to start a war, or cheat their neighbours, or lay hands on the wealth of others.

Christ's attitude is quite different. The Gospel, if looked at closely, seems to measure everything by a yardstick that is strange and para-doxical. Instead of attenuating evil in order to contain and circum-scribe it, the Gospel gives evil its true proportion. It calls sin, that is our disordered actions, an offence to God himself.

Evil has something vast, immeasurable about it; the Old Testa-ment reached this understanding of it. Jesus showed us that evil is even more serious, by telling us that sin is not only an offence against God, it is an offence against a God who loves; sin is an offence

[1] From Sermon given on Wednesday of Holy Week, 1959.

against love. God so loved the world that he gave his only Son for it; and it is against this God of love, this God of charity, that evil reacts. Weak and wretched humanity when it rebels sets itself up against a God who calls himself our Father, calls himself our brother, calls himself our consoler and our host.

In the Roman liturgy for Good Friday the action becomes almost dramatic at one point. This is when the cross, which has been so long hidden, as evidence of a crime is hidden from a criminal, is at last gradually uncovered. Then man no longer sees it with horrified eyes as the result of his own sin, but as the source of his own salvation. And now comes one of the most heart-rending appeals in the whole prayer of the Church. The crucifix seems not only to be showing us its sagging bleeding limbs, it seems to be speaking to us in a sweet, penetratingly sad, lament: '*Popule meus, quid feci tibi aut in quo contristavite?*' 'My people, what have I done to you? How have I offended you?' Answer me. I have given my life for you, I have opened up to you the good things of this world, I have called you and raised you up, given you high and noble life, chosen you as my people—and you have prepared a cross for your Saviour. I have favoured you as a people, brought you out of the land of Egypt, given you a land flowing with milk and honey, I have brought you to royal heights, and you have prepared a crown of thorns for your king. You have sucked the blood that gave you life. My people, answer me!

Now at last the people seem to understand something of what they have done, and can only answer by crying out: 'Holy is God! Holy and strong! Holy and immortal, have mercy on us!'

This shows the enormity of sin, particularly when it becomes a habit, part of our daily lives. For to sin is to kill Christ anew: 'They crucify God on their own account and hold him up to contempt,' says St Paul (Heb. 6, 6).

Our sin is against love itself; and this must be why the punishment it deserves is so appalling: hell. Hell can only be explained in terms of an enormity preceding it.

Well, if Christ did this, if he made us aware of sin's true dimensions, did he not thereby make the struggle against it harder? He has shown the enemy so great, how can we defeat it? But another paradox, another overwhelmingly wonderful truth of the Gospel is this: that only after seeing sin in its true proportions, defining it as it is, does redemption from sin begin.

For we are capable of committing sin, crime, deicide, mainly because we do not know what we do. Jesus himself wished to lessen
our blame before God; and he did so at a moment which in any
other human crisis would have been one for fierce curses and condemnations.

Think of Christ nailed to the cross, with the blood running along
his arms and down his body, in spasms and agonies of pain we cannot even conceive. And, at the very moment when the weight of his
holy body slumped and dragged at his wounds, what does he say?
'Father, forgive them, for they know not what they do.' At that
bitterest of moments our Lord finds an excuse for us, takes our side,
defends and consoles us as if it were we who most need comfort.

We are so irresponsible. That is why we are capable of such
atrocious and appalling crimes. Our Lord tried to excuse us. But he
also tried to show us the reality of sin, to touch a sensitive chord in
the human heart. Remorse, if there is any, comes from the recognition of love.

Think of children, for instance. They are often disobedient, rebellious, and wilful. But when someone says to a normal child, 'Look,
you're making your mother cry,' he will be touched, will stop,
quieten down, say he is sorry, and then run away because he cannot
bear to see his mother's tears. When we realize somebody loves us,
we are touched too. When we see we are the objects of affection and
sacrifice we are apt to yield. Such coaxing from a sincere heart can
have more effect on us than any threat.

Well, our Lord coaxed us sinners beyond the imaginable, to draw
from our complicated and erratic human minds the genuine goodness that lies deep in them. Remorse, sin's first remedy—we usually
call it sorrow or contrition—comes when we think: I have been the
object of God's thought, God's love, God's providence, God's help,
God's mercy. I have so often been forgiven, excused, encouraged,
rehabilitated, re-admitted, so often blessed by his presence, his goodness . . . yet see what I am still capable of. Peter, who had bravely
sustained his role to the very last, that night denied his Master, and
not just once. At the third denial he burst out: 'I do not know this
man of whom you speak!' (Mark 14, 71). As one Gospel commentary
says:

'Jesus, who was standing humiliated and assailed before his
judges, only turned his head and looked at him. That was enough.

Peter was horrified. He fled, and burst into tears that flowed un-restrained, until the day when three times, to offset that triple denial, Peter was able to make his profession of love to Christ, "You know, Jesus, that I love you." '

Christ's look had been enough to make Peter realize how little it needs to commit so shameful an act. The cock had only to crow as prophesied, Christ had only to look at Peter, and Peter's sinful state of mind at once melted into the most loyal and loving contrition, ending in martyrdom.

Well, is this all? Is this the only cure Christ and the Gospel hold out to sin? Is it nothing more than arousing feelings of remorse, contrition, and love? That might, after all, be achieved by human means, by a therapy based on deep knowledge of the human mind, though it would not be easy. The Gospel shows it as foreseen and immediate. But that is not all; in fact I might call it the least. The Gospel shows another remedy, the one for which we celebrate Easter. It lies in God's attitude towards sinning mankind.

What a strange, mysterious, almost unthinkable fact! But so it is. God who is insulted, but who is also God of justice, shows he is a just God. In his judgment of sinning man there is no revenge. He does not let loose on us the torrents of his justice and his punishment. Let us thank God for that fact and make the most of it.

Our Lord's attitude was so unexpected, so new, that St Paul seemed almost hesitant to announce and explain it to men. In his letter to the Ephesians he calls it 'this mystery' (Eph. 3, 3). Hidden indeed in his mystery, our Lord was not preparing thunderbolts of vengeance for our sins. He was making another plan, a plan which is now begun, though we have not understood it well enough.

Our Lord showed us his mercy. What does this mean? It means that our Lord has a plan—the Fathers call it an 'economy'—to come to the aid of man who had betrayed, insulted, and abandoned him, who had tried to deceive himself and not believe in God.

Our Lord took pity on humanity, took pity on us. Watching over us is a goodness which we can never know well enough, never exalt enough, never be moved by enough, a goodness to which no joy or happiness of ours can be in the slightest degree commensurable. Watching over us, my children, is a Father of infinite tenderness. In the mysterious depth of his thought he wants us to have what we could never deserve; a concord of justice with mercy and goodness, a response to our sin by our reparation. He did all this.

So Jesus came, with the mission of saving the world. He took on human flesh, became man, became our brother, so as to put himself in a state to expiate for us, to become our representative, to assume all our responsibilities on himself, to take on himself all the immeasurable punishment for our sins. He came to be himself the victim of the human race.

'*Ecce agnus Dei*.' He was to be the Lamb, the innocent life that assumes all the consequences of sinning humanity. That was how John the Baptist greeted Christ on the threshold of his public life. 'Behold the lamb of God, who takes away the sin of the world' (John 1, 29). There, look at him, the Lamb, look at the victim. He will have the power to annul, expiate, burn away all our responsibility and make us innocent again, children again, candidates once again for eternal life.

See how Jesus carried out his mission. He came into the world and the world did not want to receive him. There was no room for him. But at least he was born in a stable, on the level of the animals. And luckily a crib was found for the newborn baby. So he came; and his dealings with men brought him terrible adversities. Humanly speaking we might say that his mission completely failed. The rationalists say so constantly, filling pages with purely external facts about the prophet of Nazareth.

His preaching aroused a certain amount of enthusiasm, which made him implacable enemies. Finally he got what they thought he deserved. He was condemned as an imposter, blasphemer, and enemy of the people, as enemy of Caesar, of all and sundry. He was killed and sent out of this life: 'Let us cut him off from the land of the living, that his name be remembered no more' (Jer. 11, 19). That was the greeting Jesus got from the human race. And Jesus is patient, Jesus, who came into our midst, loves us.

This is an aspect of the Gospels which, once explored, should make us understand how tremendous its revelations are. However could a person so treated retain any love for those who served him so? Jesus loves mankind, in fact his love is most open and accentuated for the very people who are most fallen, the people dubbed 'publicans and sinners'.

One of the accusations made against him was that he spent his time with these publicans and sinners. Because he lived among the most abject in the society of the day, Jesus was considered a sub-verter of the moral and social order, and was treated by the law as a traitor, a disturber of tradition. Jesus was condemned by men. Yet Jesus *loves* them.

Remember how Jesus treated children, the very poor, the afflicted, and the sick. You know his message to them: Blessed are you poor, blessed are you who weep, blessed are you who long for peace, blessed are you who are persecuted. And whenever a man draws close to him in sincerity, whatever his state in life, his origin, culture, or background, he finds the Master, the good shepherd, the doctor, the friend, finds him who forgives and rehabilitates.

This is how Jesus treats mankind. We know how much confidence his heart has already given mankind. If there is such comfort, after twenty centuries, for us who are so fickle and so wretched, it is because there is one who sympathizes with us, does not despise us, waits for us, is still capable of raising us up and of forgiving us. This one is Jesus Christ, our Lord. How many souls have drawn near him, gone to him with bent heads and hesitant steps, and found our Lord ready to greet and console. Remember how this attitude of Christ and of God—for Jesus is but the pattern of God on earth—was described in the parable of the Prodigal Son. The son, before he returned home, had returned to himself; hence the remorse, the contrition of which I have spoken. Then he went back to his father. And his father, instead of rebuking him and rejecting him, threw his arms around his neck, gave him a new robe, ordered a more sumptuous and far more cordial banquet than usual, because his son who was lost had returned, his son who was dead had come back to life.

The lost sheep is an eternally moving image which tells us of Christ's, that is of God's, feelings towards our misery, if only we have the courage and humility to let him find us.

Jesus carried out his mission not only by suffering and blessing and consoling all, by healing the sinners and the sick. He sealed his mission by dying on the cross. Christ went on the cross because he himself wanted to. In no human tragedy does the victim have foreknowledge of what is about to happen to him, is certain that he will be sacrificed. Soldiers who give their lives for their country always live in the hope of escaping that death or in ignorance of what is about to happen to them.

Jesus had the clearest, calmest, and saddest foreknowledge which a human heart can have of human misfortune. Jesus offered himself of his own will, as victim and priest. When we see him on the cross next Good Friday let us think that he is there 'for us men and for our salvation'.

As if to reinforce this, St Paul reduced it to a single exclamation, '*dilexit me et tradidit semetipsum pro me*'. Redemption has become personal to each of us. Each of us is the object of God's love. Each of us has a share in the blood of redemption given by Christ for all humanity.

Yes, that is our redemption, that is the remedy for our sin.

6

ON THE CHRISTIAN FAMILY[1]

To FOUND a family needs preparation; firstly, mental preparation: one needs an overall concept of what a family is.

Since natural instinct leads to a family, it is easy to fall into the illusion that this instinct is enough to give the contracting parties an accurate idea of human love and of the social unit that results.

Many consider that emotional and sexual experience is the necessary and sufficient initiation. Countless young people are deceived by this opinion, then allow it to become a blind prejudice and a hypocritical justification for sexual licence. This attitude also gains credit from tales of romantic love. But unless such experience is guided by moral rules and raised to a spiritual level, it gives no more than a degraded notion of the sublime unity to which man and woman can aspire. Those who abandon themselves to it come up against the negations that ensue: first a sense of degradation, then of disgust, boredom, even hatred, and eventually of pessimism. Such are the inner results, coupled sometimes with outer ills, which show up the mysterious and fatal disorder of pleasure sought for itself, of so-called free love.

Mysterious and fatal disorder; for it should be realized that a radical disorder in a human being's sexual life affects his inner equilibrium more easily (and more seriously) than other sectors of human activity. Lust, with which we are all tainted, was let loose by original sin; it causes an explosion of the animal and the irrational in man, and this usually anticipates the development of reason and always tends to prevail over it, so that it upsets and humiliates our real selves, rational and sanctified by grace; it leads to experiences which pass at once from the idyllic fascination of passion to the nausea of sin.

[1] From *For the Christian Family*, Pastoral Letter to the Archdiocese of Milan, Holy Week, 1960.

Lust is very near the surface of the flesh; and it is deep in each human being, close to the origin of life, to men's fullness and happiness, to love.

It seems almost impossible to restore integrity to the enjoyment of feelings and senses.[1]

But this is just what we must do first of all. Human love must be given back the sublime dignity which it only has at its peak, that is when it unfolds according to a higher, exclusive design, the divine design.

The encyclical *Casti connubii* has good reason to begin by proclaiming the dignity of marriage; its dignity even before its integrity; for marriage is not only good, but can be morally grand, spiritually splendid.

These two aspects should be pointed out to those preparing for married life. On the one side, the ease and danger, the almost fatal degradation of sexual life when not part of the divine design; and on the other its real and ideal beauty if part of God's established order.

We must show the young what is involved in choosing between these two. They are like people walking on heights, in danger of catastrophic falls on one side and on the other the bracing joy of reaching the peak. Vice and virtue stand very close to each other.

We must teach a new idea of human love, of love raised to the sublime by Christ.

This brings us to the question of instructing the young on chastity, about which so many different things are said. There is no escaping from this subject. Experience tells us how necessary it is to warn adolescents about satisfying their natural curiosity about sex, and how difficult it is, once innocence is lost, to show what chastity is.

Pope Pius XII was very definite about the need for such instruction: 'On these matters [connected with chastity] adolescents should be given appropriate instruction and advice. They should also be allowed to speak their minds openly, to ask questions without hesitation, and receive replies that beget trust and a firm, clear, and widespread light.'[2]

We should not only instruct, we should *educate*. This is opposed

[1] Cf. Bouyer, *Le trône de la sagesse*, pp. 109 ff. (English translation *Woman and Man Before God*, London, 1960).
[2] *Discorsi*, XIII, p. 257.

by the naturalism in vogue among those of our teachers who have lost a genuinely Christian concept of man. We must boldly affirm the need for purity, and that it is both possible and useful.

This is not utopian. It is all part of a moral training, the power of which is still acknowledged by many splendid young people who exercise self-domination and respect for others, whose secret is the help of divine grace.

Christian education needs revitalizing, refortifying, perfecting on this subject.

Teachers should not only be capable of preserving youth from moral falls, often so prevalent that many consider them inevitable; but they should also show the moral and spiritual force, the beauty and serenity that come from habits of purity. They should infuse a taste for purity, and teach their pupils how to avoid the occasions of evil that can be avoided, and to remain untouched in those that are inevitable.[1]

School-teachers must make great efforts here, for temptations and corruptions of heart and habit are very powerful today.

Much in modern life, far from protecting and defending habits of purity, seems to go out of its way to produce more and more titillating stimulants in order to divert these habits and drag them down into the sad and easy experience of weakness and human squalor.

Christian teachers must not falter before such assaults, but draw from the inexhaustible powers of their religion the wisdom and strength to form men and women who are both vigorous in their virtue and aware of the reasons for it.

Since most young people are destined for family life, and the way to the family is love, the best line to pursue in teaching them is to show how good habits in matters of sex are the truest preparation for love; and as love can and should have no other aim than marriage, that these good habits give it both fullness and sanctification.

The delicate and dangerous engagement period is of great importance for this education. Reasons should be given and care taken so that this period may be one of serene, virtuous, and joyful development, a period when the two beings who are to form one whole are modelled on life's highest ideals and learn to anticipate the fusion of their souls before their union in marriage.[2]

This preparation for the formation of a family should also include

[1] Cf. 1 Cor. 5, 10.
[2] Cf. Casti Connubii, n. 41. Carré, Compagnons d'éternité, du Cerf, Paris, 1957.

instruction on health and hygiene, and on intellectual, moral, professional, and spiritual matters.

All families need to come as close as possible to perfection. Even the health and fitness of a couple are not to be ignored, are part of the perfection of every kind which is required to celebrate the mystery of love and new life.

We leave details of these to experts, pausing only on one of particular interest, the couple's capacity to carry out their future role as educators. As the first end of marriage is to create progeny, this necessarily implies the duty of educating them. Husband and wife must be well informed about this great mission and be prepared to carry it out.

It is a duty from which the modern family has abdicated far too much. Families must be made aware of their rights in this matter, which precede even those of the State, and of their duties in the education of their own children. If they cannot carry out these duties themselves, they should at least know what they are, and this can be taught in theory during the period before marriage, when they are full of good resolutions and preparing themselves for the joys, the anxieties, the sacrifices of educating their families, in this apprenticeship of noble and loving hearts.

Among matters to be considered before a marriage are 'impediments', that is circumstances which might prevent the contraction of a marriage, make it invalid (if diriment) or illegal (if impedient).

This is not the place to go into these in detail. But it is our pastoral duty to recall how wise are these restrictions on the freedom to contract marriage; some are according to natural and divine law and allow no dispensation of any kind; others are purely according to ecclesiastical law.

If certain impediments can be dispensed for just motives, nonetheless we must not underrate the reason for their existence since they exist for the sake of society and of those individuals to whom they apply.

As well as the obvious cases of the marriage of couples within certain degrees of blood or other relationship, the Church justly and severely forbids marriages in which both parties are not of the same religion. This includes marriage between parties one of whom is not baptized (disparity of cult) or one of whom is not Catholic (mixed religion).

When there is a lack of spiritual unity between husband and wife, marriage itself can become a danger to the faith of the believing partner and of the children. The atmosphere of such a home often becomes apathetic and indifferent towards religion, making it far more difficult for husband and wife to achieve 'that lively union of souls which should imitate the mystery . . . of the Church's ineffable union with Christ'.[1]

If people were to know and respect these impediments, the serious hazards to which those couples expose themselves who plan marriages without taking cognizance of their rigour and wisdom would be avoided.

Preparation for marriage would, we think, be helped if the forming of a family were presented to young people and understood as a vocation, a mission, a great duty, one which gives life the highest of aims and fills it with graces and powers.

This is not an exaggeration or distortion of reality.

Marriage is not a whim, not a momentary venture. It is the conscious and definite choice of a state of life which those who enter it consider best, a state created by both the man and the woman not only to complete each other physically but to carry out a design of Providence that determines the human and supernatural destiny of each of them.

They seek a completion that will fulfill 'humanity', an image in nature of the all-fruitful and all-loving God the Creator: and a supernatural image, to the Christian's mind, of the union of Christ with his Church.

'How splendid is the state of life that offers such fullness, such horizons! [says a contemporary writer]. Because it is so normal, the state of the majority of human beings, we must not judge it banal, not lose the sense of "vocation" that it requires. . . . This state does not derive, as with inferior species, from the instincts alone. This mutual fulfillment is the desire of the whole being and the object of a *choice*, hence of a *gift*, that are both free, both high manifestations of the human personality.'[2]

If marriage is conceived in this way it fuses in a single emotion, a single purpose, the two greatest voluntary acts of which the human spirit is capable: love and duty. Love follows its rightful path, that

[1] *Casti Connubii*, n. 30.
[2] Carré, *Compagnons d'éternité, op. cit.*, pp. 16–17.

of giving itself, pledging itself, utterly and for ever; duty reacquires its energy and force.

Such is life when presented and transfigured by Christ.

The Christian concept of the family

The Christian concept of the family must, one would suppose, be well known to everyone already.

The family is a natural institution resulting from the permanent union of a man and a woman and of the children born of that union. It begins with marriage, which is a mutual contract by which the husband and wife give themselves to each other, exclusively and perpetually, intending to procreate children.

So marriage is the 'source and foundation of the family and therefore of all human society'.[1] It consists in the 'natural union of man and woman, contracted between persons legally free to do so; a union implying inseparable community of life'.[2] 'Marriage is born of free consent given by both parties according to law.'[3]

We know also that marriage between Christians was raised by Christ to the dignity of a sacrament.

This is a doctrine which needs particular emphasis; one of the major developments in Catholic life during our century has been to give the faithful an awareness of the sacramental character of marriage.

It must be explained how a natural institution, by the fact of being celebrated between two human beings who are Christians, becomes a sacrament, is made divine, is lit inwardly by divine charity, and establishes a perennial font of grace and sanctification.

It is not the nuptial blessing which gives this mysterious quality to marriage, though this has a preordained form so that a marriage may be valid; but it must be understood that for Christians marriage is a sacred act, implying a transcendent, divine causation, of which husband and wife are themselves the ministers.[4]

Let us examine carefully some basic concepts connected with marriage, concepts which are the object of much discussion and dispute today.

Let us remember the two main properties of marriage: unity and

---

[1] *Casti Connubii* (C.T.S. translation, p. 5).
[2] *Catech. ad Parochos*, 290.
[3] Can. 1081. Cf. in Roman Law, Inst. 1, 9, 1; Dig. XXII, 2, 1.
[4] Council of Trent, Session XXIV, 1. *Catech. ad Parochos*, 292.

indissolubility. Let us keep in mind its ends, the first of which, within nature, is progeny, followed by the mutual aid of husband and wife and defence against concupiscence. Let us keep in mind the benefits of marriage, classified since St Augustine's time under three heads '*proles, fides, sacramentum*',[1] that is: children, faithfulness, the sacred bond; benefits which are at the same time the great duties of marriage.

Let us bear in mind that the Church has authority on all matters to do with Christian marriage.

The Church's teaching in this field is vast, and we can dwell here only on some areas which are most under discussion today.

First among these is the seriousness with which the matrimonial vow should be considered by all, particularly by the contracting parties.

We have already said, and we repeat, that a purely naturalist concept of marriage does not take into account either its whole nature or its mysterious elevation to a supernatural level.

What shall we say then about the easy manner in which it is publicly derided, undervalued, and insulted by superficial, worldly, corrupt modern minds, examples of which abound in the press, theatre, films, television, and in social customs?

Those who insult marriage strike at the basis of society and at the sources of life.

Marriage is not a private whim nor a matter that concerns only the contracting parties. In its origin it is a free act; but once carried out—'consummated', to use the legal term—it no longer depends on the will of the contracting parties. It is then a public act; a sacred act; a definitive act. It is a solemn act forever binding those who take part in it, before their consciences and their children, before society, the Church and God.

Woe betide those who lower or besmirch it! Woe betide those who titillate the public by wretched tales of vice or fascinate it by details of low life and the scandalous love-affairs of screen-stars, treating these as if they were mere adventures to satisfy the avid curiosity of the weak and the undefended!

And woe betide those couples who make conditions to their marriage which harm its essential aims, arming themselves beforehand with excuses to impugn its validity later, turning marriage into a mere source of pleasure.

[1] *De bono coniung.*, 24, 32; *De Genesi ad litt.*, 9, 7, 12.

Woe betide those who build castles of lies and perjuries, or deform the truth with false and subsequent versions of the facts, thinking that a judge's declaration can free them from a binding contract from which no man can free them!

We must in this connection recall the solemn words of the Gospel in defence of conjugal fidelity: 'But I say to you that everyone who divorces his wife, except on the ground of unchastity, makes her an adulteress; and whoever marries a divorced woman commits adultery' (Matt. 5, 32).

The divine law, the interpreter and founder of the deepest human needs, is very severe on this point.

Pope Pius XI wrote:

'Our Lord Jesus Christ condemned every form of polygamy or polyandry, whether simultaneous or successive, as well as every external act of impurity. But he went further. In order to preserve the frontiers of marriage perfectly inviolable he also forbade any thoughts or voluntary desire concerning such things: "But I say to you, that whosoever shall look on a woman to lust after her hath already committed adultery with her in his heart." These words of our Lord cannot be made void even by the consent of one of the partners; they are the promulgation of a divine and natural law which no human will can infringe or modify.'[1]

This language falls strangely on the modern ear, used to more and more varied casuistries about conjugal infidelity, and to expressions which soften its cruelty by polite hypocrisy.

But for us Christians this language has no substitute; we are bound to call anyone who breaks the bonds which marriage has made sacred and untouchable an adulterer.

We feel compassion or understanding for the weak, who have been drawn away from their sacrosanct duties by passion and self-interest. But we cannot allow relaxed modern habits to change our judgment on this crime, or to temper the language which defines it. We cannot resign ourselves to comfortable acceptance.[2]

So we come to the subject of divorce.

A great deal has been said about this; and we hope that you are all clear about this legal palliative, which is contrary to God's law. The

[1] *Casti Connubii* (C.T.S., pp. 13–14).
[2] Cf. St Ambrose, *In Lucam*, VIII, 2–9.

Church has rightly opposed it with inflexible energy. She is the jealous custodian of life, love, and honesty. She is the tenacious defender of the social benefits deriving from the indissolubility of the the family. She is the proud and tender guardian of the innocent children whom divorce deprives of trusted and responsible parents.

We cannot speak of this at length here. But we call on all priests, lawyers, writers, teachers, and particularly parents, to watch very carefully the ever-active campaign in favour of divorce, remembering that, to the honour of Italy and the preservation of one of life's major benefits, there is no civil divorce on our statute-book.

Let us remember that no infringement—even the so-called 'little divorce'—of the stability of the family can ever remedy the evils which a change in the law on divorce wishes to eliminate, and would only increase these evils enormously. Indeed, when the possibility of divorce is foreseen it actually helps to bring these evils about.

'The knowledge that marriage is indissoluble helps husband and wife to contain themselves within limits from which a relative happiness derives; while the possibility of a marriage being dissolved can only increase and exasperate any circumstances that make a married couple unhappy.'[1]

Leo XIII, in his encyclical on Christian Marriage, *Arcanum* (1880), listed the following evils deriving from divorce; by divorce:

'the union of a married couple becomes subject to change, mutual benevolence between them diminishes, infidelity is incited, and the well-being and education of the children prejudiced; seeds of discord are sown between families, and the dignity of woman is lowered; for after serving men's pleasure, they run the risk of being abandoned.'

Another sad topic is abortion, whether for eugenic, therapeutic, social, or any other reasons.

We do not intend to say much here about this either, only to recall that abortion is a crime because it means the direct murder of an innocent life.

However freely and carelessly discussed, abortion is forbidden, it is a sin. It is a tragedy which strikes at the very fount of life; it violently contradicts the highest and most sacred purpose of a

[1] Pastoral Letter of Mgr. Tredici, p. 238.

family; it is a dishonour, secret maybe, but scalding those who desire it and those who do it.

To this slaughter of the innocents our modern habits of mind no longer react with the necessary horror. So we beg those whose duty it is to study this delicate question in its proper terms to rectify false opinions which are spread about it and do all they can to cure this shameful moral and social sore, to fight against this among other propaganda for limiting families and against indifference or tolerance or complicity towards it.

We beg doctors, particularly, to do all they can, in the name of the law which makes every life sacred, of the ideals of their profession and the dignity of their social function.

And to mothers, above all, we cry: do not kill your own children!

Linked with this is another very serious problem of family morality: birth-control.

This problem becomes critical when the family has not the ability to guarantee a healthy birth or—as so often happens today—to provide sustenance.

We must leave this delicate subject, also, for the competent to deal with tactfully, and only mention it here in order to recall how seriously reproved every action which deliberately intends to deprive a marriage of its natural, generating function must be.[1]

God's law is particularly strict about this. It should not be forgotten by married couples or ignored by those who give advice on medical or spiritual matters.

Let us also recall that the prudence with which husband and wife avoid conception, by recourse to methods in themselves lawful, must not become a preconceived or fixed habit of will nor must it be adopted without well-founded reasons.

Pius XII's balanced teaching on this matter can be a great help.[2]

We must also ask ourselves whether too much attention is paid to this topic today, and whether this interest tends to favour limitation of births, or their regulation and blessed fruitfulness.

Selfishness very often seeks to give credit to the motives of limitation; and selfishness smothers life, fecundity, and love. We

---

[1] *Casti Connubii* (C.T.S., pp. 27-8).

[2] *Discorsi*, XIII, pp. 343-418; XX, 347-8. In English translation, see *Marriage and the Moral Law*, C.T.S., London, which includes Pius XII's address to Italian midwives, *Vegliare con sollecitudine*, 1951, and his address to the 'Family Campaign', *Nell 'Ordine della Natura*, 1951.

would like to see Catholic families preserve as far as possible their generous fertility. Large families should redound to the credit of the parents, ministers of life; they should bear witness to their parents' fidelity, love, and trust in Providence, their affection for their children, and reap, when necessary, the praise and help of society.

If limitation of births is necessary—which one presumes may be the case in every marriage given certain circumstances—then continence must be the normal means to practise it.

This virtue is not contrary to the happiness of husband or wife, nor harmful to their love and life in common. It requires training, moral and spiritual strength, and the help of prayer and grace. But this is part of the great programme of Christian life. Blessed are those who can exercise it with strength, and so feel its hidden spiritual compensations.[1]

The perfection of Christian marriage

We would like to quote here a phrase of St Ambrose's: 'The home in which a man and woman are united, is an image of complete perfection.'[2]

We must grow used to recognizing and honouring the perfection of Christian marriage, and to favouring the formation of families in which this ideal of natural and supernatural perfection can be realized. It is not true that this is impossible today. Indeed it is more than ever necessary in our time, and is already being carried out wherever Catholic life is fully and genuinely embodied.

It is in line with the development of modern Christian spirituality. That the family begins to appear as a source of grace is one of the 'signs of our times'. 'The full realization of the sacramental character of marriage is without doubt an acquisition by the Church in the twentieth century.'[3]

Let us accept that fine definition of the family as 'a community of love'. Let us restore to that word 'love', which can mean so many things, its true moral, spiritual, indeed divine meaning. We must see that human love has a genuine and worthy meaning in that state which alone makes it legitimate and sacred, marriage.

'According to the Church's concept, love is for marriage and marriage is for love, both being for the family. . . . Marriage

[1] Cf. Suenens, *Love and Control*, Burns Oates, London, 1961.
[2] *De Parad.*, XI, 50.
[3] J. Leclercq, *Le mariage chrétien*, Tournai, 1947, p. 8.

makes love moral, it is the institution by which love becomes a means of salvation . . . and allows the mass of the faithful to save and sanctify themselves. . . .'¹

The fatal deviation is to look for love outside marriage; it is then no longer love, but passion, disorder, and vice.

Conjugal love was raised by Christ to the dignity of a sacrament, as we know if we recall and meditate on the famous passage in St Paul that sets the full scope of this love. 'Husbands should love their wives as their own bodies' (Eph. 5, 28)—that is natural love; and 'as Christ loved the Church'—that is Christian love. Christ's 'husbandly' love of the Church is the model which the sacrament of matrimony reproduces as grace in husband and wife, giving them the capacity of turning their family life into virtue lived.

Total love, sanctifying love, unifying love, fruitful love, is reflected in contemporary theology.² Christ's generous and heroic gift of himself, his sacrificial love, is the epitome of that love—as it is of his love for mankind whom he longed to save, i.e. the Church.

Christian love finds its true colours in this sacrificial light. That is to say, its true fruitfulness depends on the degree to which the rule, synthesized and expressed in all Christianity, is accepted: 'He who finds his life will lose it, and he who loses his life for my sake will find it' (Matt. 10, 39).

So we should study how natural love becomes Christian love. Not only in matters of morality does the grace of the sacrament leave its impress on natural love, though this is already a great step forward, since it causes natural love to develop according to its own sense of integrity and fitness, detracting nothing but bringing out all its intrinsic value; but it does so too by making it holy and, more than anything else, by purifying it. It is a great thing to purify love!

Grace, if not resisted, leads to this. The various components of natural love: instinct, imagination, sensibility, passion, sensuality, rationality, are ordered and governed by an innate spirituality which unifies them and raises them to the supernatural.³

Natural love, prone to so many corruptions, is ennobled and becomes a channel of grace, which so pervades and informs it that it takes on the image of the greatest love there has ever been, the love of Jesus Christ for his Church.

¹ J. Lerclercq, *ibid.*, pp. 47 ff.
² Cf. C. Colombo, *Enciclopedia del Matrimonis*, Brescia, 1960, pp. 602 ff.
³ *Casti Connubii.*

A love new, pure, living, and holy.

One must remember too that the sacrament of marriage gives birth to an attitude in husband and wife which should go on developing throughout the whole of their married life so that its every aspect (household, work, job, amusements, anxieties, etc.) becomes more and more permeated by love: the mutual love of husband and wife for each other and their love for their children. In this way God's love for the family is reflected in its daily life.

It requires a sustained effort for natural love to yield to the demands of Christian love. Pronouncing the marriage vow is not enough; it must be renewed every day; and particularly on important family occasions such as the birth of a child, an anniversary, or a trial, it must be able to do battle over and over again against the temptations of scepticism, or resigned disappointment, weariness, or self-withdrawal and selfishness that usually come after some years of marriage.

The family is built up spiritually day by day; and its value comes from daily fidelity to the first sacred pledge of love.

Then we may dare to use that great word, 'charity', and say that love has turned into charity.

For this sacred pledge of love vivified by grace is in fact charity: conjugal, paternal, maternal charity; the charity which generates and demands an increase of every virtue in both Christian and family life.[1] Hence for the Christian husband and wife there comes a duty to study the spiritual life that is proper to their state of life; and with it goes a corresponding duty on the part of priests to know about this and be able to explain it to the faithful.

Let St Paul be our master. He gives us the first elements of a family's constitutional right. Its head is the husband (1 Cor. 11, 3); his duties are the most serious, to love even to the point of sacrifice (Eph. 5, 25 ff.); the wife is subject to her husband's authority (Eph. 5, 22; Col. 3, 18), but she is equal to him in dignity (1 Cor. 7, 4; 11, 12; Gal. 3, 28) and also the object of his special care (Eph. 5, 29) and admiration; she 'is the glory of man' (1 Cor. 11, 7).

We know the laws of marriage which St Paul, echoing Christ, proclaimed; the unity and indissolubility of the marriage vow were firmly taught by him (1 Cor. 1, 7; 4, 10; 4, 39–40; Eph. 5, 31). He tells of the integrity (1 Cor. 7, 28; 1 Tim. 5, 14) and dignity (Eph. 5, 15) of marriage; he reveals its sacramental character and mys-

[1] Cf. 1 Cor. 13, 4–7.

terious supernatural depth: 'This is a great mystery' (Eph. 5, 32). He
teaches its sanctifying power (1 Cor. 7, 14) and he speaks of the
virtues which should adorn the family (1 Cor. 7, 5; Eph. 5, 28, 33;
1 Tim. 3, 11), of the values of maternity (1 Tim. 5, 14; 2, 15), and
how widowhood must be honoured (1 Tim. 5, 3 ff; 1 Cor. 7, 40)
and virginity exalted (1 Cor. 7, 25 ff).

We can also find authoritative precepts in St Ambrose, remembering particularly the one that we have tried in this letter to set at
the heart of the whole doctrine of marriage *primum in coniugo
religio quaeritur*', 'the first thing to be observed in marriage is its sacred
character'.[1]

Closer to our own time we have the voice of Pius XII, who dedi-
cated many of his apostolic discourses to the family.

A series of his discourses on the subject of the family home were
interrupted by the war. Here is a quotation from one of them,
addressed to married couples:

'Imagine the perfect model of one of these homes. Everyone in
it is careful and eager to carry out his or her own duty conscien-
tiously and well; to please the others, practise justice, frankness,
gentleness, self-abnegation with a smile on the lips and in the
heart, patience and forgiveness, strength in the hour of trial
and under the burden of work. Here the parents are educating
their children in the love and practice of every virtue. In such a
family home God is honoured and served with trust, neighbours
treated with goodness. Can anything be lovelier or more edify-
ing?'[2]

Something that should be thought about and encouraged is that
each member of a family should try to complement the others in
mutual striving for moral perfection.

A man who really carries out his duties as a father can rise to great
heights of manly virtue. And how much each and every member of
his family can learn from his kind, authoritative care for them.
And a woman who is a mother in the full sense of that word
can achieve such perfection, can be a source of tender virtue and
compassion, of true unity for her husband, her children, and the
whole of her family!

Children themselves learn goodness in the school of a good
family, and can sometimes even improve their parents when their

---

[1] *De Abraham*, I, 9, 84.   [2] *Discorsi*, 5, 22–3.

simple innocence awakens in them the image of those angels who watch over them and who gaze on the face of God.

This serene and rosy vision of family life should not let us forget its inherent difficulties.

As time passes temperaments show their prosaic reality and their defects, provoke irritation which can turn into quarrels, and from quarrels into discord.

But we insist in our optimism, remembering that family life is not perfection achieved, but a school of perfection to be achieved.

From the outset husband and wife must each become adept at improving the other, correcting the other lovingly, being patient, understanding, encouraging.

They, more than anyone else, can practise that wonderful love called forgiveness. They can feel its regenerating effect, sometimes dramatically, when the family may seem on the brink of ruin.

However united the Christian family is, it should not be self-absorbed and isolated from other families, from the civil society around it or from the clergy.

The love which unites a domestic community does not cut it off from the social community, must not become group selfishness. It should create the first sense of community, but not the only one; it should determine the sense of community, not restrict it.

Certainly we do not look today for any revival of the old feudal type of family, for that would preserve only its defects and not its functions, and make a family proud of itself, jealous of others, pleased with its own privileges and generally hostile to those of others.

A Christian family is friendly to other families. It joins as widely as possible in the life and doings of the society which surrounds it. It has a sense of solidarity with its own neighbourhood; it loves the place in which it lives and its history, it loves its local church and takes part in that Church's activities; it serves the needs of its own nation, respects that nation's laws, and promotes its prosperity.

The Christian family is a school for a sense of universality; it is an initiation into humanity; it leads towards universal love, to a vision of the world.

The Christian family has its own ways of practising this: modest, kindly, but effective ways; in its choice and cultivation of friends, cordiality to guests, love of the poor, interest in good works, sociability, loyalty to its parish, civic sense, and *sensus Ecclesiae*.

All this is possible, or at least easier, if the Christian family complies with one of its most basic needs, prayer in common. Prayer gathers hearts and opens them; it brings the little domestic circle together and spreads around it the great circle of the universe and of God.

Human *pietas* becomes religious *pietas*.

During our Mission of Milan we ourselves distributed a booklet of prayers for family use. It was designed to promote meditation and comment on the great religious and sanctifying value of prayer in common.

Prayer in common also has an educative value. In the moments of quiet, when the family is united to murmur the same prayer together as if with a single heart, there is present a common search for the glory and love of God; Christ is present, the Holy Ghost is present.

Here we should add a further consideration concerning a basic state of soul in a Christian family: that is trust, the practice of the virtue of hope.

The difficulties of home life, never absent in small, growing units, are all the greater today due to social surroundings, the current profane mentality, and the uncertain future.

The sacrament of marriage will preserve our Lord's blessing on the human nucleus which he has generated and watched over. The sense of Providence innate in Christian hearts will certainly be answered by signs of loving and divine help. It is God who prepared the humble but magnificent circumstances in which a family is born.[1] It is he who permitted these two people to meet, who by the marriage blessing has protected them on the risky journey through life, and he certainly does not forget or abandon responsibility for any family that lives according to his laws.

Let us hope that you, Christian families, may feel, as your family history develops, the simple but stupendous experience of Providence; and come to realize

'that troubles often come to those who bring them on themselves, but that not even the most cautious and innocent behaviour can ward them off; and that when they come—whether by our own fault or not—confidence in God can lighten them and make them useful for a better life'.[2]

---

[1] Cf. Prov. 19, 14; Eccl. 26, 3.
[2] Manzoni, *The Betrothed*, end of last chapter.

7

THE CHRISTIAN SENSE OF TEMPORAL REALITY[1]

WE MAY limit ourselves to three observations here.

The first is that the Christian's attitude to temporal goods is *a priori* optimistic; friendly, not hostile; admiring and sympathetic, not scandalized or alarmed. It may be wary, but out of respect and an awareness of their superiority.

I find this state of mind confirmed every time in the course of my ministry I visit great works of modern industry, see over new factories and displays of modern products. I realize at once how impossible it is, especially in view of our religious principles, to ignore such works, much less reject them.

Instead I find coming to mind those wonderful and mysterious words repeated so often in the Bible, which tell how God himself admired the work of his own creation: 'and God saw that it was good'. The Creator of the universe is pleased with his work. God sees himself reflected in his creations. He admires their order, movement, grandeur, beauty, and depth. He listens to the song of praise rising from the cosmos he has made. In it he realizes his own power and his own freedom.

What a vast subject for meditation! It is almost like thinking with the mind of God! We are instantly dazzled. Perhaps, though, it will be by this route that the man of tomorrow will return to the religion lost by the scientific world of yesterday.

But all we can assume for the moment, by way of a very disparate analogy which is encouraged and authorized by St Paul, who wanted us to be imitators of God (Eph. 5, 1), is a similar attitude before the works of man—works full of ability, patience, and effort, whose results are useful, even beautiful. Surely we should applaud works which appeal to our religious sense for two other reasons as

---

[1] From *The Christian and Temporal Goods*, Pastoral Letter to the Archdiocese of Milan, Holy Week, 1963.

well. They develop God's work on our earthly horizon; they show its vast possibilities, unveil its marvels, use its powers, enjoy its benefits. And then these benefits are not only economic, but are also social, since modern industry usually looks after the welfare of its workers as well as the needs of its customers. So we admire the best human works as examples both of human intelligence and of human charity; and as such they deserve acknowledgement and gratitude.

The effort which modern man puts into trying to know, to dominate, to use nature and harness it to his own service should be considered a worthy response to God's gift of it to us. And God's primeval voice still reveals the meaning of the world: 'Fill the earth and subdue it' (Gen. 1, 28). Surrounding nature calls us to explore, conquer, and possess it.

This call, though, should not make us dwell in the domain of the temporal but press on as if we were on a road, or rather a staircase, which eventually leads back to the point of departure, to God. Our labour, and our conquest of the natural world are only part of a journey which should take us back to their first source. We must journey through the profane universe with the religious sense of a divine presence, or rather of a divine expectation, which is both very hidden and very obvious.

This journey has one great surprise: our encounter with the Word of God come into the world as man, our encounter with the Incarnation. Our knowledge of the created world is then transformed into an extraordinary adventure, a revelation. As St Paul says: 'The world or life or death or the present or the future are yours, and you are Christ's, and Christ is God's' (1 Cor. 3, 22–3). He says also: 'Whatever is true, whatever is honourable, whatever is just, whatever is pure, whatever is lovely, whatever is gracious, if there is any excellence, if there is anything worthy of praise, think about these things' (Phil. 4, 8).

The Christian does not discard the world of nature and temporal realities; he is not up in the air, is not an escapist, not absorbed in seraphic contemplation of things spiritual. In fact it is he who can have the most complete and noblest vision of temporal values, be most realistic about them, and so able to administer them best. Is honesty, for instance, which we think of as a virtue essential to Christianity, not a first requisite for the proper use of economic goods?

In the same way Christianity is not an obstacle to modern

progress, because it considers not only the technical and economic
aspects but its integral development. Temporal goods can certainly
help towards the full development of man, but can be neither the
ideal of human perfection nor the essence of civil progress. The
Christian sees temporal goods as the work and gift of God, and as
such he admires and uses them but he does not make idols of them.
He always remembers the first commandment, 'Thou shalt have no
other God but me'. And it is here that the conflict arises between
Christianity and temporal realities.

This brings us to our second observation which, being negative,
seems to contradict the optimism of the first. The Christian is
warned by his catechism that in things of this world, particularly in
the way they have been arranged by human (or diabolic) cunning,
there can be and in fact often is a deep and mysterious disorder
(1 John 2, 15; 5, 19). Neither human nature as it is today nor its
works are invariably good. Evil exists outside our own will, and is
all around us. If this were not so all the struggles for human progress
throughout history would be nonsense.

The Christian has his eyes open towards this aspect of reality too.
He is not ingenuous, full of good-will, and hazily optimistic. He has
a sense of the tragic in life, that 'the whole creation has been groan-
ing in travail together until now' (Rom. 8, 22).[1]

By the sorcery of modern man, the forces of nature can unleash
appalling threats and ruin. The atomic bomb has taught us that.
Anyone who is wise, anyone who is Christian, must be alarmed by
these grave dangers which progress itself is bound to bring with it
when divorced from higher moral law.

It is in view of these higher moral laws that the Christian is wary
about the goods of this world. They can be a strong temptation to
overthrow the moral order; not only by explosions sowing vast
destruction and confusion, but more often by insinuating an inner,
fatal, illusion; that they, these temporal goods, are the final and
supreme purpose of human activity, its paradise, its happiness. This
illusion transforms temporal goods from mirrors of the divine into
fascinations, from instruments into chains, from stairs leading upwards to stairs leading down.

That is why the Christian accepts as supremely true the words of
Christ which make poverty the first blessing of the kingdom of

[1] Cf. Gen. 3, 18; Acts 2, 19; 3, 21.

heaven. Poverty immunizes man from the deceit of the goods of this world.

It may seem absurd to praise poverty today. Wealth has assumed such importance that it seems nonsense not only to praise but even to tolerate poverty.

We must explain the poverty on which the spirit of Christianity is based.

Do we mean poverty in terms of money? Yes, that too, but with two provisos: one, that our Lord did not impose on us physical poverty, that is deprivation of the necessities of life. He taught us to ask his father in heaven for the bread we need; he himself multiplied the loaves to feed a hungry crowd that had followed him. He himself recommended alms as a remedy for indigence, and recognized work for gain and reward as a law of this present life. He himself was a 'carpenter's son'. The second proviso is: material poverty is presented in the Gospel not as a good in itself, but as a reflection of another poverty, indispensable to the Christian—poverty of spirit.

What this poverty of spirit is we must ask the saints and doctors of the Church, who have said so much about it. Here we need only recall a remark by St Ambrose, who interpreted poverty of spirit as humility of spirit.[1]

The Gospel speaks of a state of soul, of an ascetic poverty, without establishing a necessary relationship between it and a Christian's financial condition. A person in a state of indigence, who puts his highest aspirations and total trust in money, can lack Christian poverty. So too a rich man who does not take selfish pride in his money nor make it the aim of his life, can have Christian poverty.[2] Thus it can be seen that this poverty of spirit, whose seat is in the heart, can apply to everyone, irrespective of their financial or social conditions, though this inner virtue can have a considerable effect on these.

Evangelic poverty is in fact the realization of man's insufficiency and of his consequent need of God. It means denying the capacity of money or temporal goods to satisfy the heart of man. It means not to seek in this world the achievement of his destiny and the solution of his deep and fatal ills such as sin and death. It means being wise enough to see fever for money and power as an illusion, and to realize that goodness, love, charity, peace, moral grandeur are not

---

[1] *Exp. Evang. sec. Lucam*, V, 60.
[2] Cf. St Augustine, *Serm.* L, c. III and IV, *P.L.*, 38, 327–8.

reached by the way of money. It means being dignified and patient
when in financial straits and modest social conditions. It is the proper
state for working, hoping, giving, and loving, because it teaches us
to trust providence and realize the value of moral goods and things.
It is a liberation of the spirit, freeing it from the burden of inferior
goods and letting it act and love as spirit.

So we should take Christian poverty seriously, and never regard
it as an anachronism to us moderns, an absurdity to experts of
sociology and economics. We should in fact recognize and practise
Christian poverty as such, for should we eventually acquire an
abundance of temporal goods we might be tempted to forget it or
be prevented from observing it; and without this inner virtue we
cannot achieve our salvation. Christ's words are impressively severe.
'Truly, I say to you, it will be hard for a rich man to enter the kingdom of heaven. Again I tell you, it is easier for a camel to go through
the eye of a needle than for a rich man to enter the kingdom of God'
(Matt. 19, 23–4).

We must try to see why Christ treated wealth with such bitter
frankness; to see how the ease and power of wealth disturbs those
who long for it or already have it, making them think, firstly, that
wealth is an indispensable good; then that it is a supreme good, and
so that it is really the only good which satisfies all necessities, confers
all security, appeases all desires, gives all power, and makes every
happiness possible.

This is idolatry and deceit. And slavery too. Wealth owes its value
to the service it renders man; but if man does not use it with a heart
that is strong and free, that is, in a spirit of poverty, it becomes the
master and he the servant. It dominates his thought and heart, ob-
scures a true vision of life and order, dulls his feelings and embitters
his relations with others. It loads him with cares, and extinguishes his
aspiration to the higher goods which are our true destiny. It lowers
his moral stature to the mediocrity of the venal or the egoism of his
own possessions, swells him with false pride and empties him of
humility, enervates his will and throws the door open to idleness,
boredom, and vice, so that eventually he becomes hard-hearted and
forgets the joy of giving without receiving.

For in the end, to look on money in this way prevents love, and
Christianity is love; it prevents prayer, and Christianity is communion with God.

These and other ideas we may derive from the Gospel about the dangerous intercourse between the human soul and wealth may make us reflect how serious the subject is and how an honest and satisfactory solution for it must be found. But Christ's words are so solemn and decisive that they may make us wonder if ever we can arrive at such a solution, which is what the rich young man in the Gospels wondered, as he sadly turned away from our Lord after hearing these words reserved for those who seek perfection: 'Go, sell what you possess and give to the poor, and you will have treasure in heaven; and come, follow me' (Matt. 19, 21). After that incident, even the apostles themselves wondered: 'Who then can be saved?' (Matt. 19, 25).

Jesus's own words, which form the subject of our third observation, answer that question: 'With men this is impossible; but with God all things are possible' (Matt. 19, 26).

This is an important statement. It teaches us that man by his own strength alone cannot disentangle himself from the web of temporal goods, but can succeed only with God's help. And it shows us how religion can be operative in freeing us from the fascination of earthly things.

So a religious life is indispensable to man in the economic field too, if he does not want temporal goods, precious in one way, pernicious in another, to become a cargo that shipwrecks man in materialism. To a religious man, money should be only one of God's gifts, a gift heavy with responsibility but also with normal and genuine advantages for human life and even for eternal salvation. Only religion can give this healthy balance to the economic factor.

Modern science and practice has created a gap between the economic factor and morality (and so religion). This is one of the most serious errors of our time. Economics has its own specific field of study, methods, and application, but it cannot supersede the high totality of human life, which can only be given by moral and religious vision.

This basic observation suggests another by St Thomas which helps to clarify it. He teaches us that human things 'do not in themselves draw us away from God but lead us to him. . . . What does draw us away from God is to use them in an unreasonable way.'[1] And what he says about human things in general can be said about riches in particular: it is the use they are put to which classifies them

---

[1] S.T., I, q. 65, a. 1, ad. 3.

as good or bad. But as riches are useful by their nature, so by their nature they tend only to the particular and personal advantage, to the immediate interests of those who possess them, and hence to selfishness.

St Ambrose, who was so severe in his denunciation of the dangers and sins of the rich, also explicitly affirms that the evil lies not in riches themselves but in the bad use to which they are put.[1]

From this principle derive many teachings which we do not intend to repeat here. We may get some idea of the potential of this principle if we recall that it was from the concept of economic good, of its origins and scope, of its relations with production and distribution, that the so-called 'social question', which so preoccupies political and economic life today, arose.

Not for nothing has the Church, in particular, through the ministry and *magisterium* of the last popes, developed some basic principles on this question, principles which therefore reflect on the temporal economy too. We would do well to know the 'social doctrine of the Church'. Today, in the crisis of social systems, both capitalist and Marxist, founded on the primacy of economics, this doctrine is finding a warrant and vindication which confirms the faithful in their support of it and immunizes them from sympathy with other theories that are erroneous. So, too, other persons of goodwill who seek an authoritative, coherent, and human solution, find the thoughts of the Church provide a solid foundation for the reconstruction of our society.

To study these problems means clarifying certain ideas about temporal goods inherent to our theme. Is, for example, a renunciation of temporal goods, that is voluntary poverty, obligatory for the true Christian, or is it only a counsel of Christian perfection? And that call to give the poor what we have left over, or rather as the text says 'what we have within' (Luke 11, 41), how far should that be taken? What should be the measure of our alms and our charity?

Again, how and why should private property be defended? By what rights is it attributed a double function, both private and social? Why is it advisable to save? What is the relationship between justice and charity? And so on. The questions are many; and the increase of economic well-being that now seems likely acts as stimulus to new solutions.

[1] *Exp. in Ev. Lc.*, VIII, 84–5.

It will be seen, too, how under certain aspects this well-being makes solutions easier to find.

The economic preoccupations of modern man are swept now by a kind of instinctive dynamism. He is no longer so tenaciously attached to his particular interests as he once was. Now he dominates them, changes them, transfers them more easily. Plenty has smoothed the rough edge of his avarice. Trust in prosperity has made him more inclined to spend, to use his money on others, and to take risks. There is some link between this attitude towards money and a Christian mentality in so far as the former tends towards considering temporal goods as means and not ends.

But let us leave the study of these problems to those willing to undertake them, and go on to some practical suggestions useful to Christian life in the favourable economic phase through which we are now passing.

The Christian line of conduct in the economic circumstances of the modern world

We are speaking to those who understand, that is to those who have or at least want to have a sense of 'the mind of Christ' (1 Cor. 2, 16).

Our first point is more than advice or mere recommendation, it is a precept, the great precept on which the whole of Christianity is founded; and it is *love*. Love of God, with all our hearts, with all our souls, with all our minds. These are not empty words or vague emotion. They are an order, they are God's law, and they should find lively and potent expression in us. This mental attitude of loving God should be understood and cultivated today in particular when the wind of greed blows stronger, the greed which turns man from striving towards his true aim and which was called by the Apostle Paul 'the root of all evils' (1 Tim. 6, 10). We must all learn again to keep in our spirit the place which is God's—love's—due, and to reserve for this first supreme act of our religion our fullest and deepest feelings.

Then there is the love of our neighbour; another great precept which, if it has not yet become so obvious and so real as to be a distinctive sign of our Christianity (John 13, 35), and if we are still far from realizing that double equation to love one another as Christ loved us and to love our neighbour as we love ourselves, we have not yet practised as fully as we might.

If this love really did infuse our lives, what an economy, what a sociology, what a human society there would be! Here Christianity is still obviously incomplete and at the beginning of a long new road.

Another religious duty arises from today's prosperity, and this is *gratitude* to Providence which disposes things in such a way that we are called to recognize and praise it. We moderns are so blind that we neither seek nor find God's paternal hand at work behind our experience, giving it profound meaning which we may not be wholly able to decipher, but which we can always ascribe to infinite goodness, and which gives it a sense of spiritual and moral ascent.

This interpretation of the scene in which our lives takes place should be familiar, particularly to us Christians,[1] because it derives from an awareness of reality, splendidly optimistic in the light of faith; an awareness which should supplant the bleak and desperate vision of modern pessimism diffused through modern philosophy, literature, and theatre, immersed in its dark night of anguish, its Godless universe.

It is not always easy for us of little faith to thank God when we are suffering and in want. But it can be easier and so more of a duty when relative prosperity in the material order comforts us on our weary pilgrimage.

So we should get into the habit of saying a prayer of thanks to God at mealtimes, at the day's end, at happy events, and at moments of recollections such as, for example, during Holy Mass on Sundays.[2]

The habit of gratitude to God for his benefits educates us also to gratitude towards the men and women who, from affection or relationship or friendship or as a result of the civil organization to which we belong, are our benefactors. We owe so much to the love and help of others, and we forget so easily! Let us remember that much of the social mentality of today, derived from the French Revolution and spread by the cultural, social, and political movements that came after it, is impregnated with bitterness and hatred; and that in spite of progress in collective living we are still, even today, partly poisoned by an atmosphere of criticism and enmity towards the civil order of which we are beneficiaries. This negative attitude has

[1] Cf. Eph. 5, 20; and the last pages of Manzoni, *The Betrothed*.
[2] Why should we not have a day of religious thanksgiving at the end of the civil year, similar to the American Thanksgiving Day?

now become almost a habit, though dissociated from many of the reasons from which it drew its historical origins.

Modern economic and social conditions should help to overcome this morbid attitude and produce a more serene, more positive and, if you wish, more democratic attitude of mind, deriving from more equable and fraternal human relations, due partly to increased prosperity. Obviously this is what the Christian social sense, with its linking of justice and charity, must aspire to. We must try to spread gratitude and respect for a society that promotes general well-being and be, as Christians, its grateful citizens and friends.

But we must note certain objections that moderate our theoretic optimism about economic well-being, and show how inadequate this is when made the first ideal of modern life and the primary value in our civilization. We cannot praise economic well-being without emphasizing yet again our reservations about it. These fall into three headings.

Non-religion: Economic well-being tends to assume the first place in the modern scale of values. It seems to be considered the supreme good, the end which justifies every effort and fulfils every aspiration. This tendency to over-estimate economic well-being can assume an anti-religious or at least non-religious character.

Self-centredness: Secondly, the exclusive search for economic well-being tends towards self-centredness; it tends to give absolute value to the central objective—which may be the production or the enjoyment—of this well-being. Hence it can be transformed into an anti-social phenomenon, making those who enjoy it the instruments of those who become indispensable for procuring it.

Moral laxity: Thirdly, economic well-being can lead to another negative tendency, an anti-moral one. This happens when ease makes life too comfortable, reduces energy, enfeebles mind and body, standardizes everything, creating a mass-man with no originality or power of decision. This mass-man may easily seek in sensual experience an outlet from the insignificant life to which he feels reduced.

Let us now give some practical recommendations for good Christian conduct in a state of economic well-being.

Honesty: The first and foremost is honesty. By honesty we mean the probity of the ancients, the justice which recognizes and respects the rights of others over what belongs to them. We must always remember those two commandments of God's law: 'Seventh, thou shalt not steal; Tenth, thou shalt not covet thy neighbour's goods.'

Reaffirmation of the right to private property: Our society, as we were saying, is moving towards a more equable distribution of wealth, a more extensive and complex organization of the social community and a parity between economic development and social progress. So now is the time to reaffirm the concept of private property, to review its various applications and recall its two limits; that every man has a right to his own property; and that all property must have some reference to public use. Hence all have a duty to respect the possessions of others and all must play their part in the common good. Neither subversive criticism of property nor the concept or working of evolution can do away with the moral fact that property has legal rights and a useful function.

As Pius XII said:

'Anyone who wants peace to shine out over our society must give work the place God assigned to it from the beginning. All work has inalienable dignity as the indispensable means of dominating nature, and as such God wants it for his glory. At the same time it is intimately linked with the perfecting of the human personality. . . . These needs include . . . the cultivation and perfection of a social order which makes private property, however modest, possible to all classes of society. . . .'[1]

Of course the terms of property must be made clear. They must be sought in the deep human need which is called 'natural right'. And they must be determined by positive law.

On the one hand, therefore, it is our duty to promote the forms of social progress that tend to an equable sharing of economic goods. But on the other, it is indispensable strictly to observe the laws which clarify and protect the ownership of economic goods, their production and distribution.

A society with no respect for such laws is decadent, and corrodes its own consistency. So the more we desire economic well-being, the more strictly the two commandments mentioned above should be observed. Their observance should be encouraged by personal and popular education. There might have been some excuse for their violation in the restricted economic conditions of the past, but today it should be firmly and generally condemned.

[1] Christmas Message, Rome, 1942.

Honesty is a necessary law in the social order. Those who violate it harm not only those whom they defraud of their own property but also the entire community, as they disturb social trust, the indispensable basis for the honour and efficiency of communal life.

Professional integrity: We must recommend to all, particularly to our faithful, the virtues proper to an economic condition such as our own, which is developing and closely involved with the social bettering of our people.

Here we need only list the requirements of public opinion. We want incorruptible public servants. The many serious incidents of administrative disorder, of corruption in public offices, of speculation by those with public duties, afflict us deeply both as citizens and as Catholics. We would like to see scrupulous and exemplary honesty among all those with political, administrative, and disciplinary functions. We would like to see our lives as citizens always characterized by personal disinterest and loyal respect to law. Cheating in commercial transactions and in taxes, smuggling, swindling, bribery, theft, and particularly broken promises . . . must be considered by all as evils dishonouring a progressive society that is still based on Christian principles; and they should be avoided and condemned by all.

Then there are other evils characteristic of an opulent society, such as stock exchange deals that harm others, gambling, excessive luxury. . . . We have no competence to speak of these with authority, but we must deplore the moral and social effects of such abuses of wealth. And we have the duty of recalling the terrible words of Christ, 'woe to you that are rich' (Luke 6, 24).

Sobriety and austerity: We do have both the competence and the duty to recommend sobriety in the use of the economic resources put at our disposal by providence. We must never forget what should be the aim of temporal goods: an honest life, not one of pride or vanity or avarice, of fatuous or vicious pleasure. Nor should we forget the human value—in terms of study, work, suffering, others' needs—that there is in money and possessions, so that we may use them with due measure, almost with reverence and gratitude.

Simplicity, frugality, liberality in the use of temporal goods, these are signs of a spirit which can rise above them.

Here we might mention mortification. At certain times and in certain forms the discipline of the Church calls us to practise mortification for moral and religious reasons. The acceptance of these

disciplinary measures and the spirit of austerity and penitence they
inculcate not only make us closer followers of Christ, but more
capable of evaluating and making the best use of the things of this
world.

This precept to lead simple austere lives, detached from money,
superfluous comforts, and all exterior vanities, is particularly applicable to us clergy. We more than others are obliged to do so by our
closer ties with Christ, by the example expected of us, by the good
effect that our poverty has on our ministry, and by the sterility
which afflicts it whenever we are mercenary or vain.

If we want to be genuine ministers of God we must be on our
guard against all avarice, all financial speculation, all worldliness.
Nor should we allow even our attempts to finance good works connected with our ministry to become obsessive or indiscreet. Here
too we must show a limpid disinterest, as if in proof of the poverty
that moves us and of the charity which is their only purpose.

In this connection there is the vexed question of fees for ceremonies inherent to our sacred ministry. Let us remember what is
established in Canon Law.[1] Never lay down arbitrary fees. Never
allow too many ornamental appendages to religious ceremonies.
Never allow devotions to assume an aspect or purpose of financial
gain. Try to avoid the suggestion of a tax-gatherer, even when dealing with rightful fees for religious services. Remember that the
public is very sensitive and easily swayed by this, and inclined to
biting criticism of priests and their ministry because of it.

Nothing today, we think, turns so many people away from religion as the accusation, or suspicion, or calumny of peculation among
the clergy. Let us remember what St Paul said: 'We put no obstacle
in anyone's way, so that no fault may be found with our ministry'
(2 Cor. 6, 3).

But what is at issue is not simply some disciplinary canon about
sundry exterior aspects of ecclesiastical life. It is a call to all, priests
and laymen, to find that inner aspect of Christ's Church which
centres on its poverty. Let us say rather, the mystery of poverty in
the great plan of redemption. This plan, as we know, is the mystery
of love that gives itself, spends itself prodigally, and in showing itself
to the world appears stripped of all earthly goods, as if to show that
no egotism or earthly possessions should cover or quality it.

Poverty is the robe of Christ, and of his followers who want to

[1] Can. 736.

imitate, represent, and preach him. The poor are first in the kingdom of God. The society born from Christ will be founded not on
luxury, power, trust in temporal goods, but on the empty terrain of
poverty, which is supported by a virtue that is wholly spiritual, and
helped and sustained from Heaven. This is the economy of the Gospel, perpetuated in 'Ecclesia pauperum', 'the Church of the poor'.
John XXIII proposed that the ecumenical council should take this
theme for its meditation and reform.

Loving and helping the poor

We must have a special reverence, a great concern for the poor.
They are mirrors of Christ, almost a living sacrament of him.[1] They
are a spur and an object for charity (Matt. 25, 31–5). They are the
brethren whose needs, even if they were not rights, are our duties.
They are our vexation if we avoid them; our happiness if we provide for them. They are our teachers of good living if we listen to
their mute lesson. They are the travelling companions who, if
looked for, are always close by us. Jesus said, 'You always have the
poor with you' (Matt. 26, 11).

This prediction is still true, even in our present period of
plenty.

Let us look at the real state of the contemporary world, which
seems at last to be achieving a state of efficiency in providing food
for all. But does it do so? No it does not. Not in our midst, because
there are many who still lack food enough for their normal needs
and natural development. Do not let our growing prosperity deceive us. It is still not equally distributed, still not stable enough and
still does not provide for many the necessities that it should. So when
we praise this prosperity of ours, we must still urge it to produce and
guarantee enough for all.

And, as soon as we have anything left over from our well-
being, we should at once think of alms-giving. 'Alms' is an ancient
word, but a sacred one. The bible tells of our obligation to give alms
and of the powers of compassion and redemption that come to those
who offer it, and of the consolation to those who receive it. The
whole Christian tradition gleams with this flower of personal goodness and social concern. It is part of Christian ascetics, teaching, and
sociology. It is so close to the spirit of the Gospels that it is contained

[1] Cf. St Ambrose, De Viduis, IX, 54. St Bonaventure, Apologia Pauperum, VIII,
233 ff.

in the central and most authentic gospel terms: providence, mercy, charity.

Today we call it social assistance or social insurance or some other expression of the kind. But the concept remains what it originally was, that of spontaneously offering financial benefits to the indigent (not so that they should remain so, but that they should be raised from indigence and become self-supporting). And this must be given freely, from love; let us say right out, from love of God. Then a work of mercy is perfect. It draws its source and vigour from the heart of those who do it, not from fear or constriction or some hidden self-interest. It does not look for any merit or sympathy in those benefited, seeks no praise or gratitude. Enough for it that the eye of God has seen the good heart within and the secret gesture without. If we are looking for true expressions of our Christianity, we must still to a very great degree cultivate the exercise of 'charity'.

Our thoughts go to Catholic works of charity; to the activities of the Society of St Vincent de Paul in particular, which from their exercise of charity have become a school of living faith as well as such a source of humble and human consolation. And we think of the thousands of others; yes thousands, because by the grace of God there are innumerable other forms of charitable activity among Catholics. We want them all, in this period of prosperity, to be more flourishing, more co-ordinated, more operative and efficacious: and always freely, readily, generously, silently moved by the spirit of Christ.

Christians, and particularly the young among us, must listen to the urgent call of the Gospels. The young are those most tempted to make themselves their only law and to waste their money without valuing the efforts that went to making it and the uses to which it should be put. They are, however, also the most sensitive to the duty of helping the suffering, and by their own sacrifice too. Their sense of participation with the humble is personal, their forms of practical charity modern. May they become aware of the moral energy and civic wisdom to be drawn from the positive exercise of human and Christian charity. Aspiration, however noble, however helpful to social reforms, is not enough to prove the sincerity which suggests it, unless it is supported by lively direct experience of others' needs.

Let us all try to obey another related duty, the duty of imposing on ourselves a sacrifice, a saving of money, in order to have something of our own to offer those persons and institutions which cannot provide for themselves. Today when we are all becoming citizens of the world this duty broadens into 'catholic', universal, ecumenical horizons; today our neighbour can be a long way off.

The sense of universality should be highly developed in a Christian and Catholic country like Italy. And it should give proof of itself by stretching out hands and opening purses wide to unknown brethren in remote areas which are only starting on the road of modern civilization. Under this aspect Milan has its ancient tradition of charity which should reanimate us all today. And the example of the German Catholics in collective gestures of penitential saving and ecumenical charity should be admired and imitated.

Today there are still vast hidden needs whose only resource is the spontaneous one of charity. It is to the honour of the Church today that she is poor, a beggar for charitable works and purposes, which her ministry cannot abandon.

For the fact is that the Church has no patrimony proportionate to her mission; the Church is forbidden to take part in any secular, money-earning activity; the Church, in this hour of others' prosperity, is in a phase of acute need and with resources that are utterly inadequate to cope. For our own profit and our own comfort these are favourable times; let them be so too for all good works, that the time of prosperity may become the time of charity; and so also the time of justice and peace.

It is in the nature of good Catholics to consider temporal riches as opportunities for evangelical charity. If some say too many demands are made on them, then at the risk of seeming tactless or self-interested, we would point out that, compared to the works of charity needing help, a vast amount of money is poured out today on amusements and superfluities.

This overspending on selfish pleasures or comforts needs tempering with Christian charity. There are huge reserves of capital which need purifying from the dubious or over-facile ways they were accumulated. There are vast stagnant riches waiting to become fruitful and blessed by use for charitable and social ends; while at the moment they are only a responsibility for those who guard them jealously, often without knowing how to enjoy them wisely. Let us take courage and repeat again the words of our Lord: 'Blessed are the merciful for they shall obtain mercy' (Matt. 5, 7). 'Give and it will be given to you' (Luke 6, 38). Let us dare to hope that the progress of the temporal economy which has to day reached such high peaks, will not harm the society which has produced it, but be to its moral and temporal advantage.

Now, after these considerations concerning the nature, dangers, and functions of temporal goods, it is our duty to bless and encourage the efforts that go into their production, the knowledge that goes to their distribution and use, and the charity that spiritualizes them. We end by referring to the final words in Pope John XXIII's encyclical *Mater et Magistra*, in which he says that whenever temporal activities and institutions are open to spiritual values and supernatural ends, their efficiency in terms of their specific and immediate ends increases. The words of the divine Master always remain true: 'Seek first his kingdom and his righteousness, and all these things shall be yours as well' (Matt, 6, 33).

8

THE POVERTY OF CHRISTMAS[1]

LAST NIGHT we announced the joy and fullness that Christ's birth brings into the world, the 'great tidings' of the Gospel, which tell how the mystery of the Incarnation can raise men and save them, not only when their life on earth is at an end but also during their sojourn in this world. For Christ restored mankind's relations with God, the source of all life and happiness, giving them a new harmony, which is already in existence yet, in part, remains to be realized. He frees man from the supreme evil and misery of sin; urges him along the path of goodness and justice; protects him from the contagions of this world, drawing all things to his own order, and directing this order to the supreme one of the future life. Christ gives man inner support in the toils of his wretched life, joys that reveal the value of present suffering in terms of man's final destiny. Christ is light, Christ is peace, Christ is the gladness, the treasure of humanity.

But let us see how this source of incomparable joy actually began in historical reality. Let us look at the blessed scene of the birth of Christ. It is a scene of poverty.

We who celebrate Christmas amid our plenty and our amusements are too apt to ignore the dark background from which the light of Bethlehem shines out. But we know that it was a bare night scene, and that the divine guest from heaven was greeted on this earth by the harshest poverty; poverty and humiliation. Poverty was the realm of the great King. And poverty is an ugly, repellent thing; it detaches, deprives, weakens; it brings suffering and subjection. It is a fate we find appalling because it means renouncing the splendid gifts of this earth, lacking those material, economic, hedonistic things which give impetus to so many hearts, are their dream, their power, their pride, indispensable to most lives, to their

[1] Sermon given on Christmas Day, 1959.

progress and culture. They are man's earthly bread. Yes, but Jesus was born poor.

There seems a conflict here. He who appeared as Saviour of the world, as friend of humanity, as conciliator between earth and heaven, showed, on his arrival, an utter indifference to the things which we, in general, most esteem; even a contempt, that total poverty of his might make us think. Can we then ever really accept a Messiah who was willingly born poor? A prophet so far removed from man's instinctive aspirations? Can a teacher ever be listened to, followed, loved, who does not speak from the rostrum of values we accept as the only positive and necessary ones? Yes, here is our drama. Such questions are bound to find contradictory replies. Jesus appears as herald of a message which is incomprehensible for many, and difficult for all (Luke 18, 25 ff).

Here then is a mystery. Why did the Master of the Universe come to the earth poor? This is his earth after all: 'He came to his own home,' St John tells us (1, 11). He was born in a stall, and when he grew up was to be poorer than the animals and the birds. 'Foxes have holes and birds of the air have nests; but the Son of Man has nowhere to lay his head' (Luke 9, 58). Yes, what a mystery! Though the Word of God made man lost none of his divine prerogatives (*non remittens, quod erit,* says St Ambrose),[1] yet, as St Paul wrote, 'He emptied himself, taking the form of a servant' (Phil. 2, 7). We shall never really understand this mystery of his extreme humiliation unless we connect it with God's infinitely generous intention. For God empties himself and gives himself, as is proper to his inmost life of love;[2] and to show his love in the human sphere he carried to its limits the effect it could have on men by dispossessing himself in poverty. Christ's poverty is thus the proof, the symbol of God's generosity, of the riches of his love. 'Jesus Christ . . . was rich, yet for your sake he became poor' (2 Cor. 8, 9) in order that we, through his poverty, should become rich.

This mystery becomes a little clearer if we consider that the poverty with which Christ invested himself was intended to show that his work of salvation was not founded on any human means. For how in fact has he saved us? St Peter tells us clearly in his very first letter that 'You know that you were ransomed from the futile ways inherited from your fathers, not with perishable things such as

[1] *De Fede,* 8.
[2] Cf. Garrigou-Lagrange, *Dieu,* p. 510 (English translation, *God,* St Louis, 1941).

silver and gold, but with the precious blood of Christ' (1 Pet. 1, 18).
The Redemption was not achieved by any earthly means, but by the
word and the death of Christ. It had no foundation in the things, the
forces, the goods of this world; the causality of Christ's salvation is
entirely in him, entirely from him.[1]

As Fr Ceresi wrote:

'Jesus Christ, and he alone, is in himself great with absolute
greatness, with Truth, Justice and Love, which he did not
possess but which are part of himself (cf. 1 Cor. 1, 30); realities
uncreated, yet substantial, or rather a reality full and unique to
which nothing can be added or taken away, and whose light
dims if we try to see it by any light but his. Obviously if the
circumstances at Bethlehem were not merely an unlucky mis-
adventure for Mary but a calculated arrangement by God to
mark the beginning of his work of Redemption, then the fact
that the Divine Child was born in the straw of a manger was not
something that happened in spite of himself, but was willed.
Only the poverty of that birth was proper to both his natures,
the divine and the human.'[2]

The same is true of those for whom our Lord came. Christ's
poverty is a sign of the closest inner relationship he could offer men.
Jesus put himself on the lowest social level so that none could think
him inaccessible. All temporal goods, in one way or another, divide
men from each other. All property introduces a 'mine' and 'thine'
that separates men, or unites them in a relationship which as it is
not one of community of goods is often not one of community of
spirit. Jesus, though he did not abolish property, detached himself
from it completely so as to come into immediate and universal
communion with men, whom he wanted as brothers. Christ's
poverty appears then under an aspect that is wonderfully human;
it is a sign of his friendship, of his relationship with humanity. And
that part of humanity which does not erect barriers of social
position, of isolating wealth, of selfish sufficiency, to this brotherly
relationship can find him, understand him, have him for their own.
In the Gospels there is a resounding call to those who are best placed
to enter into the economy of salvation. 'Blessed are the poor in
spirit, for the kingdom of heaven is theirs' (Matt. 5, 3). As a wave
of sympathy, of preference, of love it spreads over the earth, and

[1] Cf. *S.T.*, III, 40.   [2] *Il mistero della poverta*, p. 20.

it is heard wherever there is poverty, need, suffering, and humility, that is wherever there is still room to receive, still heart to desire, still hope to pray. It is in fact the poor who have most to desire, to hope, to pray for. Christ our Lord, their poor, great brother, came for them, and for those who, like them, desire, hope, and pray.

Here, without exploring this mystery of poverty further, let us gather a double lesson from it, one which can make a good Christmas for us. One lesson is on poverty, the other on the poor.

Poverty is honoured by Christ; let us honour it too. Honour it, not detest or despise it as a state of life, whether this state is our own or one that we see in our brethren. Let us honour it as a merit, as a voluntary disposition of the soul, freeing the soul from disordered attachment to temporal goods and directing it towards goods that are spiritual and towards the practice of charity and love. Poverty today arouses much praiseworthy concern; it is studied, helped. But to honour poverty means more than to help it. Modern civilization, under the influence—silent, denied perhaps, but real— of Christianity, is certainly developing ways of helping, caring for, combating, even removing poverty. But, if we look closely, we see that our civilization fears poverty more than it loves it; judging it definitely as an evil, finding no good in it whatsoever. This modern concern for poverty is already a great and commendable thing, a Christian thing, as I have said. But that is as far as it can go. A complete vision of human life in Christ's light sees in a poor person more than someone in need. It sees a brother of mysterious dignity, a dignity which makes him someone to be respected, treated with attention and more than due sympathy. Through the very rags of the poor glows a light, forms a face, the face of the suffering Christ. Bossuet, in his discourse on the high dignity of the poor in the Church, said: 'Jesus needs nothing, and Jesus needs everything. Jesus needs nothing by his power; but Jesus needs everything by his compassion.'[1] The Incarnation reaches out to all humanity, particularly where human beings are in want; behind that want is hidden Christ. This discovery can be applied in innumerable ways, firstly in the motive force it gives for the exercise of love, charity, and generosity.

The second way it can be applied is in helping us to see a con-

[1] *Oeuvres*, 1836, IV, 4.

dition worse than material poverty, one in which men can lack a greater and better good than the bread of temporal life.

The third way is the most important and the most difficult for us to practise: poverty of spirit, the detachment of the heart from the overwhelming and tangled chains which bind us to the riches and values of this world.

This is so important because it pledges everything; and it is so difficult because nearly all of us in this modern world of ours are caught up in economic life. Not that we can abdicate from economic life; in fact we should promote it within reason and even with fervour because to us it is an inexorable law of life, more pressing today than ever before. But we must become poor in spirit, if we want to be Christians, if we want to be rich in charity and love, and if we want to be genuine and civilized people.

9

THE INTEGRATION OF RELIGION AND WORK IN THE MODERN WORLD[1]

I WANT to ask the world of labour to make a mental effort on this problem of the relationship between religion and work.

Given this mental effort it would not be difficult to achieve happy relations between religion and labour, to reach a state of happy integration, of mutual collaboration and esteem, where each respects and acknowledges the other's role and the other's liberty. How splendidly fruitful such a state could be, like a springtime of the spirit! We both stand in need of this, it seems to me, and perhaps, under Mary's protection on this feast-day of hers, we are not so very far from new and positive achievements.

Here, for brevity's sake, I will do no more than suggest three lines of thought about this problem for men of goodwill to pursue.

The first concerns the twofold expression of our religion, in doctrine and in life.

Is there anything in our teaching or in the way we live our religion, that is in the Church, that conflicts either with the scientific and research branches, or the technical and practical sides of working life? When has she ever opposed these proper and rightful forms of human activity?

Though the Church's ends are spiritual and transcendental, this does not mean that she rejects subordinate ends that conform with human nature. Such aims, in fact, receive impulse, direction, and buoyancy when seen as part of a wider vista of life than one limited by the temporal order.

Here, if anywhere, lies the only conflict between religion and labour; in the limitation of human horizons to the economic and the material. For this means depriving the worker of the wish and

[1] From *Religion and Work*, address given at Turin, 27 March 1960, to industrial workers.

the right to see beyond work and the satisfaction of material needs; it means denying him access to the higher world of the spirit and the hope of a fullness of life beyond the grave.

If work is not to become a sentence of life imprisonment, then the sky of spiritual life must open above the sphere of human action and earthly gain. And if this sky is not to be an empty unreality of dreams and illusions, it must be lit by the supreme, dazzling reality, the living God.

There should be discussion, not conflict, about theories that seek to integrate the various social problems deriving from industrial work. Need we recall all the guidance given by the Church towards rational, progressive, ordered solutions of these problems, with only the common good in view? During the last hundred years a vast body of authoritative, coherent, up-to-date thought about this has come from the Church, showing how lively and genuine is her interest in sociology.

The Church's vision on matters of economics and sociology must be recognized by the propertied classes. They must see that she respects property when it is essential and really justified, but supports a tempered gradualism in reform. They must realize she values and trusts the promoters of new businesses and industrial enterprises, if, that is, they create new sources of general wealth and property. They must accept her consistent, often severe, but always balanced warnings about the moral and social dangers of selfish riches, of the need for a more equable distribution of economic goods. They must listen to her call for a disinterested and generous contribution from them towards the bettering of the working classes, particularly of the class created by industry which some call the proletariat, by allowing them a proper share in a company's profits, and even, though this is not strictly their right, a share in its management.

The social teaching of the Church has never denied the role of private initiative in the economic order, nor the need for promoters and managers of factories or works to exercise, just as the artist must in his own field, their own particular talents and capacities. But this must not harm the human dignity or legitimate aspirations of the actual workers, the active producers. These must not be slaves, but free men and brothers.

The non-possessing classes, the workers themselves, must, on the other hand, recognize one thing above all that the Church has done for them; she has realized, encouraged and defended the need hidden deep inside them for a new and worthwhile life.

These classes, humiliated by their state of social inferiority, driven to exacerbation by subversive propaganda, eager for justice and dignity, have a right to share the developments of modern civilization.

The Church understands the hearts of the under-privileged in our modern age as she has in other circumstances in the past. Her own heart goes out to them in love. She has both helped them and educated them in innumerable ways. Again and again she has understood, supported, affirmed principles about them that have been generally accepted later. She has laid bare errors that were subsequently confirmed by experience. She has supported movements whose purity and intellectual enthusiasm were difficult to realize in practice. To the dialogue she has opened with the working classes she brings goodness, comfort, and friendship.

There is a great deal more I could say about this. But we all know one thing; whatever oscillations there may be in political or social factors, however differing may be tendencies and expressions about these among Catholics themselves, the Church will be true to her word: the word of her popes, her bishops, and her doctors. She will keep faith and remain at the side of the worker to encourage his hopes and relieve his sorrows, to defend his rights and legitimate aspirations, and to guide his steps on the paths of honesty, justice, and concord.

Certainly the Church will never take part in purely temporal controversies. She will not deduce practical conclusions from her principles, for such conclusions take many forms and include many opinions. These she will leave to be freely discussed and dealt with by those with specific competence in the social and political spheres. But by her social doctrines she will light the way for men of goodwill in these spheres too. And this social doctrine of hers, let us mark well, rests on the principle of human perfectability, that is on the idea of progress.

If this were understood it would clear away the biggest obstacles to the life-giving flow of religion among industrial and other workers, and help them to draw from religion those refreshing energies of the spirit that they have a right to and that they need.

Such is the first effort of understanding they need to make.

The second is for them to acquire a better understanding of the nature of work itself.

Work obviously leads to external, practical, economic realities. But how does it lead to these, and what are its final ends?

At this point we might put forward a philosophy of work. But don't worry; you already know it, you already practice it.

I will express this in the form of a synthesis. Work is a secular activity; but it is a human activity. Human activity is guided by a faculty of the spirit, intelligence, which puts the stamp of thought on action. Thought is the element that confers a human aspect on a finished work; it mirrors and imprints itself on this activity. Now thought, particularly scientific thought, is based on principles that postulate the absolute, that are founded on necessity.

Here, without realizing it, we are back at religion, back in the presence of God.

Galileo affirmed the connection between 'necessity' and recourse to the thought of God, its source, in mathematics (and what does mathematics not enter into nowadays). Mathematical knowledge, he said, 'is equal in objective certainty to divine knowledge, as long as it understands necessity'. It thus becomes 'a participator of divinity', by the mere fact that human intelligence is able to understand the nature of numbers.

Much the same could be said when work tends towards its best expression, towards perfection. Perfection is a concept eager for transcendence, touching on mystery, because it reflects a metaphysical harmony which sends a divine message to those who can accept it.[1]

This divine message is all the more eloquent and fascinating today, when the kingdoms of space are opening to conquests by human machines and human daring. How, one wonders, could an intelligent poet, when the first Sputnik was launched into the sky, look on it as a victory for atheism and not a call to contemplate further that universe which sings God's glory?

May it not happen that, as modern man's scientific studies progress and he discovers laws and realities hitherto buried in the mute vaults of matter, he will also find himself listening to the voice of the spirit aquiver within them? May that not be the religion of tomorrow?

Einstein himself foresaw a spontaneous religion of the universe.

[1] Cf. B. Varisco, *Dall'uomo a Dio*, Padova, 1939, p. 5.

And may that not be my religion today too? Does it not already tell me, filling my spirit with overwhelming amazement and joy, of the infinite power and infinite wisdom of the God whom I adore and love, of the true, living God?

Why preclude work from this boundless and joyful horizon, when man's labour is the most daring and assiduous explorer of God's work, nature?

Is not work already on the road that leads to religion? Why bar its way? Why make work only a means, and deprive it of reaching out towards the supreme aim? Why not allow it the sublime prize of prayer? Why deny to the life of activity the chance of crossing ways with the life of contemplation, and so moving on together towards the great common goal?

We could come to similar conclusions on very different grounds by remembering that work, however profane or material, is guided by another spiritual faculty of man, the will. This in its turn gives human activity a moral qualification; this qualification, whether we like it or not, derives its own genuine vitality from duty; and duty postulates the relationship of man with his ultimate aim, God.

Here too a mental effort is needed to free work from its mere valuation as an instrument and to raise it to its full moral evaluation which, of its nature, is proportionate to man's relationship with God.

All this shows us how the opposition which has grown up between religion and labour derives chiefly from a restricted concept often held of religion. One is apt to consider religion as just one of man's many activities, limited to a specific field, to its outer forms, to certain definite moments; such a concept would be enough for an activity that was only human.

But religion takes the whole sweep of life, all the horizons of reality, into its vision. It not only traces connections between component parts, it describes the whole arch of the general order. Nothing is extraneous to it, nothing superior to it. Everything is included in the universal conception it puts forward.

One can see why this is not understood by those who limit the sectors of their observation and experience, as do so many scholars and men of business. To deny a problem is not to solve it. To deny the problem of religion does not rule it out of existence. The reasoning of such people is restricted, their clarity illusory because it is partial. It ignores the true dimensions of reality.

One can see, too, why the world eventually comes to appear a cruel absurdity and life a hallucinatory anguish to those who think they can exclude God from their vision of life. When the supreme light is put out, darkness falls over everything. The world becomes dreary, bitter, violent, squalid. 'The atheist has lost his patrimony of joy, because joy . . . cannot derive . . . from anarchy raised to a force of universal gravity.'[1]

[1] G. Bevilacqua, *Equivoci, Mondo moderno e Cristo*, Brescia, p. 38.

PART FOUR

THE COUNCIL, THE CHURCH, AND THE WORLD

I

THINKING ABOUT THE COUNCIL[1]

WE ARE beginning this pastoral letter in Rome, where we have been called for the preparatory meetings of the ecumenical council which is to be inaugurated this year, 1962, as solemnly announced by the Holy Father Pope John XXIII in the Bull, 'Humanae Salutis', of 25 December 1961. As we now know from a statement by the Pope himself, the Second Vatican Council will open on the 11 October this year.

This event is so important that we can choose no other subject for this our main annual instruction, though the singularity and grandeur of the forthcoming council have already led to innumerable explanations, comments, and hopes, and though the preparations for it have already filled the world with facts and forecasts. 'In omnem terram exivit sonus eorum', their echo has spread throughout the world (Ps. 18, 5).

We too have already spoken a good deal about the council. From the first moment when the Pope made his announcement we have shown our surprise, joy, and hope, exhorting you to 'understand at once the hour of God'.[2]

Publications, lectures, meetings, sermons, and prayers have already spread information and aroused feelings which would seem enough to prepare us for the forthcoming event. But even so we want to ask you in this Easter message to give more thought to a theme of such scope and high importance.

First of all we must re-order our ideas about the ecumenical council; then we must deepen our sense not only of its historical and external significance but also of its inner, spiritual, human, and religious meaning. We should fully realize the mysterious and stirring implications of an event whose protagonists are not only

[1] From Pastoral Letter to the Archdiocese of Milan, Easter, 1962.
[2] Rivista Milanese, pp. 73, 101-2.

men of this world but also the Holy Spirit himself, speaking through them and animating the Church of Christ.

Let us review our thoughts about the council. It has aroused many ideas, both sound and fanciful, in most people, and particularly in the most fervently religious. Let us try to re-order these ideas and test their validity as far as we can.

The council poses many themes of the highest interest concerning both the internal life of the Church and its influence on the spiritual and moral life of the outside world. Let us mentally draw up a list of these so as to assess their meaning and importance better. Lastly we must try and realize how universal this event is. The council concerns us too, not only because in one way or another it touches on our own interests and destinies, but also because we should all, if we are really loyal members of the Mystical Body of Christ, participate in it in some way and to some extent. The whole Church is expressed in the council, and we are the Church.

We must all, singly and as a community, prepare ourselves for the council, take part in it as far as possible and then dispose ourselves to follow up its results. Without this communion of souls and intentions the council cannot entirely achieve the aims for which it was called.

Here in Rome we find this view of the extraordinary importance of the forthcoming council becoming clearer to us. We have spent most of our life in Rome. Here we tried to penetrate the mystery of the Church, while working humbly but assiduously in the offices of the apostolic see. And here we also tried to find, and sometimes to encourage under the guidance of the successor of Peter, the signs of the Church's perennial vitality. Rome always awakens thoughts that surprise and move us, thoughts that we cannot repress. So we would like to confide them in you as a preface to the precepts which we bring to your attention on the eve of the council. They seem to us all the more authentic and all the more worthy of diffusion as coming from the city of the holy see.

Indeed it seems to us that the concept of Rome must be associated with the concept of the council. Not that ecumenical councils have taken place only in Rome; in fact, most councils took place elsewhere. But obviously Rome is the best meeting place for an ecumenical council and the fact that it is held here gives it greater prominence, as well as lending to the city some of its own warmth of spirit. Rome is the city of unity, authority, catholicity, and universality; it is the city of truth and the city of charity.

And what is an ecumenical council if not the honouring of these human ideals which are realized, made eternal and sanctified only in the religion of Christ? Rome is the city of the Church; a council is a phase of the Church's fullness. Rome is the city of Christ; a council is a period when Christ's mystic presence operates in his Church and in the world.

So it seems to us that the council will give Rome a period of sublime splendour greater than it has ever enjoyed before, infusing with an unequalled vigour its forecasting of God's words to men and men's words to God. A charism of prophecy will animate Rome, and the human city will be transmuted into a city of God. Rome will become Jerusalem.

Amid the whirl of ideas and feelings that Catholic Rome arouses in those who contemplate her, two main thoughts are uppermost in my mind today. Both have innumerable subscribers, as indeed do all the other thoughts which have been expressed about her and which come so easily in this blessed place. One is of 'Roma patria communis': no-one is a stranger in Rome if he yields to her in spirit. All those who will come flocking to Rome for this solemn meeting will be her citizens, not strangers, guests, or travellers. This mysterious sense of elevation to the citizenship of true humanity is felt by anyone who comes to Rome on pilgrimage. So it will be felt all the more by those brought here to carry out this inherently universal function—the magisterium of the Church. They will be at home.

It is a wonderful thing that there should exist in the world and in history a place where all can feel at home. Even the profane, even non-believers, have this mysterious feeling in Rome. The council takes on this sense of community, of brotherhood, of family by the mere fact of being convoked in Rome. To us this seems a prelude to a better understanding of its meaning and a deeper appreciation of its value.

The second thought is hope. In Rome, though hope is not always obvious, it always seems to be seeking its domain: it has about it something messianic, something eschatological. It is inaccurate to define Rome only as an ancient city surviving as a modern capital; Rome has a destiny which projects into the future. Her history is not at an end and her present state does not fully realize the potentiality of her mission in time.

In Rome there is a logic of expectation, developing and reaching out towards new aims; there is a premise which could be a promise: here nothing is ended, all is beginning; here the petitions of human needs find their supreme court of appeal. The trust in, the art of, human perfectability have their stronghold, their workshop in Rome. Pessimism has no permanent place on her soil. Here redemption is always possible; here peace can always be achieved, human progress always pursued. A genuine humanism seems in constant development here; in the words of the bible, 'Let us make man in the likeness of God' (Gen. 1, 26)—that is, according to man's highest prototype. The effort is never satisfied by the results, and that in itself suggests a course of action; for here Christ is in the process of becoming—'until Christ is formed in us' (Gal. 4, 19). The effort, the mission of Catholic Rome is to preach and spread Christ, steadfastly, facing difficulties and persecution and awaiting his glorious final return with unshaken trust. The gathering in Rome of the council, of the whole preaching and evangelizing Church, gives us a sense of hope unfurled like a flag in the wind of history, floating like a sign of comfort and guidance above the worried and uncertain world.

The ecumenical council is a vast subject and one calling for long and varied discussion. But it is enough if this modest pastoral letter leaves you with a sense of the depth and solemn complexity of our theme and so helps you to avoid making hurried and superficial judgments.

The aspect of the council that first comes to mind is the manner of its convocation. It was called quite without forewarning, by the sole and free will of the supreme pontiff. Its announcement was enough to give the entire Church and the whole world the sense of a quite extraordinary event on the point of achievement, just as if it had been definitely expected. At once it took on the aspect and power of a universal call. It seemed to awaken and revive the entire Church.

The Pope, we learnt, had contacted all the bishops, beyond the canonical circle of the Roman Curia, in order to reach directly the great horizon of the universal hierarchy. If such an event came unexpectedly in the series of external events which we call history, it seemed to have been maturing, unconsciously perhaps, in the minds of Catholics all over the world. This vocation was necessary.

Our generation of Catholics has been through the richest, strangest, most dramatic of experiences. It has been tried by the sufferings and consequences of wars, subject in many countries to severe persecution, corroded by crises of ideas and habits brought about by the evolution of modern life, attacked by the most radical forms of laicism and atheism. But in spite of all that, it is alive, a new energy throbbing in every part of its being. There has been a renewal in thought, in faith, in sanctity, in liturgy, in pastoral care, in the missions. New organizations, new works of charity, have developed, the laity have collaborated more closely in the work of the clergy, Christian principles have shed their light on various fields of temporal society. Meanwhile, full of confidence, Catholics have been listening with loyalty and veneration to Rome, carrying out its rulings and instructions willingly and obediently. But they have often felt that there was a lack of dialogue or mutual collaboration, that the Church's unity should be lived rather than impassively accepted, that brotherhood was the pivot of unity.

In many sectors of Catholic life throughout the world there were reservoirs of experience waiting to be tapped, waiting to ask vital questions and discuss vital opinions—not only with Rome but with other Catholics.

So when the Pope announced the ecumenical council it seemed that he had sensed the secret expectation not only among the bishops but among the whole Catholic world. A flame of enthusiasm ran round the entire Church. He had an intuition, an inspiration, perhaps, that the calling of a council would arouse in her an unparalleled vitality.

Never before had a call of this kind come when the Catholic Church was in such a state of good-will, in such need to communicate with the vicar of Christ and with her fellow-Catholics scattered all over the globe. This in itself makes the council an historical fact of the first importance and of great spiritual value for all Catholics. It is a call to the great dialogue of the Church's interior unity.

How is this dialogue to take place? A meeting of such extent and complexity requires a closely organized procedure. This is the second aspect of the council—juridical and canonical—which is plain for all to see. We will not linger on this exterior and, as it were, concrete and material side of the council. But we can infer something of it from the existing laws of the Church. In current terminology the word council means an assembly of bishops. When the bishops of the whole world are convoked by the pope, then the council calls itself ecumenical, that is, universal or, one might say, truly catholic.

This is not just an assembly of friends, scholars, or fellow-worshippers. It is an assembly of ecclesiastical government, that is it deliberates on matters of doctrine and discipline. In a council the *magisterium* and jurisdiction of the Church are at their fullest and most solemn. The subjects proper to a council are therefore religious questions, that is those which concern the faith, customs, and discipline of the Church. Its purpose is the spiritual and moral good of Christians everywhere and, indirectly, of the whole world as well.

We can give a descriptive and purely juridical definition of an ecumenical council in these terms; it is a solemn gathering of the bishops of the whole world, convoked by the Roman pontiff, to deliberate in common, under his authority and presidency, religious questions which interest all Christians.[1]

A council is therefore the supreme form of the government of the Church.

It is important to understand the position of the pope in relation to an ecumenical council. The pope alone, it must be remembered, has supreme, full power of jurisdiction over the whole Church. This is an 'episcopal', that is a pastoral, power given directly by Christ and not by the Church, and it is his alone. When the pope speaks solemnly (*ex cathedra*) he enjoys the special divine help promised to him in the person of the apostle Peter; this makes his definitions infallible and therefore unchangeable. He does this by virtue of being what he is and not by consent of other bishops or of the Church.[2] This was defined by the First Vatican Council, interpreting Christ's thought and the age-old belief of the Church.[3] The pope's power is that of a 'vicar' in respect to Christ, but it is his alone, supremely and universally, in respect to the Church.

Thus the pope can act with full authority and efficacy without a council; though even when exercising his authority in this way he

[1] *Dictionnaire de Théologie Catholique*, art. 'Conciles', col. 641.
[2] Cf. Denz., 1939.
[3] *S.T.*, II, II, 1, 10, 3. Cf. Journet, *The Church of the Word Incarnate*, vol. 1.

never acts without knowing himself to be in communion with the bishops and the Church. But it is given to him, and him alone, to confirm the faith of all.

On the other hand a council cannot be valid without the pope. The pope must be the one to convoke and preside over a council, or at least ratify its deliberations. A council adds no substantial validity to the pope's authority, but for a council to have any specific efficacy, unity with the pope is indispensable. A council does not distinguish its jurisdiction from the pope's, but identifies its own with his, constituting with him the supreme power in the whole Church.[1] A council is therefore not indispensable to the government of the Church, but when a council meets round the pope the government of the Church assumes its most solemn form, manifests its greatest power and is therefore at its most effective.

Christ gave Peter primacy in his Church, as being necessary and sufficient to govern it. But he also instituted the apostolic college with power and mandate for teaching and pastoral care in communion with Peter.

When we have a council this communion of rule is shown in its fullness. The primacy in power of Peter, transmitted to the bishop of Rome, is fused with the collegial power of the apostles (of whom Peter himself was the first and not the only one) transmitted to the bishops. So a council is not just a particularly solemn moment of ecclesiastical government. It is the moment when the mystery of the teaching Church, of her distinctive characteristics, apostolic, unifying, catholic, and sanctifying, is revealed in full.

It follows that the theory that councils serve no purpose since the definition of the fullness of papal power has no basis whatsoever. To us the contrary seems the case, as the convocation of the forthcoming council already shows. Hesitation about the convocation of a council was possible when there was some doubt about a council's authority in relation to the pope's (as at the councils of Constance and of Basle). But once this constitutional truth of the Church concerning the supremacy of the pope in respect to a council has been defined, the main difficulty to the holding of an ecumenical council has gone. Now there is no longer any suspicion of possible inner contradictions, councils can become splendid sources of spiritual energy for the whole Church.

The mystery of the Church, as we were saying, is more evident

[1] Can. 228, s. 1.

in a council now than ever before. This was taught by Pope
Pius IX:

> 'It is in an ecumenical council that the holy dogmas of religion
> are defined with greatest depth, and expressed most fully, that
> ecclesiastical discipline is best restored and most firmly re-estab-
> lished. . . that links are tightened between the Church's members
> and her head, that the vigour of the whole Mystical Body of
> Christ grows. . . .'[1]

Thus the supreme authority of the pope does not annul the
authority of the bishops, as some Catholics have suspected,[2] and
many separated brethren still assert.

The bishops receive the fullness of the priesthood from the
sacrament of ordination, but their powers of jurisdiction over their
respective dioceses is conferred by the supreme pontiff.

The authority of the pope does not diminish but sustains that of
the bishops, and its honour is enhanced by the dignity and stability
of the bishops' authority. This was affirmed by Pope Gregory the
Great when he wrote to the Bishop of Alexandria: 'My honour is
the honour of the universal Church. My honour is the strength and
prosperity of my brothers. I am truly honoured when the honour
which is the due of each is refused to none.'

Many other questions asking for a reply will be answered by the
event itself; should, for instance, the times for calling a council be
fixed or should they be arbitrary; on whom and on what does their
calling depend; what about other councils that have been less
solemn and less timely; or the appeal, now certainly illegal, from
pope to council; or the question of voting in councils, etc.?

Here we might raise one question, concerning which members,
according to existing canonical law, are to be convoked today.
We know from the Bull already quoted that to the forthcoming
council will be called cardinals, patriarchs, primates, archbishops,
and bishops both residential and titular, abbots and prelates with
jurisdiction, abbots primate and abbots of the monastic congregations, and superiors-general of religious orders.

Thus a council is not like a parliament elected by the people.
It is an organism composed of ecclesiastics and invested with its own
authority. It is not an assembly of experts, of professors or theo-

---

[1] Cf. Const. *Dei Filius. Coll. Lac.*, VII, 248.
[2] Dejalfre, *Pape et Eveques au premier Concile du Vatican*, Desclee de Brouwer. 1961.

logians or specialists on Canon Law, but of pastors and doctors of Christ's Church. They assume their office not because of their personal qualities, nor by dynastic succession, nor by historical or local privilege, but because, if they are bishops, they are legitimately called to succeed the apostles and invested with powers and dignities which can come only from a call from on high and which can be made on any individual, without distinction of class, nation, or race, who is considered suitable for that high and solemn function.

The Church's authority comes from on high, that is it derives only from Christ, not from the community; but it does not fear to search all its ranks, making a free choice of its elect.

This aspect of the composition of a council also merits reflection so that we may admire God's work in this spectacular human phenomenon.

If only those sit in a council who are charged by God's Church to carry out the 'service of authority' it is understandable why other members of the community of believers, priests, religious and laity do not figure there. Yet the whole community is present in a council because there its faith is expressed, there its interests are treated and there meet the pastors who guide, interpret, and represent it.

If a council were conceived of as a meeting of ecclesiastics separate from the rest of the Church, this would deny its nature as a synthesis of the Church. The priesthood is created for the faithful, and where the priestly composition of an assembly is most marked there, too, the moral presence of the Christian people is most marked. So the whole Church will be present in the council, because neither pope nor bishops function apart from the Church.

The civil authorities will not figure at this council. They did so once and had various functions which were not, however, intrinsic to the exercise of the ecclesiastical *magisterium*. But the distinction between civil and ecclesiastical society is becoming ever clearer and more widely acknowledged, and this makes the presence of the civil authorities at the council neither possible nor desirable. The Church will appear alone, unarmed, but free in its most complete and most original expression.[1]

These brief notes could lead us on to a conspectus of the history of past councils. But this would distract us from our present purpose, which is intended to be not so much informative as indicative of the

[1] Cf. Héfélé, I, 41, n. 3, 47–8, 52, 57, etc.

forthcoming council's religious importance. So we will make only one observation from the history of past ecumenical councils, and that with reference to the collegial character of the episcopate as successor of the apostolic college.

Just as the apostolic college had Peter as its head, so the college of bishops has the pope as its head. This is the root source of the Church's structure. Therefore the meeting of the college of bishops by means of the pope, which makes up an ecumenical council, is by divine right.[1] The origin of ecumenical councils is Christ.

The long sequence of these great assemblies tells us of the Church's history throughout the centuries, shows us Christianity's most dramatic and most decisive moments, from defining the meaning of the Word revealed by God, to vindicating the Church's liberty, then recomposing her unity and bringing out her inner and genuine vitality.

Here we must look deeper into this recurrent historical phenomenon which plays such a part in the Church's life, in determining her thought and spirituality, in the strength of her integration, in her survival.

The Church is not only a visible institution composed of men, a unique historical phenomenon. It is a complex of doctrines, precepts, and rites. The Church is a mystery.[2] That is, she is a divine presence and design, a divine act.

This presence, design, and act are mysteriously visible and yet mysteriously hidden. Those who have the grace of faith and lucid minds coupled with a loving desire to accept the faith and live it, will see, understand, and rejoice in the Church. But to enter this inner and mysterious aspect of the Church will help them to see the outer and historical side of the same Church; a side which is in itself a sign, with its own unmistakable marks, of her truth.[3]

The Church is a mystery which must be sought in the mind of God. We must become used to making a humble, attentive, loving effort to seek the origin of the Church in the divine mind to finding treasure in the words of sacred scripture. And in setting off on this search we at once make this sublime discovery: even before

[1] Wernz-Vidal, *Jus Canonicum*, II, p. 444, n. 457.

[2] de Lubac, *The Splendour of the Church*, London, 1956; Congar, *The Mystery of the Church*, London, 1960; Clerissac, *Le Mystère de l'Eglise*; Hasseveldt, *The Church, a Divine Mystery*, Chicago, 1955.

[3] Cf. J. H. Newman, *Apologia pro vita sua, passim*.

we were seeking God, God was seeking us! 'He first loved us' (1 John 4, 10 and 19). And the Church, that is humanity united in Christ, is only the accomplishment of God's loving design for us. In the Old Testament it is God who seeks his people and builds his Jerusalem. It is God who forms his people according to the image of his Son, sent to redeem the world by love (cf. Rom. 8, 29; John 3, 16).

The Church in fact is the continuation of Christ in time and the expression of Christ on earth. She is his living presence. In the authority and teaching of the Church, 'He who hears you hears me' (Luke 10, 16). In the legitimately constituted community of the Church, 'Where two or three are gathered in my name there am I in the midst of them' (Matt. 18, 20). In her activity and by the apostolic succession, he is present forever: 'I am with you always, to the close of the age' (Matt. 28, 20). The mystery of the eucharistic sacrifice perpetuates the ineffable presence of Jesus among us, 'For as often as you eat this bread and drink the cup, you proclaim the Lord's death until he comes' (1 Cor. 11, 26).

The Church is his salvific action, the means, the vehicle, that is, of his salvific action, the instrument for exercising his power of order by administrating the sacraments; she is also, as a free and human secondary cause, his subordinate collaborator in exercising her power of jurisdiction.[1] The Holy Spirit is sent by Jesus to animate the Church and create grace in her by his gifts and charisms.[2] All this is recalled and clarified by an ecumenical council. The very fact of a council being held in complete concordance with Christ's original message is a clear indication that he is helping his Church.

Pope John XXIII's Bull announcing the forthcoming council is permeated with this thought:

'The restorer of human salvation, Jesus Christ, before he ascended into heaven, gave orders to the apostles he had chosen to bring the light of the Gospel to all men, and in order to give authority and salvation to the office entrusted them, he made them this promise: "Behold I am with you, all days until the consummation of time". And though Christ's help has never ceased to live and operate in the Church, it has certainly been shown the more when human society was shaken by the fiercest storms.'[3]

[1] Journet, *The Church of the Word Incarnate op. cit.*
[2] Cf. John 14–16, the discourse at the Last Supper.
[3] Bull, *Humanae Salutis*, 25 December 1961.

As we were saying before, the marks of the Church are now clearly apparent. Never before has she shown herself, as in this council, to be so united, holy, catholic, and apostolic. And never before has the divine–human conscience of the Church so expressed itself: 'For it has seemed good to the Holy Spirit and to us' (Acts 15, 28), said the apostles at the first Council of Jerusalem. And so will say the Fathers of the Second Vatican Council.

Strong in our certainty that God loves, that Christ helps, and the Holy Spirit guides the Church, as we will all, to some extent, soon see for ourselves, we must view the council with great reverence and hope and try to realize how the Pope's intentions in calling a council are themselves signs of the divine will.

What does our Lord want of this council? To understand this would be a great thing indeed. If we did, the mysterious and loving play of Providence in dialogue with history, with the sum, that is, of free human wills, preparing new destinies for souls and for the world, would be in some way unveiled. Vast panoramas would open up to us—of graces pouring from heaven, of responsibility called to make supreme choices, of new energies surging up from within human hearts, of wonderful combinations of time and fact, of threads leading from yesterday into today and on towards the future and beyond time to Christ's final coming.

It is a stupendous vision and though it is not absolutely clear the Christian is not wholly blind to it. But in order for the eye to open on this luminous half-light we must, as we have said, keep our minds on the Pope's intentions. Here too he is the reflected and visible mediator of the one invisible mediator between heaven and earth, Christ our Lord.

What then are the Pope's intentions for the forthcoming ecumenical council? Before repeating the familiar answer to this question, we might note how the announcement of the council has raised in men's minds utopian dreams, curiosity, and hopes of all kinds, and many fantasies too. Myriad wishes and hopes have also been aroused in the faithful.

This state of expectation is justified, and does honour to those who encourage it. We can expect great things from the council; graces, spiritual light and energy, renewal of discipline, of the liturgy, of the Church's administration, of her contacts with the modern world and with separated Christians.

But we must avoid encouraging desires that are strictly personal, arbitrary, and capricious. We must not think that the council will correspond to our particular views, but should ourselves enter into the general views of the council. To believe that the council will abolish human frailty and bring perfection to the Church and the world is an ingenuous dream. To believe that it will remedy the many improper practices and theoretical imperfections among Catholics, which each one of us comes across in his experience as a member of the Church or as an observer of ecclesiastical life, is too much to ask. It is also too much to believe that the council will realize all the fine ideas that occur to each individual Christian or particular religious group.

The council—it is helpful to remember—has also been well prepared by the gathering of suggestions from the whole Church. All the bishops, Roman congregations, religious orders, Catholic universities, and experts, both men and women, scholars and practical people, ecclesiastic and lay—all these have been questioned with complete freedom to express what they thought and wanted for the good of religion and the Church. Numerous large volumes have been printed to record and systematize this vast material for the use of the Fathers of the council and later for the improvement and modernization of ecclesiastical life.

Never has a council had such broad and careful preparation. We need have no doubts about the council lacking abundance of advice, experience, and aspirations. The whole Church, one can say, has contributed to supply from its faith, its piety, and its love for Christ subjects to be examined and discussed by the great conciliar assembly.

It should edify and comfort us that our Church is like this; that at a certain hour of its history the entire Catholic world in its best qualified voices is freely invited to express and present its desires and judgments of every kind to those responsible. A whole crop of publications has sprung up around the forthcoming council. Another will certainly arise after it has ended.

From this it can be seen that the so-called dogmatism of the Catholic Church does not smother but stimulates thought among its teachers and disciples. This is made possible by the cult of truth proper to God's holy Church. And this truth is expressed as a great living choir, whose innumerable voices do not fall into confusion.

The master of this choir is the Pope. He has given the forthcoming council two basic aims: to reform ecclesiastical life inwardly, and to seek reconciliation with separated Christians in the Catholic unity of the Church. Of these aims he has said:

'But the most pressing topics will be those which concern the spread of the Catholic faith, the revival of Christian standards of morality, and the bringing of ecclesiastical discipline into closer accord with the needs and conditions of our times. This in itself will provide an outstanding example of truth, unity, and love. May those who are separated from this Apostolic See, beholding this manifestation of unity, derive from it the inspiration to seek out that unity which Jesus Christ prayed for so ardently from his heavenly Father.'[1]

Let us now take the aim, so easy and yet involving so many difficulties, of the reform of ecclesiastical life. This time it is the Pope who has raised this matter before the whole Church. In the past this has been a course of action adopted by the saints, as well as a clarion-call for rebels, a subject for wishful thinking, the ambition of politicians, the deeply-felt need of contemplatives and pastors, the whim of restless and stubborn spirits. Throughout the centuries, reform has been a periodic ferment tending either to revivify Catholic tradition or to disintegrate the life of the Church.

Those who know the Church's history realize how important and how dynamic this impulse for reform has been through the centuries. We have only to recall that the great religious and political crisis which detached the Protestants from the Catholic Church was called the Reformation, and that the great effort by the Council of Trent to define doctrine and repair moral evils and the movement of Catholic restoration which followed was inappropriately called the Counter-Reformation, though in fact it was not so much a movement to defend and conserve as a true and positive Catholic reformation which has led to copious benefits from the sixteenth century until our own day.

We must clarify our ideas on this concept of reform. This is important for an understanding of the forthcoming council's ultimate aims and for a realization of its spirit. It is important too because the idea of reform has a strong and varied appeal to the modern mind.

How does the idea of reform arise? It has two roots: the observa-

[1] *A.A.S.*, 1959, p. 511. English translation, *Ad Petri Cathedram*, C.T.S., London, p. 19.

tion of a wrong and varied reaction to that wrong. Here a specious objection arises: can there be wrong in the Church? Is she not the holy, infallible Church? The answer is easy for those who see in the Church God's work and design, his divine gifts of grace and truth, and see that the Church's final purpose is with God and eternal life. Her work is holy, sanctifying, and divine in its principle, the Holy Spirit. And in certain special and specific acts (solemn definitions of dogma) the Church is infallible.

But God's work is carried out by men who belong to this world, who can be frail and fallible even if they are sustained by the grace and pledge of following Christ. We must, that is, distinguish two aspects of the Church, that of divine institution and that of human community. We could call these, in one sense, the ideal and the real; or the efficient cause, formal and final, which is the work of God and therefore perfect, and the material cause (always pervaded by the formal one) which is the Church's human composition, made up of men who are imperfect and, perhaps, sinners, but who are always sanctified by baptism.

The first aspect is that of the utterly wonderful and immaculate model of the Church conceived by Christ and loved by him as his Mystical Bride, 'without spot or wrinkle . . . holy and without blemish', as St Paul wrote (Eph. 5, 27). This is not only a model, but a reality in course of fulfilment, and its historical and concrete expression is the second aspect, that of humanity collected in the Church militant and imperfect. But she is in process of perfecting and sanctifying herself according to the model conceived by Christ of the Church in glory, reaching beyond time to her final end. So reform is a perennial effort by the Church to bring her human reality closer to the divine idea and the divine idea closer to her human reality.

So this earthly Church of ours, schooled in her human form and in process of sanctification by Christ, is and should be in a state of constant reform. The very supernatural reality of the Church calls for her natural reality to be always tending towards perfection. Jesus told us: 'You, therefore, must be perfect as your heavenly Father is perfect' (Matt. 5, 48). And St Paul counsels us: 'Be imitators of God as beloved children' (Eph. 5, 1), and urges us always to 'be renewed in the spirit of your minds and put on the new nature' (Eph. 4, 23–4). So we are called to an effort for perfection which is without truce or limits. Our lives must be in a continual state of moral tension, imbued with all the juridical discipline, all the moral teaching, all the ascetic and mystical vigilance of the Church. Reform is in the normal programme of the Church. Reform is continuous.

But when we speak of reform in connection with an ecumenical council we usually think of widespread and inveterate evils, and of various grave measures to be taken against these. This is what happened at various preceding councils. But the characteristic quality of this council, intended though it is for notable reforms, derives from the fact that its convocation is due more to a desire for good than an escape from evil. By divine mercy there are in the Church today no errors, scandals, or deviations, no abuses such as necessitate the convocation of a council.

Today the Church, always by the grace of God and the merit of so many good and holy Christians, is in a state of weakness and endurance rather than of decadence and scandal. In general the face of the Catholic Church today shows more wounds than it does sins, more need than infidelity. This makes us all the more grateful and glad that the Pope, spontaneously animated by love of Christ and a wish to help the Church further along its road of perfection, has himself, with no exterior urge, called an ecumenical council. It will therefore be a council of positive rather than punitive reforms; of exhortations rather than of anathemas.

Thus the Church expresses the needs and wishes of her children who must themselves nourish these in connection with the forthcoming council. Their needs are becoming their hopes and must become their prayers. This change in the mental climate of Catholicism is a positive result which the council has achieved before it has even opened. The Pope's optimism thus diffuses over the whole body of the Church, increasing her sensibility, without morbid or existentialist *angst*, without sterile or pharisaical criticisms, but eagerly searching for truth and trusting in good.

This eve of the council is a time for a general examination of conscience for us all. Who of us is not aware of some need, of some possible improvement in Catholic religious life? This explains the vast number of forecasts and suggestions about the council that come from every direction.

It might be helpful to give our faithful some idea, however general, of the prospects which the council opens for the fervent.

We will mention them briefly, in the hope of enlarging horizons —some individuals or groups hope that the council will satisfy their own restricted personal interests or particular tastes; there is also a good deal of wishful thinking which can all too easily grip people who are in good faith but out of touch with reality. Another reason for mentioning the prospects of the council is so that our hopes and prayers may be concentrated on some of its more likely and desirable results.

There are various expectations that belong to the Church's inner, others to her outer life, that is, to the relationships which the Church must revivify and re-establish. What do we hope for in connection with the interior life of the Church? This question has many possible answers. Above all, we hope for an ever closer union with Christ and with the Gospel; to know him, to imitate him, to possess his grace. This touches our very origin and is the proof of the Church's loyalty and authenticity. Let us hope that the whole life of the Church will grow, improve, be made lovelier in the light of the mystery which she already possesses and by which she lives, the mystery of her genuine derivation from Jesus Christ as presented in the Gospels. This mystery has been the subject of meditation for centuries and is traced as authoritative doctrine in scripture and tradition by both the *magisterium* and the piety of the Church. In a council the Church carries out a great act of love for Christ. She is a faithful wife celebrating her joy.

This great act of love for the historical Christ and then for the Christ who is in heaven moves the Church spontaneously towards his living and divine reality and towards her future meeting with him. It becomes an expectation, an invocation of the Christ to come. It generates a spiritual and mystical impetus, a presentiment, a hope already partly fulfilled. At the same time it produces an ascetic tension, a watchfulness, a moral urge which gives Christian life the semblance of a pilgrimage towards that final end which classifies and evaluates all human experience in relation to its supernatural relationship with God.

From this view of our expectations, all centred in Christ, it is easy to move on to that of his Mystical Body. The council offers the Church a mirror in which to look and see herself. The most eagerly awaited decisions of the council concern, as we all know, the Church herself. For her structure is still not wholly clear or defined.

The First Vatican Council, of course, defined the position of the supreme pontiff in this structure, and recognized in the successor to St Peter and the bishop of Rome not only pastoral functions in the diocese of Rome, but the primary functions of universal teacher, infallible when he speaks *ex cathedra*, and universal pastor with full authority over the whole Church.[1] But though that council affirmed the harmony between the pope's primacy and the authority of the bishops, the political events of 1870 in Rome prevented it from proceeding to define the proper place of the bishops in this structure.

The interruption of the First Vatican Council and the need to clarify the essence of the episcopate, its functions, powers, and obligations, allow us to suppose that the Second Vatican Council will also deal with the episcopate, showing its evangelic origins, its sacramental gifts of grace and its powers of ruling, administration, and jurisdiction, whether in the person of the individual bishop or in its collegiate expression. We can also suppose that the council will confirm the dependence of the bishops on the supreme pontiff and at the same time their community and collaboration with him. Whether we consider its doctrinal, its juridical, or its pastoral aspect, this question of the episcopate is perhaps the most eagerly awaited, the most serious and the one most full of potential benefits.

Discussions about the nature and function of the episcopate, in harmony with the Roman pontiff, may lead to a new and spontaneous affirmation of the unity, not only juridical but vital, of the Church around the chair of St Peter. This might lead, without hard feelings, to a greater and more organic internationalization of the Church's central government.

It seems possible that if the council deals with the matter of the episcopate it will also discuss the priesthood, the religious state, maybe also celibacy, the married state, and the Christian family.

It is also probable that the Catholic laity will receive explicit and honourable recognition in the council. The status of the layman in the Church will certainly be raised to the level on which he is put by baptism, which makes him a participator in supernatural life, and confirmation, which calls him to the public profession of his faith and to Christian perfection. And we might come to see more clearly the implications of the term 'royal priesthood' when applied to the ordinary layman.

Two sides of Catholic life will be mentioned, we hope, as part

[1] Cf. Constitution, *Pastor aeternus*, First Vatican Council, Denz. n. 1828.

of the layman's adult vocation; his spirituality, developed in a more and more intimate, co-operating participation in the liturgical mysteries of the Christian community; and his vocation, now officially recognized, to collaborate with the apostolic hierarchy, through which the layman too should help infuse new moral and religious energy into the body of the faithful, and so bear witness in his own way to Christ and the Church in the modern world.[1]

If this happens, then human life raised by Christ to the supernatural state will be given full consideration in the council, and appear in its high dignity and regenerated beauty.

Let us now move on to other prospects, particularly those concerning the faith itself.

Will the council give us any new teaching on revealed truth, any new dogmas, apart from those considered above?

We cannot know; and this already shows that the definition of a new dogma as part of revelation seems improbable.

But what does seem generally needed in the Church is advice, some suggestions on how we can preserve, deepen, and profess our faith today. This faith, the starting point of our salvation, is the spiritual patrimony most threatened by modern errors of thought and modern modes of life.

Then there will be a consideration of the law of the Church, Canon Law—the practical dispositions by which the ecclesiastical authority governs the visible body of the Church, her community of clergy, religious and laity.

We may expect many new developments in this field. They have already been foreseen by the Pope himself when he said, on announcing the council, that he intended to put to general revision the whole code of Canon Law promulgated by Pope Benedict XVI in 1917. Jurists will bring all their knowledge to bear on this revision, after the council has laid down its main lines.

We foresee that many reforms of this kind will scarcely be noticed by most of the faithful, largely because, as we were saying, the Church cannot change her fundamental structure or her traditional face. She cannot make a break in the coherence of her interpretation of the evangelic spirit (about the celibacy of the clergy, for instance). But a number of new measures are likely to be discussed by the council and well-received by the faithful; in liturgy, in pastoral

[1] Philips, *Pour un christianisme adulte*, Tournai, 1962. The whole volume merits study.

and missionary work, the task of the ministry and the apostolate is certain to be eased.

A word much used about the council is *aggiornamento*, the 'bringing up-to-date' of the Church's life. What does this mean? That the Church has mistaken her tactics up till now? That she is old and backward looking? That she is conditioned by exterior events? That everything about her is open to discussion? That the Church can recover a reason for existence and flourish only if she falls into step with the natural evolutions of secular history?

This obviously raises matters of great importance, such as the Church's adaptation to her times and surroundings. In many aspects she not only undergoes adaptation but desires and promotes it. Her capacity to accept man as he is, as long as he in his turn accepts God's natural and positive law, and to infuse her truth and grace into him, is part of her universality in time and on earth. But this adaptation is not absolute and does not impair the original and eternal values which the Church possesses and offers to humanity.

The relativism of her pastoral expression in history is not a symptom of weakness and old age. Rather is it the result of an inner vigour that is always renewing itself. This might be an opportune moment to study the question of the Church's perennial youth; but we need only wait for the forthcoming council to offer magnificent proof of this.

The reforming aspect of the council is bound to reawaken a sense of good-will throughout the Church. This is not a council to spread fear even if it rebukes error and evil. No, it arouses hope and love, which explains the popularity with which it is awaited.

Each one of us must look to it with hope and trust, for its success concerns us all.

But we must beware of two illusions which could lead to disappointments. We should see the forthcoming council in the great setting of the Church's historical and traditional economy, and not as a reflection of our own personal fantasies or desires.

The first illusion would be to think that the council will decree radical, overwhelming reforms in the present ordering of the Church, changing her ancient marks and turning her into an institution entirely new and what some call modern, copying, that is, the organizations of ordinary contemporary life. That will not happen.

The present structure of the Church certainly needs overhauling, but it cannot be substantially changed. This structure was not built in disloyalty to Christ, and shows no signs of decay or collapse. It is the result of historical experience, in strict loyalty to and coherence with the will and spirit of the Church's divine founder. It shows an instinctive and often loving care to keep close to the useful and honourable forms of human society. It has, that is, a tendency to a humanist view of the religion which celebrates the word of God made man. This structure has been tested in its essentials by age-old wisdom and sanctity, even where some elements have at times grown disproportionate. The council will not change the traditional appearance of the Catholic Church. But she will, we hope, return to the logic of her original pledges and make them ever more clearly, truly, Christian.

Another illusion would be to think that the council will remedy the many defects and abuses which we all, including myself, find in Catholic life. Certainly the council will try to repair imperfections in every sector of Catholic life. Not for nothing have all the persons capable of giving wise suggestions been questioned, and sub-commissions and commissions created to reduce their suggestions to a practicable form.

But the council is not a panacea. It will indeed give directives for the revision of the Church's discipline and worship, provide guidance for the correction of many aspects in need of renovation and development. Even so this will not be its immediate importance or effectiveness. The council will not be measured purely by its results in church law and ritual. It will show in the ineffable presence, the living and merciful action, of God in his Church.

For, before all else, the council will call forth a greater activity of the Holy Spirit in the whole Church. It will give the faith unanimous, solemn, triumphant expression. It will bring out great ideas and great principles of Christian life drawn from a new and impassioned study of the Gospel and from the wisdom which draws light and energy from that Gospel. This means that it will give the Church a new awareness, a new energy, a new sense of duty, a new love.

The council will give the Church an intimate understanding of what she is and what she should do; and from this deep inner awareness she will draw new capacities for expression; in her preaching, in her apostolate, in her bearing witness, in her suffering and her goodness, her art and her sanctity. But all this will not be immediate, nor will it all be visible. And what is more, this effect will not depend on the council alone. It will depend on the whole Mystical Body which is the Church. It will depend also on each one of us. So let us pledge ourselves now, each one of us, to accept the rulings of the council with prompt and filial obedience. This lofty, and to a certain extent mysterious, scope of the council was the theme of the inspired words of Pope John XXIII:

'The work of the new ecumenical council is intended to restore the face of Christ's Church to the simple, pure lines of her birth, and so present her as the divine founder made her, without mark or blemish. Her journey through the centuries is still far from reaching its transformation into triumphant eternity. So the noble aim of the ecumenical council is to pause a little and lovingly seek the traces of her ardent youth. It must recover and reveal the Church's power to win over the many who are tempted by the false theories of the prince of this world, the enemy, open or secret, of the Son of God, our Redeemer and Saviour.' (13 November 1960.)

This leads us to another consideration which completes the picture: the effect of the council on the contemporary world beyond the Catholic Church.

The world in itself has no practical connection with this ecclesiastical event. The civil authority today, unlike those days previous to and including the Council of Trent, is wholly extraneous to it. The progressive distinction and separation between Church and State excludes all representatives of civil society from the council. This is partly an expression of modern secularism, but it also excludes all pressure by temporal powers and interests in an event which is great in both religious and human terms.

The Church is holding the council on her own. She could, God forbid, be obstructed or disturbed during it, as during the First Vatican Council. But, thanks be to God, the Church is independent.

Even so the council must of necessity have some definite reference to secular society too. It is an episode of such historical importance, a human and visible phenomenon, an affirmation of principles and laws, a source of influence on thought and habit, a concentration so international in its components that the surrounding world must also in some way be aware of its singularity and might even receive some direct benefit from it.

For the council is intended to have a reference to the modern world. The Pope has said so repeatedly in words which seem to echo the prophecies of the bible. 'The Church of Christ can expect truly abundant fruits from this event, which is intended to be a service to truth, an act of charity, an example of peace proclaimed to all peoples from this high and holy See.'[1]

And in the Bull convoking the council he said:

'Although having no directly earthly aims [the Church] cannot even so dissociate herself on her journey from the problems and toils of this world. She knows how good for the soul are those means which render more human the lives of each individual with a soul to be saved; she knows that by vivifying the temporal order in the light of Christ she also reveals men to themselves, leads them to an awareness of their own beings, their own dignity, their own purpose. Hence the Church's living presence today extends over international organizations, both by right and in fact. Hence the elaboration of her social doctrine about the family, about education, work, civil society, and all problems connected with them, which has brought her *magisterium* high prestige as the most authoritative voice, interpreting and asserting the moral order, and as the champion of the rights and duties of all human beings and all political communities. In this way the influence of the council's deliberations, it is our lively hope, should succeed in investing with Christian light and penetrating with spiritual energy not only the intimacy of souls, but even the whole corpus of human activity.'[2]

The Church therefore intends to make contact with the world in the forthcoming council. Let us meditate on this. It is a great act of love. The Church will not be thinking only of herself; she will have the whole of humanity in mind. She will have it in mind and remember that she is the continuation of that Word Incarnate who came into the world to save it, whatever the state in which he found it.

Because of this she will try to become a sister and mother to men. She will try to be poor, simple, humble, friendly in her language and dealings. She will try to make herself understood, will help people today to listen and speak to her easily; and repeat to the

---

[1] Allocution to the Consistory of 16 January 1961.
[2] Bull, *Humanae Salutis*, Christmas 1961.

world her wise reflections on human dignity, loyalty, freedom, love, moral seriousness, courage, and sacrifice. For this she will try, as we were saying, to renovate herself, if need be stripping off some of the royal trappings that have remained so long on her sovereign shoulders, in order to appear in a simpler form more suited to modern taste.

For this she will call the laity, her good and faithful Catholic laity, to act as liaison between her own supernatural and wholly religious sphere and the sociological and temporal sphere in which they live. This in a way means delegating to them the arduous and splendid work of '*consecratio mundi*',[1] of penetrating with Christian principles and natural and supernatural virtues the vastness of the secular world.

Will this powerful and very wonderful attempt succeed? Will the world realize that there is an institution on earth which aims only at making the world better, healthier, happier, and more peaceful? Will the world realize that its agnosticism, its materialism, its atheism must in the end yield to a courageous and wise rediscovery of God and Christ? Will the world remain deaf to the great call to join in prayer with her which the Church will utter? Will it give a timid 'so be it' to a new and revealing spiritual experience? Will the world's victorious song to the God of the universe, to the Christ of true civilization, sound again over the earth?

We may hope so, and we are bound to desire it most earnestly. We must pray and work for it, firstly, by professing our Christianity with depth and sincerity; secondly, by trying in every way we can to give our profession of the faith vigour and brilliance.

This brings us into the trajectory of the council's highest aims. Listen to the Pope again:

'This modern age, this world of such profound outward changes, is floundering amid the fascinations and dangers of an almost exclusive search for material goods. The principles of spiritual and supernatural order, which characterized the expansion of Christian civilization throughout the centuries, languish and are forgotten. There are various points of doctrine or discipline that should be restored to the pure sources of revelation and tradition. We must give value, splendour, and substance once again to the human and Christian thought of which the Church

[1] Cf. Pius XII, *Discorsi*, III, 460; XIII, 295; XV, 590.

has been depository throughout the centuries. Meanwhile it is our duty to deplore the deviations of the human spirit, tempted to enjoy only the goods of this earth, now put within easy reach by scientific research. God guard us, however, from exaggerating its proportions to the point of believing that his skies have now definitely closed above our heads . . . and that there remains nothing more to do than shed tears on our weary road. No, we must take courage!'[1]

So the Pope, with his tonic optimism, exhorts us, comforts us with hope, and seems to be preparing us for a council which, though evil and error are condemned, encourages men of good-will rather than blames men who are astray. Those who are separated from the Church will also find consideration and love.

We come then to think about our innumerable and variously divided brethren who still bear the name Christian but are separated from the unity of the Catholic Church. This is a very delicate and complicated subject. But, as we all know, the Pope has ardently wanted this to be in the forthcoming council's field of vision. At its first announcement to the Sacred College in the Monastery of St Paul on 25 January 1959, he said that the ecumenical council was to be both for 'the edification of all Christian people', and for 'a renewed invitation to the faithful of the separated communities' to follow him 'in a friendly spirit in the search for unity and grace, yearned for by so many souls all over the earth'.

We cannot linger here over this problem, which we have meditated on and spoken about every year during the octave for Christian unity. But let us recall that this difficult but most important and urgent problem is one of the council's chief concerns. It is most unlikely to solve this particular problem; perhaps we do not deserve such a miracle yet. But the ecumenical council can prepare the way for this greatly desired solution. Under this aspect the council will be a preparatory one, a council of desire.

May God will that we Catholics can all put ourselves into this state of soul. May we all long for our Lord to grant our prayer for the reuniting of Christians around Peter and the apostles in communion with him.

We ourselves should try to be Christians of such a calibre that we change the opinion of dissidents concerning the pope and the

[1] Address to preparatory commissions of the council, 14 November 1960.

Catholic Church. May we learn how to greet honourably and in a genuine spirit of brotherhood the separated Christians who appear on our threshold. May we understand better and appreciate more what is still good and true in their religious patrimony. We must in fact hope and pray that the council will clear some of the obstacles cluttering the only road to a happy meeting between us, the road of faith, that is of the truth and reality of Christ's one religion.

Let us hope that the council will loosen the fetters of past memories that we all bear. Discussions about exegesis and prestige still hamper the energy which must one day be released. Let us pray, then, that the council will fire us with greater love, the only force which will in the end move us all towards moments of decision.

So the forthcoming council, unless it has the high good fortune of getting beyond a desire and a preparation for future reconciliation, will be a prelude to another, future council which will celebrate at last the meeting of all Christians as brothers in one fold under one pastor.[1]

These broad considerations lead us to another: each of us must try to develop himself, in order to grasp the deep meaning of the council. Some have called this the chief moment of divine action in the government of the Church; others the most salient affirmation of religion in a world which is losing the religious sense; others a great hour in which the Church finds herself; others a supreme effort by Catholicism to understand, attract, and vivify the modern world; others the total co-ordination in modern terms of apostolic and missionary forces; others a proclamation of principles which the modern world can make its corner stone for stability, peace, and progress; others the most solemn pledge the Church can make of her loyalty to Christ and her mission of salvation.

The very variety of these attempts at overall judgment shows the greatness of the event, from which it follows that our first duty is to reflect on the council.[2]

[1] Nicola Jaeger, *Il Romano Pontifice, il Concilio ecumenico ed i lontani*, Italy, 1959; Küng, *The Council and Reunion*, London, 1961; Dumont, *Les voies de l'unité chrétienne*, Editions du Cerf, Paris, 1954; Schlier, Volk, de Vries, *Unité de l'Eglise et tache oecuménique*, Ed. de l'Orante, Paris, 1961; Dacarraux, 'Catholiques et Orthodoxes devant le problème de l'unité', *Revue des deux Mondes*, 15 June 1959; Leger, *Chrétiens désunis*, Pastoral Letter, Montreal, 1962.

[2] Cf. Collective pastoral letter of the Dutch Bishops: *Le Sens du Concile*, Ed. du Cerf, Paris; Lorenz Jaeger, *The Ecumenical Council, the Church, and Christendom*, London, 1961; Cardinal Frings, *Il Concilio ecumenico Vaticano II di fronte al pensiero moderno*, Discourse, 20 November 1961.

Our other duties in connection with the council can be summed up in simple words:

1. We must keep informed about the council. This is the first purpose of this pastoral letter. It is a great event, and an event which concerns us all. There are now many books, articles, lectures dealing with the subject. We must all try to be well informed about it. Parish priests, teachers, directors of Catholic associations, writers, are all enjoined to give it the greatest publicity.

2. Let us try and see how all of us can and should contribute either collectively or individually to the council's success. It is the concern of all Christians; so during this period each one of us must revive his act of faith and give his best to his own Christian life. In this way the renewal that we all hope for from the council begins today and begins with us. The Pope exhorts us: 'We have no hesitation in saying that all our work for the council's success would be vain unless it were supported by a collective effort at sanctification. Prayer, individual virtue, the inner spirit, all become instruments of vast good. . . .' Each one of us, be we intellectuals, children, invalids, priests, must contribute in our own way by spiritual preparation. Every sort of person, every soul should feel this invitation to be a personal one. The whole Christian community must collaborate spiritually and morally in the success of the council.

2

THE COUNCIL IN THE LIFE OF THE CHURCH[1]

A GREAT deal has already been said and written about the ecumenical council since, on 25 January 1959, Pope John XXIII, 'instinctu divinitatis' to use the words carved on the arch of Constantine, as if by divine inspiration, with no public expectation or forewarning, no outward, determining event, announced his intention of calling the Second Ecumenical Vatican Council.

We too have spoken of it elsewhere, so will limit ourselves now to a brief glance at the possible meanings of any council, and of this particular council, in the life of the Church.

What does a council stand for in the life of the Church? The question requires two kinds of answers; one about the meaning a council assumes within the Church, and one about the meaning it acquires for those watching it from outside the Church and collating it with the outside world.

Let us consider, first, the importance of the council in the Church's inner life.

First of all, one cannot have any proper idea of an ecumenical council without having a true idea of the Church. One needs the Church's doctrine to understand what a council is. A council is a solemn act, a moment of great importance in the Church's life. One must know the essence of the Church in order to understand the importance and the nature of such an event.

A study of the Church would take us a very long way. But even to mention that we must clarify and deepen our ideas about her, if we are to understand what a council means for her, brings us to a first, basic, and fruitful conclusion: a council is an act of knowledge about the nature of the Church in which we are all called to participate. Then what is the Church?

This simple question creates immediate difficulties, if only

[1] Lecture given to the Catholic University of the Sacred Heart, Milan, 1962.

because of the number of possible answers. It is like the question that Christ asked his apostles at Caesarea Philippi: 'Who do men say that the Son of Man is?' (Matt. 16, 13). The variety of current opinions repeated to him about Christ, the Son of Man, by the apostles, shows their embarrassment at his question and their difficulty in formulating a clear, unanimous reply, until Simon, to be called and to become Peter, was drawn by an inner revelation to give the famous definition which stabilizes an equation, a personal identity between the two manifest natures of Jesus: the Son of Man and the Son of God.

The same question can be asked of the Church. What do you say our Church is, in which this exceptional event is about to take place? We find it a mystery. And rightly. For we must acquire a new awareness of the Church's mystery. The council makes us do so.

And to do so is to plunge into the liveliest currents of contemporary religious thought, the most exciting and advanced theological studies. For while in the past the concept of the Church was experienced rather than thought about, nowadays it is perhaps more thought about than experienced; but experienced it still will be if it is deeply thought about. Through a deep and prolonged act of self-knowledge the Church will become once again for herself, and for the world too, that which she is and should be.

Fr de Lubac puts it very well: that the Church from the beginning

'has an extraordinary deep awareness of her own being; the idea of the Church is everywhere, and everywhere shapes the expounding of the faith. In addition, at a very early stage she is compelled to begin the process of reflexion on herself. Every one of the great heresies that she has to fight forces this upon her. . . . All the mysteries which she examines, one by one, provide occasions for the same thing, for she is bound up with each and finds herself involved in all of them. Yet today we are at the beginning of an attempt at an unfolding which is at once analytic and generalized —an attempt to grasp the mystery in its totality; and circumstances have never before made necessary an effort of this kind.'[1]

And the most favourable, the most compelling circumstance for the Church to make this act of self-awareness is certainly an ecumenical council.

[1] de Lubac, The Splendour of the Church, London, 1956, p. 3.

What might cause interest and surprise is that the self-awareness which the Church is now eager to acquire does not so much concern those of her aspects which can be easily observed, such as her human composition, Canon Law, her temporal history, her exterior manifestations, i.e. her institutions, her presence in the world, her art and so on, but rather her most intimate, her deepest and most mysterious aspects. The Church is eager to explore, to sense the mystery of her own life; she is seeking her theology. She is seeking her soul, her secret, seeking within herself Christ, living in the Holy Spirit. She is seeking the mind of God, his plan, his presence, his working.

We are aware of our soul, say philosophers, only through the actions produced by that soul. The same is true of the Church's soul, of her inmost life, of the divine mystery which lives in her. We can have no better knowledge of her—except what we are already taught by divine revelation—than by experience of her life, by awareness of the power within her and of her manner of acting. Now the council is a supreme act in the Church's life; and so, while it presupposes knowledge of the Church itself, it illuminates this knowledge, develops it, celebrates it in action and through awareness.

So we may expect from the council a kind of circularity of thought on the Church. In order to accept the council as a legitimate act of the Church, we should at least start with the outline of an ecclesiology. We should, for instance, always keep in our mind's eye the teachings on the plurality and convergence of causes, from which the Church draws her life. The active cause is God, who thinks her, wants her, gives her life through Christ and the apostles, and the hierarchy which derives from them. The formal vivifying cause is the Holy Spirit, uncreated soul of the Church which by grace, created animation, gives her the breath of life in faith and charity. The material cause is humanity, called to form the Church from Adam's rib, a poor, weak thing but modelled by love, which makes her a bride of Christ. And the final cause is the Mystical Body, holy and transfigured, which is forming in time and is destined in eternity to live in the perfection and beatitude of the celestial Church.

Thus the human element, now called to fortunate but still limited symbiosis with the divine element of our supernatural life, will always be present to show the humanity of which the Church is composed. And we ask ourselves if this symbiosis, this divine help given to the Church, may not adopt some definite and tangible expression, something which will overcome human frailty, in order to assume infallible clarity and invincible strength.

The council will give a positive answer to this bold aspiration of ours. The divine element will pronounce itself through the human element. In the council men of this world, who are yet granted divine charisms, will speak according to the motion of the Holy Spirit: '*Visum est . . . Spiritui Sancto et nobis. . . .*' It is the decision of the Holy Spirit, and our decision (Acts 15, 28). Thus, through the mouths of the apostles, the very first council of Jerusalem spoke. And thus have spoken the successive councils, in the certainty of the interaction between God and man of which they are the instruments. Our knowledge that the Church is both human and divine will become a living reality, an external and an inward experience, which will bestow on our timid and laborious doctrine triumphant affirmation and virile joy.

Another basic branch of ecclesiology, to which the council will bring proof and confirmation, justifying doctrine with experience, is the social structure of the Church.

Let us give some simple examples of what we mean. We already know that the Church is a visible and hierarchic society. It is not simply a religious phenomenon, not simply a creed shared by a vague number of souls, creating an invisible, ideal communion of their human doctrines and opinions. The Church is not even a community of believers rendered visible and concrete by its uniform acceptance of teaching pronounced divine by some authority or other. The Church began by apostolic initiative, by an authority whose mandate came from Christ, and created around it a visible, organized, and governed community.

We know who Peter was and who the apostles were and who succeeded them. We know about their authority and their mission. We know how the *magisterium* and jurisdiction of the papacy has mysteriously extended, and why the keys of Peter are both necessary and sufficient to rule the Church. And we know too how the powers of the apostolic college are subordinate and coexistent with those of the Church's head. But when a council makes the Church's marvellous structure known to us not only in theory but in its living reality, in its actual functioning, then our knowledge of the Church's sovereign laws turns into a vision; and we rejoice to see in the workings of the Church the structural principles which the founder and divine architect, Christ our Lord, laid down for the building of his Church, mirrored with absolute fidelity.

The council will reveal the social, visible, organized, hierarchic, episcopal, pontifical aspects of the Church. It will be the apologia in action of the doctrine we already know. The longing to see this doctrine reflected as faithfully and completely as possible makes many hope that the Second Vatican Council will bring to its conclusion the dogmatic teaching on the structure of the Church which the First Vatican Council only partially proclaimed.

We may note that all of us, not only the Fathers who will be part of the great conciliar assembly, are called to deepen our awareness of the nature and mystery of the Church. This unique event calls every son and daughter of the Church to reflect on what the encyclical *Mystici Corpori* has already set before them:

'No greater glory, no higher dignity, no honour more sublime, can be conceived than that of belonging to the Holy, Catholic, Apostolic, and Roman Church, wherein we become members of this one and venerable body, are governed by this one august head, filled with the one, divine Spirit. . . .'[1]

The council is an extraordinary opportunity and a potent stimulus to increase 'the sense of the Church' throughout the whole Catholic world. The memorable words of Romano Guardini might have been written for these very circumstances: 'A process of incalculable importance has begun: the revival of the Church in people's souls.'

This becomes particularly obvious and desirable in reference to the ecumenical council, if we think of it as expressing the faith of the whole Church. Not, of course, that the bishops are delegates of the faithful, but because they are the witnesses and teachers of the Church's communal faith, and they themselves participate in the religious life of the whole community of believers, being the custodians of its deposit of faith.

In this connection we recall Newman's well-known passage on whether or not we should consult the faithful in matters of doctrine, not as formative sources of faith but as the index of the religious beliefs with which Christians are normally and rightly imbued.[2]

---

[1] *A.A.S.*, 1943, p. 237. English translation, C.T.S. London, p. 55.
[2] Cf. J. H. Newman, *On Consulting the Faithful in Matters of Doctrine*, London, 1961, especially pp. 62 ff.

Hence it can be seen that a council not only tends to awaken an awareness of the Church among Catholics, but also draws from the Catholic world, particularly in the course of its preparation, topics whose genuine Christian value can be judged by the Church's *magisterium*.

The Dutch bishops, in a recent pastoral letter on the 'sense of the council', which they define as an inner reform of Catholic life, affirm that 'the decisions and dispositions of a council are the potent results of active collaboration in the faith of the whole community of believers, pope, bishops, priests, and laity, accompanied by the judgment of the hierarchy, which, promoted by the Holy Spirit, examines, clarifies, and corrects all'.[1]

This leads us to consider another, still more evident, role that an ecumenical council plays in the Church's life. A council is not only an act of self-knowledge; it is also and still more an act of the fullness of the Church's being and of all her operative faculties. An ecumenical council mobilizes the whole Church. It reveals her full stature, her full efficacy, her full capacity for prayer, for doctrine, rule, inner reform, for missionary trust and eschatological hope, the sanctity she has received and the sanctity she radiates. It is not surprising that a council should throw into splendid relief the Church's distinctive characteristics, and show both those who belong to her and those watching her, unprejudiced, from outside, that she is a sign, a proof, a confirmation of divine revelation, realized and embodied in humanity.

Her apostolic mission, for instance, is obvious from those who make up a council; the assembly of pope and bishops is clear evidence of the coherent, uninterrupted, faithful derivation of the hierarchy from the apostles, and hence from Christ, and hence from God. Christ's words take shape before our eyes: 'As the Father has sent me, even so I send you' (John 20, 21), and so does his prayer: 'As thou didst send me into the world, so I have sent them into the world. . . . I do not pray for these only but also for those who believe in me through their word' (John 17, 18 and 20).

The mystic reality of the episcopate corresponds with the juridical position assumed by the successors of the apostles within the structure of the Church. This was clearly and admirably put by Ignatius, Bishop of Antioch, who was martyred in Rome at the

---

[1] Joint pastoral letter of the Dutch hierarchy, *Le Sens du Concile*, Bruges and Paris, p. 4.

beginning of the second century: 'Be subject to the bishop mutually, as Christ (was subject) to the Father according to the flesh, and the apostles to Christ, to the Father and to the Holy Spirit in a union as much material as spiritual.'[1]

The Church in council is in full apostolic strength, both formally, by the mark which the presence of the episcopal body deriving from the apostles confers upon it, and causally, by the powers handed down to the bishops in the same succession.[2]

Thus a council shows the unity of the Church in its impressive splendour. Never as at a council is the pope seen so clearly to be the head, the centre, the keystone of the Church. And it is to promote the essential need for unity that the Church recognizes as divine and providential the supernatural prerogatives which Christ gave his vicar for the ruling and government of the whole Church. At a council we see her universally converging around the successor of Peter.

Catholicity thus irradiates around unity. A council makes this evident, as if meeting the modern need to see reality in concrete terms. At a council the whole Catholic world is present, through its bishops. The universality of the Church is made obvious by the number, provenance, differing languages and races, cultures, and histories of the members of the episcopal body. If we examine it closely we will see that this representative flow is not accidental, nor is it drawn together by purely juridical links or by any attempt to co-ordinate particular interests, as might happen with great international organizations in civil life. Nor is it caused or maintained by any levelling-out of national characteristics. This unity is deeply and spiritually Catholic, produced by an identity of faith and love, which are the most personal and most living expressions of the human spirit, fused in a mysterious, divine combination in which strict fraternal respect for individuals coincides with the general harmony of all. Here the Catholic world shows the reality and full scope of her communion; this is the Church celebrating her unity and universality.

This congregation is truly ecumenical, perfect in its aims, universal in its rights and even to a large extent in reality; the universality of Christ's true Church is finally consummated in faith and love.

[1] *Ad Magnesios*, 13, 2.
[2] Journet, *The Church of the Word Incarnate*, vol. I.

Will sanctity, that final, most lovely, and most desired of the Church's qualities, also be apparent at the council? For those who believe in and can see the reality of grace, sanctity will indeed emanate and irradiate from the fullness of the Church's presence in council. Let us remember Christ's promise that where the apostles meet in his name, he himself is in their midst; and that the help of the Holy Spirit is never so fully invoked as when the teaching Church is met to speak in his name. But, apart from this supernatural sanctity, the council will illustrate another sanctity, a moral one, which it will try to indicate and arouse in the Church through legislation, through reforms in the thinking and way of life of clergy and people, with all the wisdom, all the authority, all the encouragement and efficacy which it has at its disposal.

The Church in council is in a state of moral tension. The will and judgment of the responsible hierarchy is at its fullest, and is then passed on to priests, religious, and laity.

The council, from this aspect, is a search for the authentic faith and way of life that Christ willed. It frees the Church from the sediments left by time and temporal events on the spotless robes of the Bride of Christ. It releases energies dormant in the Church's heart and recharges souls, inundating them with grace and renewed will. These are the fruits of an ecumenical council, which the First Vatican Council put in these terms:

'There the holy teachings of religion are defined with greater depth, expressed with greater fullness; there ecclesiastical discipline is restored and more firmly established . . . there the link is drawn closer between members and head; there the vigour of the whole mystical body grows; there our zeal is stimulated to spread the kingdom of Christ over the world, even if we have to give our blood for it.'

But does this extraordinary vital act have other effects on the Church? Yes. An ecumenical council is not only a time of intense clarity in the ecclesiastical conscience, not only a time of visible and sensible experience in the Church's life. It is also a time of extraordinary action. A council is the supreme operative organ of the authority of the entire Church.[1] It is the moment in the Church's life when her powers are displayed at their highest; two powers in

---

[1] Can. 228, 1.

particular, *magisterium* and jurisdiction. In an ecumenical council the Church becomes a teacher, a ruler in the fullest sense of the words.

The powers of Christ come into play in a supreme form and measure. St Charles Borromeo, authoritarian though he was, often advocated councils and synods and gave proof of this in his pastoral work; and it was usually this aspect that he put forward to show that ecumenical councils are beneficial and necessary. I will not dwell here on the relationship between the power of the pope, whose infallibility in teaching and sovereignty in jurisdiction is recognized, and the power of the bishops which, to enjoy the same prerogatives, must be in communion with, convoked by, presided over, or ratified by the pope, just as the limbs of a body must be joined to the head in order for the whole to function. This is common knowledge, particularly since the First Vatican Council, which explicitly defined this point of ecclesiastical constitutional law and of the theology of the mystery of the Church.

We may, however, note that the exercise of the supreme powers of the council has had different objectives in the past, by which I mean to say that particular circumstances and needs have required the intervention of the authority of an ecumenical council. This is the same as saying that each ecumenical council has its own history and these, in fact, in great part make up the history of the Church. The main events, the decisive moments, the most characteristic and formative manifestations, the most painful and the most victorious dramas in the Church's life have been in its councils.

In this connection I recall a remark by Monsignor Jiacinto Gaggia, a great bishop, a man of vast culture, intelligence, and will-power, to whom among many other benefits I owe my ordination as a priest. When as a young priest I timidly asked him what to read for the studies on the life and history of the Church I thought of making at that time, he replied at once: 'Read the history of the councils. Take your Héfélé [eighteen heavy tomes!] and study those; you can find everything there,' he said: theology, philosophy, spirituality, politics, humanism, and Christianity, errors, debates, truths, abuses, laws, the strength and the holiness of the Church. The history of councils is an ecclesiastical encyclopaedia. That shows the place councils hold in the Church's life. They pervade, sum up, clarify, and direct the whole.

They are the great pillars that support the living Church's history: the milestones on her path through time.

3

THE IMPLICATIONS OF THE COUNCIL FOR THE WORLD[1]

THAT THE forthcoming ecumenical council called by Pope John XXIII is an important event in the life of the Catholic Church has been said by so many people and in so many ways that public opinion, particularly its highest and most vigilant sectors, can be considered well, or at least quite well, informed about it.

It is not easy to foresee, though, the importance of the ecumenical council outside the Catholic Church. This is a question worth considering since the council, however it may be evaluated, does have international, indeed global dimensions, and concerns many who are vested with great authority and equipped with considerable erudition as are the prelates and members of the future council. It concerns also so many others who call themselves the faithful and who will set much store by the council and its doctrinal and practical conclusions that will certainly be felt beyond religious circles.

I would therefore like to say something about the position which the ecumenical council is assuming in contemporary international life.

The first observation that occurs to me in this connection is the difference between the position of the forthcoming ecumenical council in respect to civil society today and that of past ecumenical councils.

We can say at once that a council, this extraordinary and, under certain aspects, major event in the life of the Catholic Church, is wholly extraneous to the life of civil society. Cardinals, bishops, abbots, and prelates with canonical jurisdiction, superiors of religious orders of the whole world will be meeting there, gathered around the pope, without whom a council has no ecumenical character.

[1] From Address given to the Institute for the Study of International Politics, 27 April 1962.

About five thousand persons, if they all come, will discuss religious and moral, liturgical and pastoral questions, study the great and complex problems relative to the reintegration of the separated churches, Oriental, Protestant, and Anglican, with the Catholic Church. They will give encouragement and instruction for the spread of missionary work in the world and the consequent introduction of basic Christian principles (most of which are the same as those of our civilization) to peoples who are strange to Christianity and to nations in the process of development. They will also give rulings about the Catholic way of life, of priests, religious, laity, various social classes, the family, the young, as well as about salient phenomena of Catholic life itself, its culture, for example, its education, arts, and amusements. The Council may perhaps even clarify the premises for relations between the Church and modern states. And civil society, even the state authority, will be completely unaware of this episode in our contemporary history.

By unaware I mean it will officially be a stranger to it. Of course the diplomatic corps, together perhaps with a few special envoys accredited to the Holy See, will be present at the inaugural and marginal ceremonies. There will certainly be present many journalists, photographers, artists, pilgrims, and tourists. But all of these will be outside the conciliar assembly itself; outside it not only bodily but in practice, that is without any 'voce in capitolo', deprived of any interference or influence in it whatsoever.

We heard with pleasure the courteous words of the President of the Council of Ministers, when introducing to parliament the government now in office, about the forthcoming ecumenical council. One of the reasons why we are all glad to hear such declarations is that they express and confirm that the civil authority wishes, as it should, to remain outside the intrinsic development of the council.

The Church is on her own in holding these great meetings. She is utterly distinct from the state. The Church is another society, free, independent, juridically self-sufficient, potentially perfect. The distinction between Church and state is now complete, even where —as in Italy—there is no division, because of the solemn mutual agreements between the two. Church and state are two societies. Both enjoy sovereignty, each in its own sphere. Both, willingly or not, seek to work together to bring to the lives of their people (and both are concerned with the same people) means for betterment and for achieving the aims of human life; one supernatural the other natural, one eternal the other temporal.

This state of things is a most important achievement in our historical evolution. It would itself be a theme for much thought, if we were seeking the ideal principles from which the reciprocal emancipation of Church and state originate. To seek these principles would mean passing from the historical and juridical fields into the philosophical, and noting how the Church's concepts about the general ordering of human affairs has brought her to deepen this distinction. The Church has been and always tends to be friendly towards the state. She recognizes its powers and sphere of competence, endeavours to stabilize its functions and promote its well-being. But we must also note the anti-religious dialectic springing from profane ideas gradually being assumed by various state regimes, until the distinction between the two entities changes to a relationship of separation and opposition.

The present situation can be evaluated in various ways. But it undoubtedly has the advantage of making the Church reassume her essential native features, her basic structure, as Christ her divine founder conceived it in the purest of ideals, as his Church.

Thus it might seem both logical and respectful of the citizen, the politician, the layman, and the statesman to detach himself from the council as something which does not concern him at all.

Not all states will be merely detached from the Church's gathering of her bishops; some will actually be opposed to it. In spite of all the proclamations of freedom today, and of the proofs of loyalty offered by the Catholic Church to any state which allows her to live her own life and carry out her spiritual mission, we know that there are still states which do not understand her position and deny the historical reality of breadth and dignity in Christ's Church.

The bishops of countries under Communist rule will not be present at the council, even if still alive.

This is not only a political fact; it is a spiritual or ideological fact. And its gravity leads us to consider not only the external and juridical position of the Church and the council in the contemporary world, but also its moral, ideological, or more properly religious position. Under this aspect too, at first sight at least, we find detachment. Our secular society draws instinctively apart from a manifestation of ecclesiastical life, which it considers ritualized and esoteric. Our modern world is 'busy about other things'. The pre-occupations of everyday life silence any response to religious events of this kind. When the idea of religion occurs to the common run of people it is in the spiritual terms of a religious community quite different from those gathered from all over the world to re-evoke the word of revelation and to legislate by the light of the Holy Spirit.

Yet we would disregard various fascinating aspects of human reality today if we did not glance now and again at the deep, perhaps unconscious, yet positive attitude of our generation towards religion, and so towards Christ and the Church of which the council is the salient expression.

This is a vast subject, I know. I dare not attempt—I won't say an explanation, but even a description of it. I can think, though, of two adjectives which may help to define this general attitude: sceptical and demanding. By sceptical I mean that it suspects and opposes any idea of the transcendent, that it is self-absorbed, and convinced that the only reality is in the confines of experience, whether of the senses or the reason; confines that may be capable of spreading, but are always controllable subjectively. It is an attitude which puts man alone: alone with the exterior things he possesses, knows, and enjoys; alone with his wealth, his discoveries, his business; all things that are mute, and say nothing to him. Alone with his disquiet, with his insufficiency of thought, with a growing weight of responsibilities due to his material conquests, and with an ever increasing uncertainty about his capacity to affirm any values whatsoever. Alone with his secret *angst* (how fashionable this word has become), with the progressive disintegration of all logic and morality (think of the modern theatre!). Alone and ever in search of himself, incapable even of any clear awareness about his own thinking and reasoning, as subjectivists and agnostics were in the past.

The outline I have traced may seem gloomy. But perhaps it is less so than certain other creeds of the modern spirit, where the rejection of the supernatural is wearing thin.

'This anguish [writes a contemporary] is a first contact, negative though it is, with the essential in reality. . . . In its struggle to return to reality it tends to abandon the priority of thought. . . . While the sciences celebrate their triumphs over nature, despair spreads like a patch of oil. A new contact is being sought with reality. Already man is being offered new philosophies born of the basic instinct natural to man . . . to believe and trust in existence.'[1]

Modern man may not yet have achieved a new certainty: but he does feel its need. He needs, he thirsts for a reality that is not only physical, not only economic, not only scientific, not only rational, but spiritual too. Reality; not a myth.

That is why the world now looks with amazement at the Church, which seems to be rich in just this reality; and that is why it is not wholly deaf to her summons, ringing with this reality, to the council. Public opinion and curiosity is awakened, people are watching this event closely. People with thoughtful minds are beginning to reflect on the council and those with good in their hearts to be hopeful.

Our modern world, avid but spiritually empty, has not been deaf to this event. If nothing else, it has realized that the notion of the separation to which it has been so well conditioned, the separation of the Church from profane society, does not actually exist. The Church, the old Church, only survivor of the hundreds shipwrecked throughout history, is not outside the world but inside the world, our own world; she is inside our history, inside our life. Indeed if one grasps the primary meaning of the council one realizes that the Church is not only inside the world but is for the world. As Pius XI said: 'The Church came into existence for no other reason than to make all men participants in the Redemption and to spread the kingdom of Christ everywhere.'[2] John XXIII said the same thing in his admirable speech to the preparatory commissions of the council (cf. p. 246–7 above).

One conclusion must be that the council is not only an internal event in the life of the Church, but is intended to be, and could turn out to be, an event for the world too; a hope for all.

If this is so, there are two different prospects to consider; that of the council seen from outside, from the world; and that of the world seen from the council.

On the first prospect I have little to say. In fact I confess that this is something I should prefer to hear about and discuss. It would be very interesting to know what those who observe the Church

[1] L. C. Baas.   [2] A.A.S., 1926, p. 65.

from outside expect of the council. Hostile observers will say, nothing or rather nothing good. The indifferent will ask: what can
the contemporary world gain from an ecclesiastical event of this
nature? The cultured, the intelligent, the well-informed will have
many suppositions to make. And the simple and the good will
have imaginings and hopes, maybe some ingenuous and impractical
ideas. The enquiry is open.

A pamphlet has been published in Germany with eighty-one
answers to the question: what do we expect from the Council?[1]

Another enquiry has been made in France among Christians
of different denominations, called 'Ideas for the Council'.[2] The
Annual of International Politics published by this Institute, also
gives examples of the interest and importance accorded to it.

For my part, looking over the world in expectation of the
council, I can only say that if there is to be contact between this
ecclesiastical event and the society of our time, it will not be on any
political level. This observation of mine may disappoint professional politicians, or those who expect the political scene to be
swept by some prophetic flame, or to find the Vatican calling
representatives of all peoples together to discuss their differences
and make peace between them. But my observation seems sound
to me.

It does not undervalue, I think, an event whose greatness is in
quite another sphere than the political one. What is more, I do not
think the council is even likely to remedy the errors of theory and
the many moral evils there are in the world. It can diagnose them,
prescribe and indicate remedies. But the council will not be a
miraculous medicine with immediate effects, the inaugurator of an
epoch that is holy and happy.

The council, I think, will thunder no curses on the world, though
it may speak in the firm sharp tones of truth. This too may be
something new in the style of councils of the Church, who, usually
in history, has used the authority of her *magisterium* to make negative
condemnations in defence of positive truths. St Augustine in his
great book *De civitate Dei* in fact observes that the Church's doctrinal
thought has been stimulated by impetus of contrary errors, 'ad
adversario mota quaestio discendi existit occasio'.[3] The Church will

---

[1] *Umfrage zum Konzil*, Herder, 1961.
[2] *Esprit*, December 1961.
[3] 16, 2.

indeed appear in her majesty and gravity, looking the world in the face, but in the attitude described by Pope John XXIII in his recent solemn document, as *mater et magista*, mother and teacher.

So in the council we will see the Church in her greatest effort at religious affirmation, both internally and externally. We shall see her pledging herself to strict loyalty to the Gospel, to revelation, to God's word, to her living tradition, to the coherence of her teaching, in all of which she finds both her reason for existence and the secret of her perennial youth. But the outer world will find things of concern to it in the very process of the Church's inner restoration.

First will be the council's call to separated Christians to enter Christ's one true Church. This, as we know, is intended to be one of the ecumenical council's main aims, together with the Church's inner reform and a firm affirmation of the true Christian religion. Perhaps this aim, this hope, was the first spark to light in the Pope's heart the idea of convoking a council. To trust in the full achievement of this aim by the council would be an act of love as bold as, in human terms, it would be rash and futile. But love is never futile; and trust in Christ is never rash.

If the council does not succeed in celebrating the return of the separated brethren it will at least succeed in opening the doors of the family home to them, in smoothing the way, in sending out its warm appeal for their reintegration in the one truly apostolic and Catholic Church. Ecumenism will become an integral part of the Church's desires and prayers and structure. This will be a great thing for the world's peace and for establishing that spiritual foundation without which union between nations becomes so difficult and precarious.

Another thing about the council that the world might note will be the Church's efforts to make her message as comprehensible as possible, so that the world can at least listen to it before one day eventually it accepts and lives by it. The Church, in her scrupulous loyalty to her mandate as custodian and diffuser of the sacred *depositum* received from Christ, has wrapped it in ritual, language, and customs which serve in part to keep it immune from the corrosion of time and possible changes due to subjective interpretation. These must also partly help to define the *depositum* itself, make it comprehensible and capable of assimilation.

Now the Church's apostolic mission has always meant that her message should be adapted, without any loss of content, to the intelligence and also partly to the tastes of generations whose speech and habits have changed in the course of centuries. Now it is a question of clearing away the dead wood and rejuvenating religion's exterior dress, of allowing it possibilities of circulation through the language, culture, and art of our time. This the council will do, though it may defend Latin as a sacerdotal language throughout the world, and keep our immortal liturgy in its genuine and marvellous expression. There will also be other things, I think, of interest to this world of ours.

The council, that is, will not only try to make our religion understandable, but practicable too. It should not be thought that the Church will ever change the basic laws that God willed to preside over human life. It can be expected, in fact, that the Church will be their inflexible champion at the council itself. But there are also ecclesiastical laws, and some of these are out-of-date and not applicable to the needs of modern life. That is why there is talk of revising Canon Law, the only legislation today which, apart from statutes for international communications, is still worldwide.

Let me add one last remark about the ecumenical council in its relations with the contemporary world. We will find in the Church met in council another attitude of the greatest interest, the assimilation of the profane but human forms in which modern life expresses itself. To understand this attitude would need a long talk on its own; but some slight knowledge of history is enough to grasp the idea. As the Church at the time of pagan and Hellenic–Roman civilizations rejected whatever was idolatrous and inhuman about them but kept, purified, and assimilated their treasures of classical art and culture; as the Church in the period of feudalism opposed the barbarism and violence that was part of the story of new peoples, but gathered, corrected, and ennobled the positive forces of medieval man; just as the Church at the time of the Renaissance checked the raptures of resurgent humanist paganism and raised the artistic powers of the time to incomparable heights; in the same way, I dare to think, the Church, though still denouncing the materialism of all kinds typical of our era, will not anathemize the vast and marvellous civilization of science, industry, technology, and internationalized life of our time. She will try to 'absorb' it, that is give it, at its base, the principles it still lacks and, at its peak, open the horizons of spiritual truth, prayer, and redemption which only she can truly give.

She will try to do today what she has been doing for centuries; give human beings peace and brotherhood and make them children of God in Christ. She will try, as she always has, to give the world a Christian soul.